UNDER COVER:
THE ADVENTURES OF A REAL LIFE GIGOLO

Born in a small town in Western Australia, Luke Bradbury was brought up to enjoy the simple things in life, especially the outdoors. He decided to come to London after the death of his father. His many hobbies include Australian Rules Football, swimming, soccer and generally staying in good shape. He plans to move back to Australia one day.

To find out more about Luke go to www.AuthorTracker.co.uk for exclusive updates.

D0835215

LUKE BRADBURY

Under Cover:
The Adventures of a Real Life Gigolo

With Catherine von Ruhland

AVON

This is a work of non fiction, but some names, character and place names have been changed to protect identity.

AVON

A division of HarperCollins*Publishers*
77–85 Fulham Palace Road,
London W6 8JB

www.harpercollins.co.uk

A Paperback Original 2008

3

First published in Great Britain by
HarperCollins*Publishers* 2008

Copyright © Luke Bradbury 2008

Luke Bradbury asserts the moral right to
be identified as the author of this work

A catalogue record for this book is
available from the British Library

ISBN-13: 978-1-84756-108-4

Set in Minion by Palimpsest Book Production Limited,
Grangemouth, Stirlingshire

Printed and bound in Great Britain by
Clays Ltd, St Ives plc

Mixed Sources
Product group from well-managed
forests and other controlled sources
www.fsc.org Cert no. SW-COC-1806
© 1996 Forest Stewardship Council

FSC is a non-profit international organisation established
to promote the responsible management of the world's forests.
Products carrying the FSC label are independently certified
to assure consumers that they come from forests that are managed
to meet the social, economic and ecological needs
of present and future generations.

Find out more about HarperCollins and the environment at
www.harpercollins.co.uk/green

Acknowledgments

I would like to thank Diane Banks, Maxine Hitchcock and the Avon team for making this book happen. I would also like to thank Catherine for her many hours' hard work. Thank you for believing in me from the beginning and helping to get my thoughts onto paper; you have become a real friend and you have helped in getting me to where I am today as a person.

To 'Pretty' for all your love and support.

All in a day's work

For fuck's sake, how much longer? Ring the bell, you bastard!

There's me and this gorgeous girl at it on the floor. Carrie or Emily or something, I can't remember her name. It's a bit of a blur by number six. It's not as if she isn't good at what she does. She's been hired, after all, same as me. So she knows all the moves and is fit to boot. It's just I don't know how much longer I can keep it up. Literally.

I'm trying my hardest. And both of us are into our stride. Hammer and tongs, wearing the creaking floor away. It's like we're swimming together in our sweat, our damp bodies sawing against each other. We're barely coming up for air, and a strand of her long blonde hair is in my mouth, and everything else is drowned out except for our panting, heavy breathing and thumping heartbeats.

And all I yearn for is the tiny silver jingle of the bell, held between Brian's index finger and thumb. He's silent. Watching us.

When he finally shakes it, satisfied, both of us collapse, dead spent. As we catch our breath, Brian comes out from behind the curtain and tosses us both bathrobes. I help the girl to her feet, my arm around her narrow shoulders.

'You okay?'

'Yeah,' she mouths through a half-smile, catching her breath. She's pretty. She must be about twenty-three. Same as me.

1

'Luke, you stay here a while,' Brian instructs, tightening the belt of his dressing gown. 'Emma, come with me.'

Emma. That was it.

Brian guides her out of the room. I look at her go, her bare legs glistening.

As they leave the room, Emma turns to me. 'Nice meeting you, Luke. See you again, maybe.'

'You too, Emma.'

Maybe.

I stand there, waiting. A short while later, the front door slams shut, and I head to the bathroom and wash Emma off my skin. The warm jet of water is like a curtain between her and the next one.

Is that it for tonight?

I step out of the shower and dry myself down and wrap myself in the bathrobe again. I like the feel of its softness against me. I'm still tying it up when I enter Brian's lounge again. He pulls his armchair out from behind the curtain and sits low down in it, his legs stretched out before him. He raises his beer bottle to me.

'Cheers!'

'Bloody hell, Brian, I thought you were never going to ring that damn thing!'

'I thought you enjoyed sex,' he teases.

I sit down in the other armchair across the room, and pick up the open bottle that's been sitting there since before Emma arrived.

'Up to a point. It's easy for you. You don't have to put the effort in.'

'Guys your age are supposed to be gagging for it!' he smirks.

I lift the beer bottle to my lips and knock some back before answering.

'Well, yeah,' I laugh, 'but even so. That doesn't mean I don't need to come up for air!'

My muscles silently scream in agreement.

With Brian, I gave as good as I got. We'd built up a rapport since I'd started working for him. Let's face it, we'd had to. Because although he hired both me and some girls, we weren't all there on an equal footing. Because Brian was a voyeur. Which, I suppose, made me his Tester.

Brian had once hired me as many as twelve girls in one night. He would call me early evening and we'd have a drink together, and then he'd phone for a girl for me. And the bell was his method of communication, of control. If he wanted the sex to stop, he'd ring the bell. It might be after twenty minutes, it might be after five. She'd go, I'd stay, have another break, and then Brian would phone the agency for someone else for me. And a quarter of an hour later there'd be another girl on the doorstep.

Brian never joined in. All he wanted to do was hide behind the curtain and watch. And whatever else he got up to back there. Everyone gets their kicks some way. Sometimes the sex went on for so long that, like with Emma, I was willing that damn bell to ring. You can have too much of a good thing . . .

Still, I couldn't quite believe I was getting paid to do this. My mates would be up of a morning to go to work in offices, schools and cafés, whereas I could lie in bed all day or do whatever I wanted to. Until the evening. When I might have sex with five different girls Brian had selected for me. And earn in that night what my mates would in a week. It was almost too good to be true.

Brian was looking at me. His beer bottle was empty. Mine was still half full and held in mid-air on the way to my mouth. I could tell what he was going to say. He was pushing back the armchair with his bare feet even though he was still sitting in it, even as he was opening his mouth to speak. He held his mobile in the other hand. He'd put the agency number on speed dial so it took no time at all.

'Right, Luke,' he said with a wolfish leer. 'Get ready for number seven.'

Beginnings

'We've been shafted, the bastards!'

Mark spat the words out across the kitchen table. He'd just shown me his bank statement, and the evidence was there in bright red. I looked down into my mug of tea and nodded. I knew what he meant. But the truth was, we well and truly hadn't been. *That* was the problem.

'Meet loads of girls. You'll be sent out on six dates a week, and make £90 an hour . . .'

That was what the freesheet ad for the internet escort agency had promised us – and no doubt hundreds of other guys like Mark and me. Guys with too much male pride and not quite enough money to live on, who just assumed there would be women falling at our feet, and who were mugs enough to fork out £180 to register.

But in the three weeks since the two of us had coughed up our money, not one girl had called for Mark's services. Nor mine.

I took a sip of my tea and looked across at Mark. It wasn't even as if either of us was that bad-looking. Not that I'd ever admit I was *good*-looking. You got a clip for that in my family, for puffing yourself up. I'd been told that I looked a bit like the *Spiderman* actor, Tobey Maguire. Which was good enough for me. I was six foot tall with dark blond hair that bleached easily in the sun back home in Australia, while Mark's hair was brown and he was slightly shorter than me. We worked out. Both of us had a reasonable Saturday-night success rate.

Mark shook his head. 'This is London, for God's sake. Where are all the girls?' He took a digestive from the packet upended on the table and bit into it. He had a right to ask. It wasn't as if we hadn't seen enough of them falling over each other on any of our weekends out on the piss.

'Not choosing to call out for a guy, presumably. That's what blokes do.'

I could see the callbox windows in my mind's eye, completely covered from floor to ceiling with brightly coloured 'whorecards'. Blocking out the muted sunlight. That'd been my introduction to England nine weeks ago, dialling my mum to let her know I'd got here in one piece.

'We can get a number for a girl from any phone box. But they can't . . .' I was working out the problem with our plan as I was saying it.

'But that's what the internet's for!' Mark spluttered, spraying crumbs. He swept them off the table with his forearm.

I ran a finger along the edge of the pine tabletop until it hit a dent in the wood. I drew my nail again and again through the groove and looked Mark in the eye.

'Yeah, but they're not looking because they're not even aware that there's a service for them. They take their chances on a Saturday night.'

Mark nodded: 'Or go without.'

'Exactly. And even if they knew there were guys they could pay for via their PCs, that doesn't mean they'd do anything about it.'

I picked up my mug and took another gulp of tea, and thought of the callbox again and all the sex phoneline ads in the freesheets that I'd seen when I was trying to find somewhere to live. That'd been a grim time, sleeping on friends of friends' grimy floors

6

while all the while I could sense they didn't really want me there. Sharing a room with Mark in this house for the past month had been a damn sight better than *that*, even with the beer cans clustered on the floor round the bin from when we hadn't thrown straight. He'd been looking for someone to make up the rent and I'd seen his ad on Gumtree. It'd helped that the two of us had hit it off as soon as we'd met over a drink. Same small-town Aussie background, I suppose.

'I mean, have *you* ever phoned for a hooker?' I raised my eyebrows at him as I said it.

He shook his head. 'Course not. As if I need to . . .' he crowed.

I put my mug down. 'Well then.'

And that's when it hit me. *What had we been thinking?*

There was not even a market for sex with straight guys. Or not one that involved money changing hands. On the girl's part anyhow.

'They've well and truly buggered us, haven't they?' I sighed.

A grin crept up Mark's face. 'Thankfully not. And that's something to be damn grateful for.'

We both laughed, but it couldn't disguise the fact that each of us was seriously out of pocket. We'd taken a gamble on making easy money and lost.

'Well, at least we can't be the only ones who've fallen for this scam,' said Mark. 'Think about it. There must be hordes of guys across London,' he continued, flinging his arm out as if to embrace the whole city and not just our poxy kitchen in a crappy area of West London, 'just like us, weeping into their tea at what might have been!'

I sighed. Surely it was the ultimate part-time job. Screwing girls for cash. We could have waved goodbye to the crummy minimum-wage waiting and bar jobs and selling stuffed pittas while hung over from a stall at Camden Market for friends of friends who always paid shit money. God, London certainly hadn't turned out to be all it was cracked up to be.

I looked down at my half-full mug and felt the cogs whirring even as he was saying it.

'Well then, that's how we make our money back, isn't it?' I suggested.

'What?'

'Look, there's clearly enough money out there to make it worthwhile setting up an agency that gets guys to pay to sign on.'

Mark's face momentarily fell. 'What, and rip people off just the way we were? Come on.'

Miserably, I nodded. 'I agree it's not exactly ethical.' I thought for a moment. 'But then it's not exactly *not*. What if we *were* to set up an agency, y'know, advertise our services to women, and ask guys to sign on? The blokes cough up, and of course we'll give them work if there's enough going, but we'll always have first call. What *is* wrong with that? We can't lose.'

Mark cocked his head to one side and shook it. But he was also smiling. 'God, Luke. A couple of months in this country and you've turned into a London spiv!'

I smirked back. He raised his mug to mine and we chinked.

My mind was already in overdrive. We'd advertise in the London freesheets. We could do it cheaply, surely. Advertise for clients, and put something on the internet to draw in the men as well. And photos. Me, Mark and the lads, to give the girls something to choose from.

'Face it, Mark. We're broke. We might as well make a go of it. We've got nothing more to lose.'

I suppose I expected it to happen overnight. But of course it didn't. And when it didn't, it meant it didn't seem real. It was just mates mucking about. Even after I'd spent fifty quid I couldn't really afford on a box ad in a London magazine; even after we'd put a whole lot of our pictures up on the net. Seven of us had spent an afternoon taking photos of each other, all of us with a big grin on our faces in front of the drawn curtains in our lounge room so it looked like we'd hired a studio or something. So we were able to still kid ourselves that we were only having a laugh.

But we weren't, were we?

Or, as it turned out, I wasn't.

The phone rang. Mark and I were lounging on the sofa with our cans of Stella and having our last-night debrief. We looked at each other for a beat, and since he didn't get up, I did and sauntered across the room.

'Hi?'

'Male Escorts Esquire? I saw your advert.'

Shit!

I pulled up a chair and sat down, half out of shock. The name we'd come up with wasn't the greatest, but it had clearly done its job. I struggled to get my head into gear. She was the first to call – though I wasn't about to let her know that, of course.

'Hello, how might we help you?'

What have we got ourselves into?

'Uh, I've never done this before,' she mumbled. 'I was wondering if you might be able to send me someone tomorrow evening?'

What was I thinking? *I can't do this. This isn't for me.* That was why I'd volunteered my phone number in the first place, so I could act the receptionist and palm off anyone who rang onto one of the others.

It was one thing to fantasise about girls phoning you for sex, it was quite another to be faced with the sheer reality of going with whoever happened to ask. Suppose she sounded better than she turned out to look? What did you do then?

This one wasn't too young – I could tell by the tone of her voice – and she was clearly nervous.

Join the club.

I sat up straight on the dining chair and went into professional mode.

'Is there anyone on the website you liked the look of? Sorry, your name is –?'

Mark's ears pricked up. He stared across the room at me with excited saucer eyes and a smirk. I shook my head as a sign to him to ease up, and tried to focus on what was being said to me.

'Jenny,' she replied. 'I don't have a computer.'

Ah, definitely an older woman. Okaay.

'Nice to talk to you, Jenny, I'm Luke. That's not a problem. What would you like him to look like? We have a range of young men on our books.'

Mark stifled a guffaw and I shot a glare at him.

'I'm not – I'm not sure,' she stuttered.

So, she was indecisive. That wasn't a problem either. All I had to do was make sure she was satisfied with the service. She didn't sound as if she could cope with someone too bullish, like Simon, our resident rugby player. She needed a gentleman who wouldn't frighten her off.

'You sound nice.' She laughed nervously. 'Are you available?'

Fuck!

'Thank you, Jenny, but, sorry, I'm not.' I tried to sound calm and friendly though I felt out of my depth. 'I tell you what, though, I'll make sure you have a pleasant surprise.'

I took down her details and we said goodbye to each other.

As I put down the receiver, Mark started clapping.

'Congratulations. You've just nailed our very first client!'

'Yeah, and now we've got to decide which of us'll have her. Will you go?'

I sat down beside him, and picked up my can from the floor.

'What's she like?'

'She sounded old enough to be my mother.'

Mark grimaced.

I laughed. 'You've just discounted Madonna.'

'Er, yeah.'

'All angles and humourless. Fair point,' I agreed. 'Hang on, I know who.' I got up again and returned to the phone.

'What? Who?' quizzed Mark.

I pressed the buttons and put the receiver to my ear, leaning against the wall. 'Rob, of course. He's always game on. For one thing, he could do with the cash.'

'Well, yeah,' shrugged Mark. 'He could always do with the cash. Isn't that his problem?'

Rob had never quite got the hang of money, especially since his bank seemed so keen to give him more of it whenever he wanted. Except they had now decided to call in the debt. The magic had fallen out of the plastic.

Come on, Rob, I prayed. *Pick up, pick up.*

He eventually picked up.

'Hey, Rob. It's Luke. How'd you like to make a fast buck? We've had a client call for an escort and your name came up.'

Flatter the guy.

Across the room, one of Mark's eyebrows arched up. Rob was up for it too. I could sense his excitement down the line.

'I tell you what. As this is your first time, forget about the commission and just come back and tell me all about it and buy me a beer.'

I took a swig from my own can, and set it down on the seat of the chair beside me. I couldn't help noticing that, across the room, both of Mark's eyebrows were now up his forehead. The sense of that anger was a distraction even as I gave Rob the details. I ended the call, and confronted him.

'What?'

'How's the business supposed to survive if nobody puts any money in the pot?' he steamed as I sat back down.

'Aw, I know, but if you can't help out a mate, eh? Anyhow, it *is* our first ever call – not that Rob knows that. It won't happen again.'

We sat in silence and drank our beer. Then Mark grinned, his spirits obviously lifting.

'God, Luke, we're officially launched. Can you believe it?'

I smiled and nodded. We high-fived.

Rob called after I'd finished at the café the following evening and was putting together my dinner. I could hear pub clatter in the background and hoped he wasn't soaking up too much Dutch courage before his assignment.

'Luke, I'm not sure about this. I don't know if I can go through with it.'

Don't get cold feet on me, Rob.

'Don't worry about it. Think of it like any other date. You meet, have a drink, you go back to her place . . .'

I picked at the peeling wallpaper around the phone. A previous tenant had used the plaster to jot down numbers that I sometimes wondered if I should call just for the hell of it.

'Yeah, but I *fancy* my dates,' Rob flung back. 'What if I don't fancy her?'

'Well, that's where the dosh comes in. Just think about the money!'

I thought of nervous Jenny wanting someone who'd treat her well, who wouldn't ride roughshod over her. *No, it wasn't just about the money.*

'Look, Rob, everyone gets nervous their first time. Of course they do. She'll be just as anxious. Take it easy.'

A slither of wallpaper came away in my hand, and I let it fall to the floor.

'Did you get nervous, Luke? What was it like?'

I gulped. He had no idea he was the first of any of us to test out our escort scheme.

I evaded the question. On the carpet beneath the phone was a growing pile of peelings that needed a good vacuum. If we'd had a vacuum cleaner.

'It's different for everyone. You've got to go out there and make your own mark. Be every woman's dream!'

'Yeah, right,' said Rob, not sounding at all confident.

'You know what to do, of course you do. You're used to scoring, yeah? Just be a bit more of a gentleman when you go about it.' On second thoughts: 'Unless of course she requests otherwise.'

There was a chuckle on the other end of the line. That was better.

'Okay, okay.'

'Don't worry. You'll be fine,' I reassured him. 'Just be careful you don't drink too much beforehand. You want to make a good impression.'

'Will do.'

'And I want to hear all about it afterwards. Now, go forth and enjoy yourself.'

When he called back around ten thirty, Rob was clearly back in the pub. He sounded as if he'd won the Lottery.

'Easiest hundred and fifty quid I ever fucking made,' he shouted over the bar hubbub.

'Told you you'd be fine,' I laughed, caught up in his high spirits.

'Nah, you'll never believe it. She didn't want to go through with it.'

'No!' I was gob-smacked.

'You bet. We met at Dunkin Donuts, like you said. Off Piccadilly. And it lasted about forty minutes and we just had a cup of coffee. And that was it. We never even reached the hotel. And she still paid me!'

The jammy bastard.

'If it's that fucking easy, send me out to every woman you get,' he burbled.

'If it's that fucking easy, Rob, I'll keep them all to myself.'

Jenny called the following week. The only call we received. We weren't about to make a living out of this game just yet. Nor escape my shifts at the café and the pub anytime soon.

'Hello, Luke, it's Jenny.'

My mind went blank for a second. *Jenny?* I'd been so rushed off my feet with the waiting this week I'd almost forgotten about our advert. But then it all flooded back, and I went into receptionist mode straight away.

'Hello, Jenny, it's lovely to hear from you. Rob told me he enjoyed meeting you last week.'

Didn't he just.

'He was very nice.'

'See, I told you I'd give you a pleasant surprise,' I boasted.

'Yes, thank you. Um . . .'

There was an awkward silence. I jumped in feet first. This was a business we were running, after all.

'Is there anything we can do for you? Perhaps you'd like to see him again?'

When she spoke next, her voice was halting and quiet:

'The thing is, Luke, I'd like to meet you.'

You fucking bet. Rob's just made one hundred and fifty quid. Count me in.

'Is that allowed?'

This time I was ready. But first I had to cover myself so Jenny didn't start wondering why the last time she called I was just the receptionist.

'Well, Jenny, as it happens, we do have a policy when there's a run on the boys.' *Like heck we do.* 'We'd hate to leave any of our clients waiting.'

'So we can meet?' There was a hopeful girlishness to her voice.

'Certainly, Jenny.'

I began mentally spending the money on some decent jeans, a couple of CDs, and putting something towards the phone bill. The calls back home cost a bomb. And she'd even be paying for the coffee!

'Oh, I'm so glad. Because this time I want to go through with it. I want you to make love to me, Luke.'

14

There was a screech of brakes in my head.

Just my fucking luck.

'When would you like me to visit? And if I could take your address,' I asked, through gritted teeth I hoped she couldn't detect.

I scribbled down her details, said goodbye and hung up.

Yep, we were officially launched, Mark. Well and truly fucking launched . . .

Jenny

I caught my reflection in the tube window opposite but I couldn't look myself in the eye. I glanced down at my hands, gripped together in my lap to stop them shaking.

I don't need this stress in my life. I don't have to meet Jenny. I could get out at the next stop and go right home again.

This was it. My Day of Reckoning. My first time of making a go of the escort work and I was damned sure it showed on my face. I bit my lip and forced myself to look up at my fellow travellers, like what I was about to do was the most normal thing in the world.

I realised I was staring straight at a woman. I'd been so caught up in my thoughts I hadn't even registered her. I turned my head upwards to view the ad above her head. It told me which number to ring if I wanted to hire some air-con. I slipped a glance back at the girl. She was a couple of years older than me and was engrossed in her copy of *Metro*. She had dark eyes and smooth shoulder-length brunette hair with a fringe, and was better than average looking. An English rose.

You could, couldn't you?

That was the crux of the matter. I slipped a glance at all of the women on the seats around me and weighed up whether I would shag them or not. And wondered whether any of them looked anything like Jenny.

The tube drew into Shepherd's Bush and I got up. I swallowed back my nerves. I didn't want to think too much about what I was about to do. I turned left out of the station until I reached Jenny's street.

The further I followed the curve of Jenny's road, the seedier the terraced houses became. Her address had all the hallmarks of a cheap multiple occupancy. An unkempt front garden that nobody took any responsibility for. Check. Tatty labels taped next to the doorbells. Yup. Makeshift curtains at some of the windows. You bet. Rob had *so* had the better deal.

This was my very last chance to split. I braced myself and pressed Jenny's doorbell.

'Luke?' A tinny voice came through the intercom. 'Come on up.'

I pushed open the front door, crossed the scuzzy hallway and mounted the stairs two steps at a time while being careful not to slip on the worn floral carpet.

Jenny was waiting on the first floor at the entrance to her flat. She was dressed in an oversized navy jumper turned back at the cuffs and a calf-length striped cotton skirt.

'Gosh, you're a good-looking young man,' she blushed.

'Better than Rob?' I teased.

She looked down at her slippered feet. I cursed myself. Maybe she didn't want to be reminded that she'd done this before and bottled out.

I was as much trying to relax myself as her. It wasn't as if Jenny was ugly or anything. But she wore no makeup, and looked as if a harsh life had carved itself into her face. Her hair was short and black with white streaks and her colouring was mixed race, though I couldn't for the life of me make out where she came from. Yeah, I could do her.

'I liked how you sounded on the phone,' she said.

'What, startlingly handsome?'

What made things difficult was that she was closer to my

17

mother's age – she was in her forties or fifties, I couldn't be sure which, and that was a whole new ball game altogether. *That* kind of business hadn't been in either my or Mark's head when we'd decided to get into this lark. We thought we'd be inundated with requests from hot young chicks, desperate for no-strings sex, or busy career women without the time for a relationship. I still hoped we would.

Jenny's flat was sparsely furnished, aside from piles of unopened boxes. They were everywhere, and getting to the sofa in her living room was like wandering through a maze.

'Would you like a cup of tea?' she asked.

'Yes please,' I said, and stifled a laugh. Within a couple of days of getting here I'd realised that *that* was the Brits' answer to anything.

She went out to the kitchen, and I sat down among the cushions on the seen-better-days sofa, stretched out my legs and tried to make myself at home and calm the rising sense of dread.

An ancient tabby cat appeared at my feet from behind a box tower and rubbed itself up against my ankles. It was followed by a younger one, which settled itself on the worn rug in the middle of the room and licked its paw, watching me as if it were sizing me up.

Jenny came back into the room. This was going to be tricky, I could see. It was one thing to talk about sex with my mates down the pub or kicking a ball around in the park. It was going to be quite another to switch my brain into a gear that could talk about such stuff with someone like her.

And then I remembered what I'd advised Rob. To 'be every woman's dream'. To do what he always did but just to be a bit more of a gent as he went about it. That wasn't bad advice, even if I thought so myself. Mind you, it wasn't as if he'd had the chance to test it out.

Jenny had two matching floral china mugs in her hands, and

handed me one with a hesitant smile. She sat down a few inches from me.

'Thank you. That's a pair of handsome cats you've got there,' I said.

'Do you think so?' she blushed, as if it was a long time since anyone had complimented her on anything.

We drank our tea for a few horribly silent moments, until I placed the mug down beside my feet and gently took Jenny's hand in mine. She gave me a bashful smile, the lines around her eyes creasing a little, and funnily enough taking years off her. She reminded me of some scrubland creature you could only get up close to if you took it step by step, real quiet and slow.

No wonder Rob hadn't even got to first base.

I wasn't quite sure what the next move should be. But at least Jenny and I knew why I was in her home. And though I couldn't quite see it now, clearly she had a thread of steel running somewhere through her to pick up the phone and make the call in the first place. And not just once. She knew what she wanted, even if the challenge remained for me to move on from the friendly small talk without scaring her off.

'Shall we go to your bedroom?' I all but whispered.

Jenny bit her lip and nodded and we rose to our feet together. Still holding her hand, I remained a step behind her and followed her around the wall of boxes into a room off the hallway.

It was a bedroom only in name. There were more boxes but not even a mattress. Just sheets and a duvet and matching pillows set out on the carpet in the corner of the room. In place of a wardrobe were a couple of open suitcases draped with her clothes.

Jenny must have sensed my disquiet, much as I fought to hide it.

'It's not as if I get much sleep anyhow. I work all hours.'

'It'll be fine, Jenny,' I replied, and squeezed her hand as I stared down at her makeshift bed and wondered how we'd get from here to the actual sex. I chewed on the inside of my cheek, then took a deep breath and turned to face her.

'Would you like to sit with me on your bed?'

She nodded and I made an ungainly move towards the duvet and trusted she'd follow my cue.

Head in the right direction and somehow we'll get there. Surely.

We were sitting beside each other now. I threw her a tight-lipped smile as I gave her the once-over and worked out a plan of action. I didn't say anything but reached out and took hold of the hem of Jenny's jumper and raised it a couple of inches.

She looked back at me with her deep, dark eyes for a beat, then took the hint and stretched her arms behind her back and drew the jumper over her head. She shook it out, folded it and placed it on top of the pile of clothes in one of the suitcases. If we kept at this speed, the hour would be up before either of us got naked. Maybe that wasn't the worst that could happen. For either of us.

Jenny ran her fingers through her hair. Removing the jumper had taken pounds off her. She wore a short-sleeved cream blouse. I still had my shirt on. Which meant that we were sort of on the same page.

'I tell you what,' I instructed as I reached for my own top button, 'I'll undo my shirt the same time as you undo yours. Okay?'

Jenny nodded in response but she still didn't say anything. Her fingers fiddled with the little button at her throat and the cloth slowly parted. Her fingers dropped to the next in line but she kept her eyes from mine the whole time.

When she'd finished, her blouse was open and I could see her white bra beneath, but her head was still down and she was looking at her hands in her lap like she was ashamed.

I'd peeled my own shirt off without thinking. That's just how it was back home. The climate made it easier to remove your clothes, not that you didn't have to mind the sun. I'd been told about the Page 3 girls the Brits had in their papers before I came, but the people here didn't seem like that at all. They wore layers because the weather changed so often. It had to be a *really* hot day by their standards for them to relax and strip down, and then it was like they did it with a real relief. Here with Jenny, I could see that it was vital that I respected a client and how comfortable or not she felt at every stage. The way to do that was to mirror her speed of undressing – though to take care to chivvy her along if I had to.

There was nothing I could do, it seemed, but spell out to Jenny what was needed and only hope that I didn't scare her. I feared that if I went at her pace we'd never get anywhere. And the longer it took, the more gruelling it'd be for me too.

'Jenny, slip off your skirt and underwear, will you, and while you're doing that I'll get myself ready.'

There. I'd said it. I'd made it clear what came next and there was no going back. I pulled off my jeans and my Calvins, and fished in a pocket for a condom. By the time I'd turned back towards her she was stretched out and waiting. She'd taken her blouse off but kept her bra on.

I realised I'd had nothing to worry about. Jenny wasn't bad for her age, I could say *that*. She had the soft edges I'd expected, something to hold on to, which wasn't the type of woman I was used to, but wasn't something that repulsed me as I'd feared either. I was still going to have to give myself a helping hand though. She hadn't stirred me *that* much.

Jenny's eyes were fixed above my waistline all the while I nestled down beside her. I wrapped my arms around her and held her close for a few minutes to put her at her ease. One of her fingers drew a little nervous circle round and round on my chest.

'I'm just going to protect myself,' I whispered as I pulled myself gently away from her, 'and then I'm going to make love to you.'

Just then I realised that the words I used and the way I spoke were as important as the sex act itself to Jenny. She was as nervous as hell and it was up to me to take account of that and make things good for her. But it wasn't just about Jenny. Whatever happened after this, *this* was my first professional job. If I thought too much about that, I knew my performance would suffer – and Jenny's enjoyment. Yet if I forgot I was providing a service, it wouldn't be fair on her either. It was a fine line to walk. I fixed my mind back on my client. That was surely the key.

I took as much care as any guy can when he's jutting into a woman. Jenny gasped and clung tight to me as my body lapped and battered against her then juddered to a halt.

I lay against her saying nothing for a couple of minutes and she stroked the back of my head.

'This isn't my first time, you know, Luke, though I'm some-what out of practice,' she said in a quiet but matter-of-fact voice.

That took me by surprise. It was as if the sex had broken her silence. I propped myself up on one arm to look at her lying there beside me.

'Don't diss yourself, Jenny. You were fine,' I lied. She'd barely moved the whole way through, though it wasn't as if I'd been expecting some sex-tiger anyhow.

'I used to work in nightclubs, y'know. My boyfriend owned one and was a big promoter too. But that was a long time ago,' she said with wistfulness. 'It didn't work out. And that was that. There's been no one since.'

She made it sound so final. Which I suppose it was. Life had been hard.

'But you've nothing to worry about, Jenny. You're a lovely lady.'

I wasn't lying this time. True, she needed more experience and a whole boost to her confidence, but she didn't seem to have any edge to her. She was genuinely nice.

When Jenny spoke again, it was as if her mind was on another track and she sounded like she was somewhere else in her life.

'And after him I fell ill, and by the time I was back on my

feet, all my hours were taken up making ends meet. Still are. I haven't had the time for anyone since.'

I sat up, my legs stretched out across the carpet.

'So, it was quite something to call me and Rob out, then. You could have put the money towards a new bed.'

I regretted it as soon as I'd said it. Jenny looked at me, pained, and I wanted to swallow the words right back. Shit. It was none of my business. I'd stepped horribly out of line. But Jenny, to her credit, collected herself admirably.

'I saw your advert, Luke,' she said, stroking my arm with boldness, 'and it reminded me of all I'd been missing. Not just the sex, but someone else's touch and the tenderness. You've given me that this evening. It's been lovely.'

'My pleasure,' I replied. And meant it. She hadn't been what I'd been hoping for, but in a small way I felt proud. I'd helped out someone who obviously needed it.

We slipped off the duvet and got to our feet. I hugged her, and as I did I checked my watch. She had ten minutes left and I still had to get dressed.

'I'm going to have to be leaving shortly,' I said as I picked up my clothes.

'I'd like to see you again, Luke. But not for sex or anything.'

I didn't get it. Hadn't she just told me that it was the tenderness she craved?

'I'd like just to meet you for tea, and for us to talk, that's all. Like I did with Rob? I'd pay you for your time. Isn't that what escorting is about?'

'Yes, but . . .'

Jenny held up her hand to stop me – 'Wait a minute' – quickly pulled her clothes back on and left the room. I got dressed. She returned a few minutes later with a wad of notes as I was buttoning up my shirt. She counted out the £150 onto a box lid and I scooped it up and folded it into my wallet. The easiest money I'd ever made.

I thought of how Rob had felt he'd won the jackpot. Which he had, for a mere chat over a coffee. Wasn't what Jenny was now offering me the simplest part of this job? But it didn't seem right.

'I'd just like to see you for half an hour, before I go to work?'

'Look, Jenny, I can't have you pay for just that.'

'But you're not going to meet me for nothing, are you?'

She had a point. I was running a business, wasn't I?

'Well, no . . . But even so.'

Jenny took my wrist in her hand, and spoke without looking in my eyes.

'I won't hear another word, Luke. I'll give you fifty pounds. How's that?'

And then I got the message. She needed to pay *something*. She might have been hard-up but she had no need of my pity.

'It's a deal.' And just like that I had my first repeat customer.

'So, she was a right little goer, was she?' leered Mark when I met him later in the local. He had just returned from the bar with our two pints. He set mine down in front of me and grabbed a chair, and I looked down into the mouth of the glass and the deep liquid. I lifted the beer to my lips and took a gulp. I didn't know what to say. Because Jenny was outside what either of us had imagined, that was for sure.

'Well?'

Mark wasn't going to let up. He was facing me across the table, and this felt like an interview.

I set down my glass and flashed a 'don't go there' glare.

'Oh, come on, Luke. We're in this together, aren't we? You can tell me.'

I cradled my jaw in one hand, the other wrapped around my pint.

'Look, the thing is, you weren't there with me in the room, were you?'

'Oh, if that was what she wanted, she only had to ask!' he grinned, before knocking back more of his beer.

I shook my head at him and chuckled. For a second.

'God, Mark. Be serious. It wasn't like that. *She* wasn't like that, y'know.'

There was a glint of anger in his eye.

'What, suddenly you're Mr Professional Escort all of a sudden? After *one* paid lay. Don't make me laugh.'

'No, listen. I didn't mean that,' I pleaded. 'It was just . . . Jenny, she . . .'

'*Jenny*,' he sneered.

I ignored him. 'Jenny is just someone who needed a bit of TLC.'

I spoke into my glass and heard my own voice grow quieter. I looked up at Mark and I could see he was listening.

'And don't we all,' I sighed.

Jenny was hovering outside the Starbucks in Piccadilly. She hadn't yet seen me approach. Her feet were turned slightly inward, and she was focused on the paving stones in front of them. One hand gripped the other against her thigh.

'Jenny, it's lovely to see you.' I touched her shoulder and she turned towards me, a huge smile lighting up her face. I hugged her and felt her body relax against mine.

I ushered her into the café and went and ordered coffees for the two of us. She said nothing as I placed them on the table in front of us and sat myself down, but there was an expectant warmth across her face.

'So, I didn't put you off ever seeing me again, then?' I smiled.

'Oh, no, Luke.'

A tinge of pale pink washed across her face.

I flicked a look around the coffee shop and to the milling crowds in the street outside. We couldn't have been more anonymous. *I might even be mistaken for Jenny's son.*

'So, do you have family in London?' I asked.

She fiddled with the handle of her cup, and shook her head.

'I've got a sister but I've lost touch with her. I've been trying to track her down.'

She changed the subject. 'And you? That's not an English accent.'

'No.'

'Well, it's not as if you'll ever be alone in the Big City. There are plenty of Australians here.'

'Yeah,' I grinned back.

God, had I found that out. When I was out with Mark and our mates it was sometimes hard to remember that we were anywhere else but back home.

I switched the focus back to her. I was on her time after all.

'You said when we last met that you'd be off to work after this.'

She nodded. 'Yes, just round the corner. I'm a cleaner at a number of the clubs round here,' she explained. 'I spruce them up before they open, and afterwards when everyone's left.'

Grim, tough work.

'You see a different side of the city, then.'

She cocked her head at me. The words hung in the air. She didn't want to talk about work. This was her break.

'Tell me about yourself, Jenny. Have you always lived in London?'

That was the cue for her life story. It poured out. How she'd never been quite good enough. The rest of her family were teachers but she'd gone into the clubbing scene. And how when that'd fizzled out she'd ended up cleaning other people's clubs. She just wanted to talk. Just needed someone to listen.

Jenny's time was up. But it was she who made the move to go. She was the one who was racing against the clock. I, on the other hand, had plenty of time to kill until my evening shift at the pub.

She gripped the table as if ready to stand up. And then

slipped back down in her chair like she had just thought of something.

'Luke, I've got to go to work. And we haven't had much time together.'

'It's flown by, hasn't it?'

She reached into her shoulder bag and pulled out a small roll of notes and gathered them in her hand and scrunched them into my own in the hope that no one would see. I pushed my clenched fist and its contents into the back pocket of my jeans.

'I'd like to see you again, Luke.'

'Would you like me to come to your flat again?' I fished.

She looked at me and pursed her lips. 'When I said I wanted to meet you for tea, I didn't mean it to be a one-off. I'd like to see you again. To talk, I mean.'

'You mean here again? Like today?'

She nodded. 'On a weekly basis. Before work, like today.'

I let her see me weigh it up in my mind, like I was working out if I could fit her into my busy schedule.

Like hell I could.

But at the same time I couldn't help thinking that Jenny wasn't what I'd quite bargained for when I'd decided to offer sex for sale. She clearly needed someone to talk to. A listening ear, then, was going to be another vital organ in this game.

A Bit of Give and Take

The joy of sex is that it's not just about *your* pleasure. Consider the other person in the relationship and the benefits will be felt by both of you. As an ordinary guy, I know what guys tend to want, but having made my living as an escort, I've learned what brings the most pleasure to women too. Follow the tips through *Undercover* and it'll be win, win for everyone!

1. Introducing yourself

So, you see someone you like the look of across a crowded dance floor or bar.

- Smile, go and say 'hello', relax and be friendly.
- Focus on *them*, find something to compliment, flirt with your words, eyes and hands.
- Guys, don't talk about the latest football scores, mistake joke-telling for a GSOH, or try too hard to impress with magic tricks and the like.
- Girls, retain some mystery. Hold back on the life story and any problems you have. Find a mutual interest but don't fake it; he'll see right through it and it'll sound desperate.
- The sooner either of you gets to talk about sex, the more up for it you'll sound. You'll certainly grab *his* interest!
- And if you get the brush-off? Hold your head up high, put it down to experience – and *their* loss – take a deep breath and live to love another day.

Clare

Mid September

The phone's ringing was crashing through my head. I'd only got in from the pub a couple of hours ago, and I had to crawl out of bed to go and answer it. I checked the alarm clock as I stumbled out of the room: 5.20 a.m. And I was due back at the café at ten. My brain hurt just thinking it.

'Hello, my name's Clare. I saw your advert. I'd like one of your escorts to come over. Now.'

Please, God, no.

Of course, I could have told her that it was just not possible, too short notice, and gone straight back beneath my duvet. But Clare was only the second woman to call in three weeks. And if we were going to make a go of things then we needed every client who came our way.

But please, not at this time of the morning.

'The thing is, Clare, it's just gone five. I can't see any of the boys being free to come out to you at this hour. Later today, or this evening, it'd be no problem.'

I stifled a yawn. I could barely keep my eyes open.

'That's a shame, because I do really want to see someone now. I guess I'll just have to call another agency.'

Why couldn't you have done that in the first place and then I'd still be asleep?

29

But now I'd answered the phone it made good business sense to do everything I could to keep Clare sweet. It was important people came off the phone feeling good about us. I racked my still mashed brains.

'I tell you what. I'll ring round and see. I'm sure to be able to find one of the guys to come right on over. I'll get back to you as soon as I know who.'

Like there were going to be any contenders at this time of the morning. It was going to have to be me or Mark.

'Thanks for your trouble.'

'All part of the service, Clare, all part of the service,' I grimaced, and put the receiver down. I stumbled out of the living room and back across the hall to our room. I hovered at the doorway. Through the darkness I could see the duvet mound of Mark's dead-to-the-world carcass. He'd had the good fortune not to have been woken by the phone. I was tempted to give him a good kick just so he could suffer as much as me.

But I didn't. I took a deep breath and shut the door with a quiet click and went back to the phone.

'Good news – I've got a guy for you. If you can just give me your address, I'll pass it on to him. He should be with you by seven, is that okay?'

I hung up, and went and made myself a mug of strong black coffee.

Clare lived out in the north-west London suburbs, Greenford way. The roads were quiet and the morning sunlight beyond the cab window was pleasantly subdued for my bug eyes. There was a feeling of space, of wide streets and grass verges, and long front gardens. Hardly anyone was about.

I walked up the path and opened the door to the porch, stepped in and closed it behind me. The doorbell chimed against my hangover. Through the mottled glass I could make out the svelte figure of Clare coming towards me.

She pulled open the front door.

'Luke, I presume. Do come in,' she smiled.

My spirits rallied. *That's more like it. I'd have happily gone home with you last night for free.*

I don't know what I'd been expecting, but she wasn't it. Someone more *suburban*, I suppose, whatever that meant. Clare was in her late twenties, and given the unearthly hour of the morning she had a sexy glossiness about her. She had shoulder-length brown hair and a classic beauty, like Lauren Bacall. She was wearing a scarlet silk dressing gown over a floor-length cream nightdress. I, on the other hand, felt – and suspected I looked – like garbage.

She didn't seem to mind though. She looked up at the staircase but it was as if she had second thoughts. She swivelled on her kitten-heel mules.

'Come on through to the lounge.'

I stepped through and she closed the door firmly behind me. The sharp click of the latch was like a switch in my brain. It was a split-second sense of unease. Probably my lack of sleep making me jittery.

Smarten up, Luke. Look at where you are.

I was in a sexy woman's front room, in a nice house in suburbia, and she wanted to sit down and feel comfortable and relaxed and have a drink with a guy like me. That was all.

'I'm having a whisky and soda. Would you like one?'

'Yes, thanks.'

Hair of the dog. And some.

She gestured me towards her leather sofa and I sank into it as she fixed the drinks. The respite was all fine by me, because I needed to ease into the right groove if the sex was going to go well. The alcohol would help kick-start my confidence.

How many clients does it take before it's all water off a duck's back?

Clare handed me a glass, and stood before me and watched me take a sip, then took a sip of her own. She ran her gleaming white teeth over her top lip.

'Look, you don't mind if we don't use the bedroom?'

I shook my head. 'Nope. Wherever you're happy,' I smiled, trying to put her at her ease.

She looked over at the closed door. 'I like to keep the noise out, you know.'

Clare bent her head towards me and drew the hand that wasn't holding her whisky glass up my neck so my upturned lips met hers.

Actually, I didn't know. Okay, people would start leaving their homes about now to go to work, but apart from the odd slammed door and cars passing the house, it wasn't exactly Piccadilly Circus around here.

Then she tensed and pulled away from me as if someone had walked across her grave. And whoever it was, at that moment they'd walked over mine too.

What is it? There's something not quite right about this set-up.

My head was in no fit state to make much sense of what the hell was happening, but a moment later Clare had gathered herself together and it was as if any unease she'd just felt now spurred her on. Falling to her knees, she set down her glass by my feet and grabbed at my belt and unbuckled it *fast*. She was dragging my jeans from my hips even as I was pulling off my shirt.

Clare's hands were around my dick and she was drawing her open mouth to it and I was scrabbling around in my pockets for protection while all the while my body couldn't have given a damn. And I held the condom out to her and those inviting lips of hers halted in mid 'O' and she flicked an evil grin up at me from between my legs. 'Sixty-nine,' she growled, and grabbed at my waist, and we struggled and tumbled together onto the rough of the carpet.

Hers was a damn practised mouth that jackhammered me to my senses and slewed off my shattered drunken skin. I drew her nightdress up from her ankles along the length of her legs towards me and buried my face in its silk before burrowing beneath it with my tongue. Clare writhed with pleasure as I licked her clean.

I flickered licks and kisses over her belly towards the uplands of her breasts and she rose on her elbows to meet me and I wiped my mouth on the back of my hand and kissed her. I kicked my legs from under me and entwined them with hers and drew her down towards the floor again.

I ran my hand up her smooth thigh and she eyed me with desire.

'You're my birthday present,' she whispered as I leaned back and ripped the wrapper off another condom with my teeth.

'What?' I raised my eyebrows.

'I celebrated with friends last night but you're my private party,' she grinned.

'Happy birthday,' I replied as I thrust into her.

She gasped, and her legs on reflex buckled upwards, caging me between them. Her hands on my back gripped tighter. I got into my stride, my eyes all the while intent on her. The rise of her breasts in unison with my own rhythmic drive towards her, the taut honeyed length of her neck, her handsome jaw-line jutting upwards, her closed eyes and the healthy thickness of her hair. And half a metre away was the telly on a corner-stand, and below it the DVD player, and on the slim shelf between them a revolver.

What the fuck . . .?

I'd never before seen a real live gun. Or maybe it was fake. But the point was, I had no idea. And Clare was within reaching distance.

She could clip me right here and nobody would know. All my friends are asleep. I could just vanish into thin air, and nobody would ever know.

It wasn't as if she even looked in that direction. She was too busy being pleasured by me. But if she'd got a gun in the house, what on earth was it for? Protection against me? Or against someone else? I certainly couldn't concentrate on the sex any more. I just wanted out of there.

The lovemaking slowed to a halt and Clare and I drew apart. I tried to act as if nothing was the matter. Our session would soon be drawing to a close – the minutes were ticking by. We settled back on the sofa.

'Would you like a coffee?' she asked.

'No, no, I'm fine.'

'I could certainly do with one. You stay here.'

No, you stay here. I don't want you anywhere but here.

If she remained with me then I had some chance of controlling the situation. Out of my sight, I hadn't a clue what she might be up to. But I couldn't say anything without alerting her suspicions and she left the room.

So, my hunch earlier had been right and not just a figment of my drink-addled imagination. There *was* something out of kilter about this place. I tried to avoid looking at the gun but it had a magnetic appeal. I anxiously looked away. I didn't want Clare to come back in and find me staring at it.

The more I thought about it, the more I was certain it wasn't just the two of us in the house either. During the sex, I'd had the distinct impression we were being watched, even though the door was shut. I hadn't a clue how anybody could see us, but I just *felt* it. It gave me the creeps.

Or maybe I was just imagining things. You could scare yourself shitless if you wanted to. I flicked another look over at the ledge beneath the telly. The gun was still there. I damn well wasn't imagining *that*, that's for sure.

Suddenly, I heard muttering outside the door. My whole

body stiffened. I didn't give a damn about the money. I just wanted to collect my stuff and get the hell out of there. Seconds later, Clare came back into the room with a mug of coffee in her hand. I tried to act as if nothing was wrong. We even had sex again because I just wanted to do what was needed to get out of there as quickly as possible. The gun in my head I had to force into the shape of my cock battering Clare's pussy so I could perform. I didn't even need to wait for her to call a cab. I could do that myself once I was down the street and away from here.

But I didn't need to. She'd already arranged it for me and gave me my fee and the fare. When the cab came to collect me, I took one last wary look at the gun under the telly. I was back in the porch before Clare asked if she could phone for me again.

'No problem,' I muttered. 'No problem.' Hoping desperately that she wouldn't. And I walked out into the early morning sunshine, hurried down the garden path without a look back, and climbed into the car and was out of there.

'So, how goes it, stud?' Mark threw at me across the grass as we lounged around after our regular evening kick-around in the park.

Mark knew perfectly well how things were going with the escort work. I'd gone to bed as soon as I'd got back from a gruelling stint at the café to catch up on the lost zeds and told him about my time with Clare when he came in later from his temping job. He'd seemed impressed with the combo of hot sex and danger. He was just asking now to pique the interest of the other guys.

It worked. There was an incredulous look on one or two of their faces.

'Stud, Luke? Since when?' teased Simon as he rolled the ball from hand to hand.

I rested a foot on the opposite knee and picked at the caked mud on the sole of my trainer with a lolly-stick I'd found in the long grass.

'Since my balls dropped, mate. But you wouldn't know about that, would you?' I flung back, to laughter from the others.

And was rewarded with the football hitting my head, knocking me sideways.

I rolled to the ground in mock collapse and stretched out, held my hands behind my neck, and watched the clouds shift high above me. The image of self-satisfaction. For a split second the fading sun and the sky were blotted out as Rob passed within inches and went and collected the ball. He looked down at me.

'Have you seen Jenny again?'

'Over a cup of tea.'

I didn't feel the need to say anything more than that.

Paul looked at Rob and then at me and back again like we had some conspiracy going on.

'Jenny? Who's Jenny?'

'Oh, Jenny's an Older Woman. She answered our ad,' smirked Rob. 'I've *met* her,' he crowed as if he wanted people to consider him as much the stud too. Like meeting a client for a cuppa was real hot sex-work.

Mark was far more interested in the girl and the gun.

'Luke was called out at *dawn* yesterday morning. For sizzling suburban sex!'

There was a chorus of *No?* and *Really?* around me. I did a couple of sit-ups and then sat up to survey the lot of them.

'Oh yes, my friends,' I grinned.

'You've *actually* had replies to the ad? I just thought it was a bit of a laugh,' admitted Simon. He had the ball again and had stood up and was bouncing it up and down.

At least he was honest. I wasn't quite sure how to take it. I shrugged my shoulders and looked up at him, my arm above my eyes to cut out the fading sun's glare.

'Well, y'know, we made a serious enough effort to get the women calling.'

'I couldn't do it . . .' Simon stuttered. 'Imagine if it came out that a local schoolteacher was on the game? I'd lose my job. I'd have to go back home with my tail between my legs.'

He pursed his lips as if he was thinking up some further excuse not to get involved, and resumed his bouncing. He didn't realise that he didn't need to. I understood.

'No worries. That just means all the more clients for everyone else!' I beamed, trying to make it easier for him to back out.

'You know I can't get involved,' blurted out Mark. 'Before I started going out with Natasha, yes. But not now.'

Mark had only been dating his new girlfriend for a few weeks but he was already getting serious about her. So he was into escort work by proxy, then. I let his words hang in the air. I saw no point in making an issue of it.

'So, this suburban sex siren. What was she like?' piped up Rob, who wanted to get back to the crux of the matter.

'Oh, how you'd expect a suburban sex siren to be,' I replied, with as enigmatic a smile as I could muster. 'It was her twenty-ninth birthday the day before, but I was her own personal gift to herself. Waiting to be unwrapped.'

Rich sighed a high-pitched whistle and shook his head in disbelief. 'Hang on,' he countered. 'If there *are* girls out there who are willing to pay for it, how come *you're* having all the fun? What about passing on some of these gorgeous hordes to the rest of us?'

'I met Jenny,' reminded Rob. 'Easy money,' he crowed.

I drew my legs towards me and rested my chin on my knees. It was time to come clean.

'That's just it,' I said. 'Jenny and Clare have been the only callers.'

Rich whistled again. 'When did we do the photos? A couple

of months ago?' He looked at me with genuine concern. 'Fuck, Luke. How are you supposed to live? I hate to break it to you, but an average of a client a month is hardly great – there's no way you can survive.'

For a few minutes nobody said anything. When Rich put it like that, the escort life had very little going for it.

'Well, it's early days yet,' I rallied. 'It'll build up gradually. That's how it works. It's sure to. The girls'll come *flooding* in. It just takes a while for things to get going. Y'know, like any business.'

I heard myself say the words and for a split second wondered if I was trying to convince myself as much as everyone else.

'We didn't expect it to be an overnight success, did we, Mark?' I looked directly at him, willing him to back me up on this.

Mark replied with a sympathetic smile.

'But don't give up the day jobs, eh?'

'The day *jobs*,' echoed Paul. 'I don't know how you juggle it, Luke. How you'll manage if – sorry, when – the work starts pouring in?'

'I'll cross that bridge when we come to it,' I murmured in response, trying to look on the bright side. I hadn't yet worked that out myself.

'I'll stick with the temp work, if you don't mind,' continued Paul. 'I want to have something decent to put on my CV when my work visa runs out. Something to show for my time here.'

The sun was going down and had got stuck behind a cloud. There was a definite chill in the air. I shivered. Each one of them had dropped out of our grand scheme. If they'd ever dropped in in the first place.

And then it hit me between the eyes. Out of the guys I was the only one who seemed to consider this business was in any way worth pursuing. Suppose none of them had been truly into it in the first place? Even Mark, who'd only just started dating Natasha, had been a bit *too* quick to change his mind.

Oh fuck. They were joking?

A cold shiver passed through me again. The mucking about for the photo shoot. It was all for the hell of it. And there was me presuming I was the reticent one hiding behind the phone so I could pass the buck on to someone else.

I swallowed back a breaker of nausea, and trusted that nobody could see through the evening gloom what I was only now working out. Even Rob, my one-time partner in crime who'd at least dipped his toes in the escort pool, would be leaving to continue his Europe walkabout in a couple of weeks.

'I've got to go,' said Simon. 'I've got some marking to finish off. I'll see whoever can make it here tomorrow?'

It was the signal for all of us to go our separate ways for the night. Simon picked up his ball. I pulled on my jacket and got up to leave with the others.

I didn't sleep very well that night. What the guys had said in the park had been playing on my mind. I checked the time on my alarm clock: 6.05 a.m. I had just under an hour before anyone in the house got up. I sat on the side of my bed to collect my thoughts. My gaze fell on the adjacent hulk of Mark, still fast asleep. Looking as if he hadn't a care in the world. Whereas I was facing the worry of figuring out how to make my new line of business work. Because there really were only two choices. I could throw in the towel right now with the lot of them. That would be the easy option. I'd work my way out of the crummy jobs into something that would at least have some currency when I went back to Australia. Or I could carry on the way I was heading. Alone.

Because, for all Rich's genuine concern that I might be heading nowhere fast, I remained convinced that I *could* make a business out of escort work. After all, hadn't Jenny and Clare proved to me that there was at least *some* work out there in London? Even if so far it had just been the two of them. I had no one to compare notes with, but getting two clients in two months in a market that clearly nobody was sure was even out there, wasn't the *worst* that could happen.

Or maybe Rich was right and I wouldn't be able to survive. There simply wasn't the business out there. The girls weren't biting because for some reason it simply wasn't their bag. Jenny and Clare were the exception to the rule.

I pinched the bridge of my nose to sharpen my thoughts. I knew what I had to do. I was in one of the biggest cities in the world, and there were definitely plenty of women out there who had money to spend *and* were sexually up for it. You could see that on a Saturday night at any club you found yourself in. Most, if not all of them, used the internet. Which meant that the key was for me to somehow get their web attention.

I rose to my feet, took a deep breath to clear my head, and padded through to the lounge. I sat and faced the computer screen, my hands hovering above the keyboard as I wondered what to type. My fingers slid over the keys, not entirely sure what my next move should be.

Almost without thought I logged into the Male Escorts Esquire site and scrolled down the pictures of me and the guys. I shook my head and winced at how amateur and half-hearted they looked. What had we been thinking? Frankly, we'd been lucky to have even had *two* clients. Our gormless pics and a couple of tiny ads in the London freesheets were never going to be enough. If I was going to be serious about this then I had to up my game. And I'd *have* to be damn serious, since running your own successful business as an escort counted for nothing in the job market. While my friends were building up their work experience, I would be effectively opting out. Any people skills I picked up in this game would count for absolutely nothing. Which gave me all the more reason to promote myself damn hard and squirrel away as much cash as I could, so I had something to show for myself when I eventually returned home.

I had to cast my net wider.

I recalled something I'd said to Mark back when we were just thinking about advertising our wares. That the girls weren't looking because they weren't aware there was a service for them. And that's where we'd been going wrong.

My fingers set to work. I googled London Escort Agencies. The first page that came up was enough evidence that there was plenty of work out there. For the women and the gay guys, anyhow. As far as I could see, the straight male escort line was all but untried. From my next Google nationwide search, there seemed to be a grand total of three other gigolos working across the whole of Britain.

Not that any of them really used the term 'gigolo' these days. 'Escort' was the catch-all phrase, but the trouble was that if a guy called himself an escort then it was invariably assumed that he was gay. *Or at least up for it.* If you were only catering for girls then you had to stress your hetero-ness. And from what I could see, that alone made you stand out in the crowd.

I accessed a guy called Greg Allen's site. He was based in Birmingham. Miles away. He looked serious about his escort work. Professional. I couldn't tell how successful his business was, but one thing I had over him was that I wasn't living any place due north.

I logged into Male Escorts Esquire again and homed in on my own photo.

Could do better.

But with the right photo I knew I had as much to offer as the other hetero male escorts out there. I already had a pretty successful hit rate at most bars I went to. I'd never quite stuck around for my dates to develop into girlfriends, but that didn't really bother me. I wasn't the settling-down kind, for now at any rate. The sex was fun, and the girls had been up for it. I could see no reason why it shouldn't be the same for me in this game.

41

I entered a few escort sites to see if I might learn something from their approach. There were *hordes* of stunning girls available. And they clearly knew how to sell themselves. They spent decent money on their pictures, you could tell, but what's more they had a whole range of them done to give potential clients a good idea of what they'd be getting. Portraits, full-length shots, semi-naked. And in-your-face ones. And crucially these escorts got signed up with internet agencies so that they didn't have to do all the spade work. I'd presumably have to pay them something, but at least they'd get me started.

One or two of the girls, I noted, had their own websites. Like Greg Allen. That was something to think about further down the line. But for now it was enough to get my name around.

I homed in on a couple of the girls' introductory shots, the ones that were on the agency's main page. The taster pics. They were mostly full-length portraits that hinted at what was to come. All I needed for starters would be some decent photos taken of me that I could circulate with a potted biog to as many of these agencies as possible. And once I started making money I'd be able to afford to get more pictures done. All being well, the pics would end up paying for themselves. If I was one of only a handful of guys on the site advertising my wares, then so much the better.

I reached for a biro and a scrap of paper and began to list what I had to do. Pictures. A basic outline of who I was and what I had to offer. Plus, find the names and contact details of as many agencies as possible.

I logged into Gumtree, which had served me so well when I was looking for a room. A photography student was offering free portraits so he could build up his portfolio. That was *exactly* the deal I was after to help get me launched. I emailed him immediately.

Buoyed up, I grinned to myself. The guys would be made to eat their words! I knew *exactly* what I had to do to make a success of this thing. They might not have faith, but I'd always had some level of hope that there was the work out there.

Lots of sex, and money to be made. What guy wouldn't kill for a job like that?

Louise

Louise was lying on her bed looking up at me, as pleased as punch with herself. I, on the other hand, was straddled over her having just deflowered her.

'My boyfriend's going to thank you for this, Luke. Not that I'm ever going to tell him, of course,' Louise grinned.

'No, you wouldn't want to do that.' I shook my head and dismounted so I was now lying beside her. 'I don't mind helping a couple out. But I'll have you know it's not my brief to cause any break-ups.' I winked.

Louise was proof that it had been worthwhile sending my details to the agencies. I'd quickly had to get used to them not quite understanding where I was coming from or who I was offering my services to. It seemed to me that the managers were as unconvinced as my mates that there was a female market out there. They hadn't found one to date, they told me, yet they were at least still open to giving me a space to see if there might be. Just in case. If they already carried a male escort section on their site, it invariably gave off a strong gay aura. The offer of sex was explicit, the photos left little to the imagination. My picture, on the other hand, looked as if it had been taken by some respectable high-street photographer. I was fully dressed for one thing, and standing looking friendly at the camera.

44

Louise explained how she'd trawled the escort sites looking for help. She'd seen my picture on the Dream Lovers website and liked what she saw of me.

'Some of those other men scare me a bit,' she'd told me when she'd called.

I knew exactly what she meant. They scared *me* too.

'Well, Louise, you're talking to the right person. I can assure you that I'm not in the business of terrifying anyone.'

There'd been a marked silence at the end of the line. When she'd next spoken her voice was quieter.

'It's just that I've never done it before,' she'd stammered. 'I don't mean calling an escort. Sex, like. Never.'

'I've got a boyfriend!' Louise blurted out, like it was damn important that she made *that* clear.

It was just after I'd arrived and she was sitting scrunched up in the corner of her sofa, her arms wrapped round her legs and her chin on her knees. And as I sat next to her I wondered how the hell I was going to get her to move to her bed and get on with things without scaring her off.

I reached out my hand to grab hold of hers, which hung limply beside her calf. She gripped tightly and turned to look at me from behind her fringe with huge blue eyes.

'Pete and I have been going out for eight months and we've kissed and everything but we've never *slept* together,' she explained, sensing I needed to hear the story. 'I can't keep telling him that I don't feel ready. But the trouble is that I'm embarrassed to let him know I've never had sex. *At all.*'

Louise's hold had lightened as she spoke as if it was somehow a relief to tell someone this stuff. And I could see why. I nodded back at her in an attempt to reassure her.

'And the longer you leave it, the harder it becomes to let him know?'

She nuzzled her kneecaps in silence, and then she addressed them.

'It's my friends too. They all did it *ages* ago, and I'm twenty-two and by now . . .'

Louise's words petered out but I knew *exactly* where she was coming from. Because everyone was 'at it' these days, weren't they? In the papers and celeb mags and on telly. So, if you still hadn't got over that hurdle you had to ask yourself what was keeping you. Let alone find the words to begin to try and explain it to someone you cared about.

God, I'd been a late starter myself as far as my group of mates were concerned. When I was seventeen, I'd lost my virginity at a high-school party to an older girl I'd hardly known, just to get it out of the way. Back then I'd been as shy about it as Louise was now. But the older girl had been good for me, the experience a positive one. And I'd sure made up for lost time since.

'But you've done something about it. That's why you called me, isn't it?' I smiled across at her. 'You've got nothing to worry about, Louise,' I half-whispered. 'I'm going to take care of you.'

That seemed to do the trick and unlock any fear Louise might have had. She unfurled her long legs out beyond the sofa's edge and sat up. She took my hand and reached towards me and kissed me with a boldness I wasn't expecting. She was signalling that she was only a complete novice when it came to the sex itself. Or at least that was the impression she was trying to give.

It was to be my job then to be the practice run, the stabilisers on the bicycle. Or that was at least how I'd decided to see myself. And if there were other reluctant virgins after Louise, then I'd treat those girls just as well – and trust that their guys would enjoy the change in them too.

God, I should charge the boyfriends commission!

I stood up and Louise followed my cue. Hers was a studio flat and she'd used the back of her sofa to create the boundary between her bed space and her 'living room'. I took her hand and led her round the furniture and sat her down at the end of her bed.

'I'm going to undo your blouse. I'm going to take it *real* slow,' I reassured her. My fingers reached for her top button and I sensed Louise's whole body stiffen beside me. I mentally pursed my lips and wondered what other way might help ease her into the action.

'I tell you what, Louise, I'll take your hand in mine and you lead me through it,' I suggested.

It was a gamble – spelling every action out loud might deaden our time together, but at the same time it was important to let on where I might be heading with things. I didn't want to shock her into going no further. Hopefully we'd get to a point where the lovemaking gained its own momentum without the need for words.

It became almost a game, Louise undressing herself beneath my hand. And as she reached some level of confidence, she began to undo the buttons of my own shirt. While she was engrossed in that, I removed my hand from hers and got rid of my jeans. Her hands and eyes were now exploring my chest, and I wrapped my arms around her and pulled her down onto the bed with me. I held her to me and softly stroked her belly.

'If at any time you think I'm taking things too fast or want me to stop, you just let me know, okay?'

I bent my head towards her and kissed her full on the lips and her mouth opened for me. I felt her whole body relax.

I pulled away. For a split second a flush of disappointment swept across her face.

'You were all right with that? You're doing fine, Louise. I've just got to get myself ready.'

She lay there patiently while I removed my boxers and sorted out the protection. Being responsible for both my own *and* my client's sake was all part of the job. I stocked up on the condoms at my monthly check-ups at the sex workers' clinic. And I'd made damn sure I stuck to *those* ever since Day One with Jenny. If Louise was telling the truth about her inexperience – and I had no reason to believe she wasn't – then I wasn't expecting to catch anything. But I had no way of knowing if she was on the pill.

I was all geared up. And then Louise's hand pushed flat up against my chest like a *Stop!* sign. She looked deeply worried.

'Just a little while longer,' she murmured.

'No worries.'

Louise bit her lip. I knew time was ticking away. She would be paying me and the agency £250 for the two-hour session and I was determined to make every minute count for her. It wouldn't be just about the sex but the level of tenderness too. 'You never forget your first time' went the saying, and I was damned sure that she wouldn't do – and for all the right reasons. This time together was meant to be special.

I nibbled Louise's earlobe, then flickered my tongue in the dip where her jaw met her neck and traced a line of kisses from there down to her cleavage. She stretched back in pleasure. As I nestled between her breasts, I swept one hand over her midriff's smooth skin to the far side of her lithe frame so I had her waist between my fingertips. Her body arched up to meet me.

As I entered her, she let out a rasp of air between her teeth, then sank back with a pained relief. It was a tense moment for me too, hoping that the sexual experience I was giving her over-rode any of the inevitable soreness she'd feel. That it'd be more than just her ticking off a To Do list. That was where the holding and the tenderness came in. So she could look back and see that in spite of any hurt I might have caused her when I took her virginity, there had been pleasure in the mix too.

Louise closed her eyes, then opened them again and looked up at me looking down at her. There was a brightness in her gaze.

My mind flipped to Pete on the sidelines somewhere. If only he knew what his other half was up to. An image of bike stabilisers flickered through my mind, and I mentally gave Pete a tilt of the head.

Technically, mate, I suppose this doesn't really count.

My hands were full of Louise's tits. I bent towards her upturned face and kissed her lips again.

'You feeling better now?'

Louise's face beamed. 'Very much so, thanks.'

'No need to thank me. I enjoyed myself. You've got nothing to worry about when you next see Pete. You're fine.'

Although Pete wasn't in the room with us, it was important to acknowledge that this was all for his benefit.

Louise wrapped an arm around my neck and pulled my lips to hers, and I sank my tongue into her mouth. We corkscrewed around each other on the bed.

Pete's going to have a rare old time of it.

When we came up for air again, she was splayed across the mattress, her eyes pierced with raw longing for me. Time, however, was running low.

Oh, all right then, one more for the road. A first-timer freebie to get her hooked.

I allowed myself a couple of minutes' grace to re-sheath myself, and then gripped the sides of Louise's smooth torso and drove into her one last time.

'You'll let yourself out, Luke?' she murmured afterwards, pointing at the wad of cash poking out beneath a jewellery box by her dressing-table mirror. 'I want to stay right here.'

She lay there bathed in a glow of pleasured contentment. I picked up the money and went to the bathroom to get dressed. On my way out of the flat, I poked my head round the bedroom door.

'Goodbye,' she purred, tilting her head at me as she said it. The rest of her body nestled into the bed. I noted she hadn't shifted at all since I'd left her.

Jenny again

Jenny waved at me as soon as she saw me approaching.

'Luke,' she beamed, hurrying up to me and giving me a playful hug.

Both of us had relaxed a great deal over the weeks we had been meeting. I got pleasure out of seeing how much Jenny's confidence had grown. And for me, still feigning experience with any new client, it was a relief to meet someone I already knew. An advantage of regular clients, I was quickly realising. Because for all the meeting and greeting I did in my new line of work, there was an artificial mateyness about meeting my clients. On one level there *had* to be for my own protection. My job was to provide the minimum niceties along with the sex, get paid for it, and get out of there. Which was fine most of the time. But the downside of *that* was that all the new people I was meeting meant very little to me. And I to them. Like they say, you can feel alone in a crowd.

Not with Jenny, though. I opened the café door for her and followed her in, and she sat down at our regular table while I ordered the coffees. Once I'd joined her, she had my undivided attention. That was part of the job description all right, but Jenny was also a means of honing my craft, though it was important to me that she felt our time together to be like time out from the stresses of her harsh working life.

50

Jenny looked me up and down. 'Gosh, Luke, you look more handsome every time I see you!'

I winced inside. The way she said it made it sound like one of my mum's friends saying it. The older woman admiring the young man, but with barely a sexual thought between them. Clumsy as it was, I knew it took all of Jenny's limited arsenal of boldness to say it.

'Why, thank you, Jenny,' I replied, while trying not to think of my mum's friends and what they'd all think if it got back to them what I was up to on the other side of the world. I didn't give a rat's arse what anyone else thought, but I knew it would worry my mum. She just wanted her kids to be safe and happy in whatever job they ended up in but I somehow doubted that escort work had ever figured in her hopes.

I twisted my mug so its handle was facing me, and wrapped two fingers around it. 'Tell me,' I continued, 'how have you been since we last met?'

I brought the mug to my lips and kept my eyes on Jenny. The truth was, I had a very good inkling about what she'd got up to before I even asked. Because Jenny's life didn't alter from week to week. It was a long hard slog from one cleaning job to the next, just to make ends meet. Yet, the very fact she'd got her act together to see me on a regular basis, never mind the expense, filled me with a sneaking admiration for her.

'It's tough at times. At the end of the week I feel like I could sleep for a thousand years. But do you know, Luke, knowing you has brought a real ray of sunshine into my life!'

I set my mug down. 'I don't know what to say, Jenny.'

I really didn't.

There was silence between us for a few minutes.

'Tell me, how are things going with you? Is work picking up? It must be, surely,' she encouraged.

I'd confessed to Jenny about her being my first client, my first regular one too, the last time I saw her. She'd looked surprised at first. 'I'd never have guessed, Luke. You were so *professional,*' she'd said with an air of wistfulness in her voice. She couldn't bring herself to mention anything more sexual than that, I'd noted at the time, and then wondered whether I should risk angling for another go at it. She might have struggled to find the cash, but then again she had her own flat while I was struggling to pay the rent on a room. But I'd bitten my tongue.

I'd told her about sending out my CV and photos to any agency I could find on the net. She really had no idea about computers at all. But she sure as hell knew what trying to find work was about.

I ran my finger round the bottom of my mug and gazed across at Jenny. 'I've had a few emails from people. I reply to everyone and hope they might book me some time or other. You never know.'

Though when I said 'everyone' I didn't mean *every*one. I gave the timewasters a wide berth. They proved pretty easy to spot. The ones who called me 'Big Boy' or told me what they wanted to do to me. Or the letters from girls but with a guy's name in the email address. I'd caught on pretty quickly that the nervy, tentative messages were the genuine article, from women who felt awkward or embarrassed at what they were doing. Once I'd replied to *them*, they soon relaxed and were able to tell me what they were after.

That was a basic requirement. To make everyone who showed the slightest inkling of interest feel like they had my full attention. Because you never knew what that might bring, whether it was next week or some unknown time in the future. It was all potential work.

'You're getting your name around. That's the main thing.' Jenny nodded with enthusiasm in her eyes. Like she was gunning for me.

I knew I had to hope things would pick up. Because if I didn't do that, then what was the point of even bothering? And don't all small businesses struggle at first? I rubbed my finger across my closed lips and surveyed what I could see of the coffee shop behind Jenny. It was a busy afternoon, but for all the customers these places had, nobody really noticed anybody else as far as I could see.

I focused on Jenny again with a muted smile. I valued the fact that she was interested in how my own life was going. And there seemed no reason not to tell her. It wasn't as if she was going to tell anyone, was it? That was the element of security there was in my job. Hiring an escort wasn't something women tended to crow about.

The truth was that Jenny and I had realised that we could tell each other *everything*. It was as if this half an hour in our week was time out from where we each found ourselves at this point in our lives. Both of us were, to a degree, alone in the Big City. She had no family to speak of, and I was on the other side of the world from mine. I had mates, of course, but there was other stuff that I only told Jenny. We were each other's sounding board. Like a comfort blanket, I suppose. It felt sometimes as if my mates were now on a different path in life to me. I'd had to wise up fast to suit the work I was doing. They knew what I now got up to when I wasn't at the café, but they didn't altogether *get* it.

It wasn't as if what I was doing wasn't legit. Prostitution was within UK law. But it somehow remained something you weren't supposed to talk about here, never mind openly admit to indulging in. And while I had no qualms about my work, since I wasn't hurting anyone and, in fact, could see the good I was doing my clients, I was sort of 'the embarrassing mate'. What I was doing with my life was only seen by Mark and co. as 'a bit of a laugh' or 'every guy's fantasy' in the right circumstances.

Jenny, however, gave me the space no one else did to talk about my work without being judged.

Our half-hour was up. We stood up and hugged, and she squeezed my hand and passed the cash to me. I gave her a warm smile and brushed her arm. Jenny's whole life was running against the clock. But when the weekend arrived, she'd crash out and attempt to catch up on all the zeds she'd missed during the previous week, though as far as I could tell she was fighting a losing battle. Permanently running on empty.

I walked Jenny to the coffee-shop door, held it open, and watched her hurry out and disappear into the crowds. I returned to the table and finished off the dregs of my drink. Jenny needed this breathing space in her life, that was for sure. But the truth, I knew, was that I was getting as much out of meeting her on a weekly basis as she was.

<u>Good communication</u>

It's been said that when it comes to sex, the most import-ant organ is the brain. That's where things get really fired up! But when you and your partner are *talking* about what you both want to get up to, it's the *ears* that count.

- Listen with your whole body. Be sensitive to what your partner wants and desires – or doesn't.
- But don't assume you know what your partner is thinking, or read too much into their actions. Talk together to confirm each other's desires.
- Remember to listen to and acknowledge what does and doesn't turn *you* on too. And let your partner know.
- Discuss protection. Don't leave it to chance and hope that your partner has it sorted.
- Don't let sex talk become a clinical experience. It's foreplay. Keep the lights low with music in the back-ground and talk slowly and seductively to each other.
- Make your partner feel as good and sexy about themselves as possible by sincerely complimenting them. It relaxes things and leads to better sex. Anybody can find *something*. Tell them they've got nice eyes, how good their skin feels to touch, or how they look better with their clothes off . . . Guys espe-cially need to remind girls that what worries them about their bodies is rarely an issue for us.
- Call a spade a spade. Swear words can have real potency, especially if normally butter wouldn't melt in your mouth!
- Share your sexual fantasies, but take account of the level of trust there is between you. Would you want them to become the subject of gossip?

- Be careful if you choose to act out your fantasies in role play. Fantasy is most often best left to the imagination.

Sasha plus one

Sasha called me out to her apartment in a luxury new development beyond Tower Bridge around about midnight, though I was pretty much ready for my own bed.

I was knackered, but when you're just starting out you've got to accept practically every call no matter what. They could turn into regulars, and obviously that's what you're after. Jenny was the start, but if I wanted to succeed I needed more repeat meetings than *that*.

It was October, and as the cab passed London Bridge Station and made its way along Tooley Street I could see by the spotlighting of the wall-like brick buildings we ran between that this was an old part of town spruced up. The gold haloing cried out about the money that had clearly poured into the area but the night's darkness couldn't completely shake off the grime. These stolid, heavy buildings petered out, replaced by brand-spanking-new luxury flats and office blocks with river views. The tilted glass and metal egg of the London Assembly building seemed designed to bask in its reflection in the Thames. Across the way, the ancient Tower of London stood upright and proud. Like it had seen it all before; that all that brashness and cash was wafer-thin, fleeting and not to be trusted.

The cab passed a half mile beyond Tower Bridge to draw up at a brand new glass and metal block. A figure appeared out of the dark. I paid the fare and climbed out of the car, and she stepped forward to greet me.

'It's Luke, isn't it? I'm Sasha,' she smiled, and shook my hand.

Even in the dim light I could see Sasha was gorgeous, maybe a few years older than me, in her late twenties. And she had the most striking brown eyes. I followed her through the door of the apartment block and into the lift. The doors glided shut behind us.

Sasha turned towards me. As she did her coat fell slightly open, and I caught sight of the curve of her naked breasts. I all but gasped.

I swallowed and focused on her face. It was framed by glossy short brown hair. She was one of the prettiest women I had ever seen. She had almost airbrushed features, as if she'd walked off the cover of a fashion magazine.

Sasha looked back at me, and swung her coat further apart. She was wearing nothing underneath. She was slim and well-toned with wonderful rounded breasts. Like a swimwear model.

This can't be right. This can't be my luck.

My jaw tightened and I automatically clenched my teeth.

Aw, man. Keep your cool. Keep your cool.

My teeth had begun to ache.

The lift doors parted and we stepped out. We entered her apartment and she led me into the sitting room. As I stepped through the door, I froze.

Sitting on the chocolate leather sofa in front of me was a naked girl, about twenty-two. Her tits were like little foothills and her svelte body had a bronzed sheen. She reminded me of Bambi.

'Luke; Chloe. Chloe; Luke.'

Chloe smiled. 'Hello.'

I nodded, struck dumb.

This is too good to be true. No one can be this lucky and be paid for it.

If Sasha was almost a 'ten' – and she was – Chloe was more than a 'nine'. But that was just splitting hairs. Both were gorgeous. Head-turners if you saw them walking down the street. Except they shouldn't have been walking down the street. They were too *perfect*.

My God. This isn't right. This is what some guys pay a grand for. Just let me get home and tell my mates.

'Do you want your money now?' Sasha asked, taking my coat. I hadn't moved from the doorway.

'Huh? Money. Oh, afterwards is fine,' I garbled.

'Would you like a glass of champagne?'

'Yes, please.' I wasn't quite sure where to look.

'You make yourself at home. I've got some chilling in the fridge.'

Sasha went to the kitchen, and I hovered before making a beeline for the nearest armchair and perched on its edge.

'Come and join me,' Chloe beckoned, her hand patting the sofa beside her.

I crossed the room and sat down. My hands sat on my knees. Neither of us spoke for a couple of minutes. I looked around the room; anywhere but at her. The deep-pile cream carpet seemed to go on for miles. A plasma-screen telly filled the far wall. The dark brown of the furniture was broken up by pale pink cashmere throws. A couple of chrome high-end speakers added a sharp modern twist. Like its owners, it all could have stepped off the pages of some style magazine.

'You didn't have trouble finding us?'

My focus fell on Chloe. She had long blonde hair and grey-blue eyes and there was a sweet youthfulness about her. And she was deliciously relaxed in her nakedness.

'No, the cab driver knew where to go. But when Sasha told me on the phone that it was just beyond Tower Bridge, I had a mental block. I know it isn't, but it's like that's where you fall off the edge of London.'

She looked at me, curious: 'What, here be dragons?'

'Yeah, just about.'

'Well, don't worry, Luke,' she stroked my denim-clad thigh, 'we won't eat you alive.'

'Not, of course, unless you want us to.' Sasha had come back into the room. She set down a tray on the coffee table from which she handed me and Chloe a glass of champagne each before sitting down in the chair opposite.

Veuve Clicquot. The good stuff.

'So, Luke, where did you say you came from?' Sasha asked, pouring a glass for herself. She was wearing, I noted, what looked like a wedding ring.

'Out West London way,' I mumbled, and took a gulp of the drink.

'Where the dragons *don't* roam,' added Chloe.

'Yeah, something like that.'

A voice in my head was telling me that it was *my* job to ask *them* about themselves and help *them* relax. I'd just about felt comfortable chatting to Chloe. But the two of them together was too much. Their beauty left me tongue-tied.

The girls chatted, and I sipped my champagne and desperately tried to join in. It was a relief when eventually Sasha rose from her chair, picked up the bottle of champagne, and reached out her hand to take Chloe's, before turning to me. 'You'll join us in the bedroom?'

'Yes. Okay,' I nodded, a bit too eager. A good escort was supposed to suggest the next move too, but I wasn't about to argue the toss.

Chloe stood and, taking her hand out of Sasha's, slipped her arm around her girlfriend's waist. It was like they'd melted into each other; you couldn't have got a card between them. I was like a lost sheep trotting behind. Or a lamb to the slaughter. I wasn't sure which. I'd seen girls together on the telly of a night with the lads, but those girls weren't a patch on these two in front of me. I was mesmerised by their naked butts. Yup, Sasha and Chloe were the type who featured in my wildest dreams.

The girls slipped onto the bed together and stretched out before me like a pair of Siamese cats. Sleek, their lithe legs entwined, watching me. I felt like I was having an out-of-body experience. Like the very fact that I was looking on at this dream scene meant it couldn't *really* be happening. I breathed out again and I was too, too aware of myself standing there, fearing they'd caught me out of my depth.

'Now, Luke,' announced Sasha, her tongue running across her teeth, 'it's *your* turn.' She stole a glance at Chloe, and then both of them, heads cocked in parallel, watched me undress.

'*Slowly,*' purred Chloe, tracing her middle finger from just above her cleavage gently up to her top lip and drawing it back down again.

That brought me to my senses. This was first-base stuff. Easy as pie. I peeled off my jacket and placed it on the steel-grey chaise longue in the corner of the room. I turned squarely towards the bed and fixed my eyes on the two of them. With one hand on my hip, I unhitched a button and allowed the seconds to tick away before reaching for the next in line. With the final button undone, I placed the other hand on my hip and let the shirt fall open.

'Wow!' Sasha blurted out. 'That's one fine body.'

'You know just how to exercise, and just when to stop, don't you?' chimed in Chloe.

I was secretly flattered but kept schtum. All those extra hours at the gym and playing footie had paid off. I unzipped my flies, let my jeans fall to the floor, and stepped out of them.

'Miaow,' yelped Chloe, eyeing my dick, which was now straining to be freed from my Calvins.

'Luke,' Sasha beckoned with the bottle, 'get your glass and come right here. Now.'

I grinned, peeled off my boxers, and slid onto the bed beside the girls. We chinked glasses.

'You enjoying yourself, Luke?'

Chloe was younger than me but she was doing her best to make me feel relaxed. For all my naked bravado, she could still tell that I was winging it.

I could feel myself blushing: 'Yes, I am.'

It came out quieter than I wanted it to. If they were going to try and get me talking more, it wasn't going to work. I still wasn't up to having much of a conversation. It was just enough to sit with Sasha and Chloe, and enjoy being with them. And then a second later, they were kissing, their hands running down each other's body.

Oh God.

All I knew how to do was to sit there within inches of them and watch. This was heading way beyond any sex I'd had before. My own body yearned to join in but my mind was wondering how to go about it. Sasha's hand reached out and stroked my leg, willing me to be part of the action. And the next minute Sasha went down on Chloe, and Chloe writhed deeper into the bed – and I felt as if I might as well not have been there. Except, except, there was something almost stage-managed about the sex. Like they *knew* exactly what they were doing to me.

God, it was working.

I shifted closer and readied myself. But still I held back. They were so caught up in each other.

How do I join in on this without ruining the moment?

My focus shifted from Sasha to Chloe beneath her, and then back again.

Who do I go for first?

I was on the brink of every guy's wet dream – ready to jump the chasm.

Just go for it, Luke. You've just got to get in there somehow.

I felt the lull in my storm. All the attention laser-beamed onto my suddenly limp dick.

NO! Don't do this to me. Kick in, you bastard. Get your damn act together.

'You're not gay, are you?'

Everything else in me stiffened. I looked up. Chloe had spoken but both she and Sasha, embracing horizontally, were now watching me.

'Oh God, no,' I laughed.

Beyond them, I could see a sliver of a window through a gap in the burgundy curtain that ran the length of the room. A split-second urge swept through me to dive through the glass and down to the cold stone floor however many storeys below.

I clambered off the bed.

'I need to go to the bathroom,' I muttered, avoiding catching their eyes. My self-esteem felt like my dick.

I closed the bathroom door behind me and breathed out.

What the fuck's going on?

I turned on the cold tap and cupped my hands beneath it and looked at myself, tight-lipped in the mirror. The glass reflected back the shiny oxblood tiles behind me, which when I looked from the right angle appeared to line up exactly with the tiles on the wall I faced. Like I was bricked in. I washed my face and gripped the marble washbasin and wondered what Sasha and Chloe were thinking about me. Sniggering, no doubt. Or angry that they weren't getting what they'd bargained for. I was experiencing what every guy says 'never happens to me' when it does.

My dick was making no effort to rejoin the party. I looked down at it, frowning.

What are you playing at? Why NOW?

I gave it a damn hard helping hand.

Come on, come on. Oh, congratulations. About bloody time. Where the fucking hell have you been?

I returned to the bedroom, spirits and cock revived. In my

absence, the girls had decided to carry on without me. They were so wound up in each other that they barely noticed me watching their every move as I walked towards the bed and climbed onto it beside them. Sasha was on her back and Chloe sat astride her with one hand behind her as if she was riding rodeo. Sasha bucked in pleasure.

Thank you, God. Fantasy made flesh.

Chloe caught my eye and drew her girlfriend to a canter and then to a gentle halt. Her gaze didn't waver from my face as she climbed off her mount and made her way on all fours across the bed towards me. Her hand reached out to encircle my prick, and I took a deep breath. She sat back on her haunches to steady herself, and neither missing a beat nor taking her eyes off mine, she stretched out her other hand towards her lover.

'Condom, please.'

Out of the corner of my eye, I watched Sasha in turn stretch out her hand to fish around in the drawer of the bedside cabinet, pull out a rubber and slip it between Chloe's finger and thumb. It was a practised move.

They've done this before.

It was now Sasha's turn to lean on an elbow and watch, her other hand between her thighs.

Chloe brought the packet up to her mouth and ripped the corner of the wrapper away with her teeth. With a deft hand she pulled out the condom and placed it between her lips, and this time dropped her eyes. Her hands ran gently down my dick, guiding it into her mouth at the very same time as she drew her mouth up the shaft.

Oh God, yes.

I closed my eyes to both savour and withstand the breakers.

My eyes jarred open in shock a moment later. I was losing it. *Again.*

No, it can't do this to me. It can't get worse.

Chloe was doing her utmost to tantalise me. I willed my dick to harden.

What's wrong with me? With these two and I can't keep in shape? Of course I'm not gay. Am I? No. No. So what the fuck's going on? This ain't supposed to happen. What do I have to DO? God Almighty. Work, damn it.

My dick wasn't listening to a word of it.

Chloe pulled away, and shot a glance at her lover. They were looking at each other, but not in a good way. I sat there feeling completely deflated.

'Is everything all right?' said Sasha.

I braced myself and lied through my teeth. 'Oh, it's fine, it's fine.' Then bashfully I looked at both of them sitting there, and decided to admit defeat.

'Look, my dick's not working for anyone. You two are just *too* good.'

They smiled back at me and said nothing. My words hung in the air.

'Would you like another drink?' Chloe asked, and shifted off the bed to collect the bottle and our glasses.

'Thanks, love,' replied Sasha.

'Yes, please, that'd be nice,' I said.

I watched the golden elixir fill my glass.

'Cheers,' we said, almost in unison, and sunk one and then another.

Whether it was the alcohol, or just that I'd got the worst out of the way, I couldn't be sure, but my whole – yes, *whole* – body felt like it was back in the swing of things.

Welcome back.

My prick and I were back on speaking terms.

Sasha pulled herself across the bed towards me and nuzzled my neck, and then we kissed and I could taste the champagne sweetness on her lips and in her mouth. The flute slipped out of my hand. I held her in my arms and savoured her sculpted athletic plains and then laid her down on the bed and rammed into her. Hard into hard. Chloe stretched herself alongside us and watched as she stroked her girlfriend's arm.

'Sash . . .' she breathed.

As I rode her, Sasha turned her head towards Chloe, and her face was lost behind the blonde curtain of her lover's hair as they kissed. When I relaxed into Sasha's arms, Chloe in turn twisted a lock of hair behind her ear and turned her profile to me, and our lips met and my tongue entered her mouth even as I remained inside Sasha.

I felt my way. My right hand journeyed across Chloe's soft belly and slipped around the curve of her waist. My left hand cradled the weight of Sasha's right breast, and then swept up to her neck where I let my thumb stroke her throat. Her head was stretched back deep into the pillow, and I could have sworn she purred.

Nothing was said. As I drew myself away from Sasha, Chloe's hand pushed into my chest and forced me onto my back. I'd barely had a chance to work out where she was going with this before her clasped hands ran a condom down my cock and I willed myself not to come just yet, and she straddled me. Sasha's hands gripped my jaw, and she thrust her tongue into my mouth.

Chloe orgasmed first, her back arching and both her hands clawed into the back of my legs, my own hands clasping her breasts as she leaned back with the ecstasy and screeched into the night.

Chloe caught her breath and threw Sasha an evil leer and they immediately swapped places. Chloe's melting softness and Sasha's angular beauty had fluidly become one and my body could no longer tell the difference. Or wanted to. My nervousness had long fled and the newness of sleeping with two girls together had fallen away. My eyes were wide open and I was completely awake, not believing my fucking luck. Sasha and I climaxed simultaneously.

We took a breather, but the bottle of champagne was almost

empty. Chloe climbed off the bed: 'It's okay. I'll go and get some more. I'll refill the ice bucket too,' she said, picking it up and swishing it round. 'It's all water.'

She left the room. Sasha got off the bed and busied herself collecting our glasses from around the room and placed them on a scarlet lacquered chest of drawers ready for Chloe's return. I kept quiet and observed her, presuming things would get going again then too.

Sasha turned and looked directly at me.

'Come here, Luke.' It was a gentle request but it took me unawares. Yet I found myself standing as she spoke. I stepped towards her, mesmerised.

She's truly stunning.

I stood there and let her hands play over my chest, exploring. Her fingers traced a trail of pleasure. I stroked her fringe away from her forehead and kissed it, and she leaned back her head and I kissed her mouth and she kissed right back.

'Hey, you two.' Chloe's words bit into the moment as she entered the bedroom and set the ice bucket down.

I turned on my heel taking Sasha with me, so both of us were now facing Chloe. My arms were wrapped around Sasha's waist, and my chin nestled on her shoulder. Chloe's face was lit up, and she was holding out two filled champagne flutes. We both took one.

'Thanks,' we said.

Chloe picked hers up, and we raised our glasses.

'To one hell of a night!' I grinned.

'I know what I want to do next,' giggled Chloe.

'Yeah, do it,' nodded Sasha beside me. 'You've always wanted to.'

I sensed a conspiracy. I turned my head to look at Sasha, who looked full of deep warmth for her girlfriend. I looked back at Chloe. She looked even more of a dream.

''What is it?'

The night had turned and I felt up for anything.

Sasha unlinked herself from me and went to the curtain and began pulling at its cord even as Chloe spoke.

'I've always wanted to make love to a man on the balcony, looking at the bridge and the river.'

'Consider it done. And Sasha? You want it too?'

She unlocked the glass door and opened it. The blast of cold air was refreshing against the bedroom's closed-in warmth.

'No, I'm just happy to watch. It's more Chloe's fantasy than mine.'

Fantasy? Okay, I'll give her fantasy.

I took Chloe in my arms, and lifted her up so I was cradling her.

She squealed. 'What are you doing? Put me down!'

'I'm carrying you over the threshold, of course. We've got to do this right.'

I stepped out onto the balcony, and the dark and the view hit me.

'Wow.'

Chloe was looking up at me with her back to the river but she knew what I must be seeing.

'It's amazing, isn't it?'

Tower Bridge was edged in lights, and through it you could see the glint of the river and the city's lights beyond the water's edge. I set Chloe down, and she leaned against the wall beside me and together we peered upstream. I looked over the balcony. *God, it was a long way down.*

Sasha hovered by the door with her glass in her hand.

I nestled closer to Chloe and put an arm around her. She turned her head and kissed my shoulder, and I ran my fingers through her hair and we embraced. The pair of us shifted away from the full glare of the bedroom to the subdued corner of the balcony closest to the bridge. It loomed before me as I entered her. Nothing but the two of us in its shadow. And as I kissed the curved length of Chloe's neck I watched beyond the strands of her hair, the bridge's pair of pale stone towers, each topped by a hard gold tip that glinted in the night.

My focus shifted with my quickening rhythm to the guns jutting out of HMS *Belfast*'s shadowed hulk in the waters just beyond the bridge. They had the range of London's suburbs. I gave Chloe my full force. My cartridge spent, I collapsed against her.

And farewell Uxbridge.

We buried ourselves in each other, holding on until each had regained their breath. The chill air was balm on our hot skin. Sasha had already wrapped up, and handed us each a warmed bathrobe.

'God, you look like two boxers after a round. Get those on and come in.'

I put mine on, and helped Chloe on with hers. She looked up at me with a Cheshire Cat grin as I gave her myself as an extra layer. As we stepped back inside, I took one last look along the river as far as the eye could see. Far to the east in what for me were uncharted waters, there was a slither of red.

'Hey, the sun's coming up. Is it really that late?' I shook my head. 'Or early? Or whatever?'

Sasha closed the window behind us and drew the curtain.

'I'm going to take a shower, and then I've got to go home. I've got work today,' she explained.

Sasha had sealed the session's end. Chloe slipped out of my arms and began to tidy up. That was it then. A wave of tiredness swept over me. It had been a fantastic night but I yearned for my own bed. I picked up my shirt from the arm of the chair.

I was putting on my jacket when Sasha put her head around the bedroom door. She'd showered and had slipped on a dress and heels and touched up her makeup. Our night together really did feel over. The end of a ravishingly hot dream.

'Look, I'm going in a minute . . .'

I was as ready to go as she was. I took the bait.

'We can share a cab if you like,' I suggested.

'That makes sense. Make yourself at home in the lounge, and I'll call them.'

I came out into the corridor and followed her towards the living room. As I passed the kitchen, I looked in. It was chrome and dark marbled slabs and curved edges.

'It's been lovely to meet you, Chloe.'

It was code, the business part. She hung up the tea towel.

'Ah yes, I'll get you your coat. You just take a seat.'

I sat back down on the sofa and put on my shoes. Everything had a different gloss on it. It still looked like it was out of a colour supplement, but I could see Chloe in it too.

Chloe returned to the room and Sasha was steps behind her, already in her coat. We'd come full circle. Chloe handed me my own coat and slipped me a padded envelope as she did. I put on the coat and put the money in my pocket without looking at it.

'Thanks, for everything.' I smiled at Chloe.

She patted my arm. 'No, thank *you*.'

'Hey, love, I'll call.' Sasha wrapped an arm around her lover and they kissed goodbye.

We took the lift back down, and walked out into the early morning light. Everything had a crisp glow. I opened the cab door for Sasha and climbed in after her.

'Notting Hill, please,' she instructed.

We said nothing. London's streets filed past in a blur. I was dog-tired, spent. I put my brain into cruise control.

Her words broke the silence.

'Luke, do you want to come back and stay at my house for a while?'

Aw, man.

I was torn. God knew I needed some sleep. And I was desperate to get home and tell my mates about tonight.

70

Sasha crossed her leg. Her mule hung off her foot like a hand beckoning me. My eye was drawn up her leg to the hint of floral cotton peeping out from beneath the thick navy wool of her winter coat. Not like last time.

I know exactly what's beneath all that.

'I'll go back with you,' I nodded.

I looked out of the window. We passed rows of white Georgian terraces that reminded me of wedding cakes.

'I'll pay you a thousand pounds for coming over,' she announced quietly.

Hang on. How many hours is this going to go on? A couple at most, surely?

I'd already been paid for my time, and I sure as hell knew that I wouldn't be able to keep up that same level of service. For one thing, I was exhausted by the stress of giving the impression I knew exactly what I was doing.

'That's not right. I don't want that much money.'

We looked at each other, neither of us quite sure where to go from there. I decided to take things into my own hands.

'Look, you pay for my taxi home afterwards and I'm happy.'

We were somewhere behind Portobello Road. The cab edged along two sides of a fenced-off garden square and stopped outside one of the doors of a tall flat-fronted house. Sasha paid the driver and I watched her as she did and felt bad about how I'd dismissed her money and, what's more, sold myself short.

Get with the programme, Luke. That was damn unprofessional. You're not giving it away. And neither is she.

Sasha let us in and led me into a small lounge off the hallway. The room felt more relaxed than Chloe's place with a couple of comfy armchairs facing another massive flat-screen telly above a square fireplace.

We'd barely got through the door before Sasha had stripped me of my coat and I of hers. I tore her dress over her head and raced to unbutton my shirt as quickly as she was tugging it off me. She gripped me by my waistband and flung herself into one of the chairs and pulled me on top of her.

The armchair was made for cramped, hard fucking.

Afterwards, we curled up together, she on my lap with her legs over the chair's arm, and I held her hand and played with her fingers. I fiddled with her ring.

'You're married?'

In for a penny . . .

She looked into my eyes and nodded.

'As good as. In March,' she smiled.

Ah, letting off steam before he puts the lid on it.

The index finger of her other hand traced an ever-decreasing circle above my right nipple.

'We're having the wedding in Jamaica – on the beach – and we're flying out all my family and friends too.'

'Wow.'

She gazed up at the ceiling. 'He gave me all this. This house. I'm doing it up. I've got the workmen coming in this afternoon. That's why I had to get back. It's something to do, you know.'

Gave it to her? He must be loaded.

She looked back at me. She knew what I was thinking.

'Money *drips* out of him. I knew that when I first met him, except he didn't know I knew . . .'

Eh?

I shuffled on the chair to make myself more comfortable.

'He'd been seeing my best friend. She's a stripper at the same club as me, and that's where she met him.'

My ears pricked up.

A stripper. Can it get any better?

'But she was also seeing someone else who she didn't want to lose,' Sasha continued, 'so we decided to get him interested in me. We arranged a lunch date, and I paid instead of him, which

72

got him intrigued but also meant I could start pulling the strings. I've done it before.' She shrugged her shoulders.

Sasha had me hooked too. I listened wide-eyed with my jaw on the floor as she told me of her complete set-up designed to snare the poor rich sucker. The plan was to reel him in, marry him, and a couple of years down the line to divorce him for every penny she could get. She told me how, when they'd first started dating, practically all her money went on him though she could barely afford it. Whatever she killed, that's what she was eating. And when the relationship began to get more serious, she chose to mirror everything he did. The way he brushed his teeth, the way he put his toothpaste on the brush, the way he put the brush back in the cup. Every little thing.

'And then he bought me this place to keep *me* interested. Ha! It's something to play with. I mean, I don't have to work now. It keeps me occupied,' she smiled.

I didn't know what to say.

'Shit.'

'I know,' she went on, revelling in what she was getting away with. 'He gave me a card to shop at Harrods too. I treat myself to the designer labels, keep the receipt, take it back a couple of weeks later and cash it in and bank the money.'

My mind was spinning with the sheer audacity of it all. I shook my head a couple of times as if to clear it, and put an arm round Sasha's shoulder.

'So how does Chloe fit into all this?'

'Not easily.' She quietened, looking down at her hands. 'We've known each other since back when she was working at the club.'

Shit! I've been paid a grand tonight for sex with two strippers in a lesbian fantasy.

I was quickly brought back down to earth.

'Look, my fiancé. He's away a lot on business. He is now, but he has people looking out for me, checking up on me. But he doesn't know about Chloe. He *can't* find out.

'When he's here, I tell him I'm going to visit my sister, but go off and see Chlo,' she continued. 'I've got clothes 'n' stuff dotted round at friends' houses and in the car for my Great Escapes, like tonight.'

Sasha's mood lightened, and her whole body relaxed in my lap, but she couldn't quite disguise the trap she'd got herself into even while she'd been busily weaving a web of her own for her future husband.

'He can't find out about Chloe,' she repeated, half to herself. She then looked up into my eyes to make sure I got the picture. 'If he ever found out that I was seeing someone else, he'd have us both killed without giving it a second thought.'

It chilled me how it rolled off her tongue, like it was the most natural thing in the world. I held her closer to me, and for a few minutes we sat together in silence.

'Are you okay?' I half-whispered, brushing her arm with my thumb.

She nodded. 'If I paid you another thousand, could you stay longer?' she asked, in a quiet voice she was only just succeeding to keep steady.

'I'm sorry, Sasha, I wish I could but I can't.'

I took a sideways glance at my watch. It was 6 a.m. An extra grand was tempting, I had to admit. But not tempting enough. I thought of the run of late nights and missed sleep I'd rung up, and wondered how I was to catch up with myself. Tiredness threatened to engulf me, but it was mixed with a fear of all I might get myself tangled up in if I accepted this girl's offer.

'I've got to go home, Sash.'

I closed my eyes for a second. She slipped off my lap and I rallied myself.

'I tell you what. You've got my number,' I told her. 'Call me this evening and we might be able to arrange something some other time.'

I pulled myself out of the chair and we both put our clothes back on. She paid me the grand. In cash. I didn't challenge her.

'Luke?'

It was late afternoon and I hadn't been up long. But I recognised her as soon as she spoke.

'Hello, Sasha, you've had a good day?'

She was standing there sexily in my mind's eye, her head cocked to her mobile. 'Yes, I have, thanks. Hope we didn't tire you out.'

'Not at all,' I lied. 'It was a pleasure.'

It would be an early night tonight, though I decided to be professional about it and not let Sasha know. But the tiredness was mixed with the warm glow of satisfaction of at last ticking off my first handful of sessions.

'It was a good job you left when you did. The cleaner turned up half an hour later.'

There was more to it, I knew, than the fuel for a bit of idle gossip among the staff. Sasha's fiancé owned *everything*. Anything untoward that happened in his girlfriend's gilded cage would get right back to him. I shivered.

'I'd like to see you again a few times before I'm wed,' she continued.

For a split second I considered the danger, but it was swept away by the sheer fantasy made flesh of this girl. And so we made a date.

Mark

'You're kidding me!' Mark gasped, his eyes like saucers when I told him about the night before last as we geared ourselves up for a game of pool. Our work shifts were so out of synch these days that it was the first time since then that we'd had chance to catch up. I didn't reply, but leaned against my cue and raised my eyebrows.

'Fuck,' he breathed out, as he stretched himself over the table and lined up for the break. He turned his head away from the job in hand and looked over at me, bemused. I threw my head back and roared with laughter. Mark frowned at me, confused.

'What?'

'I bet you wish you hadn't given the game up,' I gloated, a wicked smile across my face.

'You know what, when I hear stuff like that, bloody hell, *no*.' He shook his head and returned his attention to the table. 'Two naked gorgeous lesbians. Fuck me.' He fired off a shot and the balls went ricocheting around the baize.

I'd been burning to tell the guys what I'd got up to with Sasha and Chloe ever since it happened – from the moment I'd walked into Chloe's flat, to be honest. *That* was exactly what I'd got into escort work for. The night had been everything I could have dreamed of – and a lot I hadn't dared imagine. Even my nervous cock was just a blip when I cast my mind back over all that had gone on.

But I wanted to tell Mark first – he was my best friend here, and he had been good to me since the time I'd moved into the house. He'd shown me around London when it was still all so new.

I watched him pot the balls. He was good at pool, but I noted that tonight he was off his game and there was an element of envy or regret or something in his eyes, though he was avoiding catching mine.

When Mark spoke again, he didn't even cast a look at me.

'I was wrong, wasn't I?'

I didn't quite understand what he meant. Wrong not to have believed enough in the possibility that there might be work out there? Wrong not to have stuck it out until the work started coming in? Or wrong to have started going out with Natasha?

The truth was that neither he nor I had had a clue how things might turn out. And for all the fun I was now having, I wasn't yet out of the woods as regards to making any kind of living from the escort work.

I watched his orange ball rim the pocket and fail to fall in.

'Well, it didn't happen overnight,' I shrugged. 'It's been a while coming. They're only number five of my clients, you know. And I sure had to wade through a mixed bunch before I met them.'

Mind you, had Sasha and Chloe been my *first*, they'd have scared me off ever working again. My cock would have been terrified into submission. Not that I'd let Mark know *that*.

Mark stood out of the way and let me take my place at the table. I chalked the tip of my cue.

'But five is more than I assumed there were out there,' he said.

'That's true,' I nodded. I shifted down the length of the table so I could check out the best line of fire. I looked across at my friend, his cue in one hand and a pint in the other and a rueful look on his face. I thought of Rob, and how when we were first starting out I'd let him have first dibs at our client

77

list, even though none of us had a clue if we'd ever get a call again.

Mark had been miffed then at how I'd effectively given some work away by allowing Rob to keep any money he made. But now I'd proved that there *was* work out there if you made the effort to find it. And Mark now had a girlfriend. So he'd missed out again.

I potted the '10' and stood up and looked across at him. He was miles away.

'Mark!'

He gripped his cue, ready for his turn.

'No. I haven't finished yet. But I was thinking . . .' I took a step back from the table, still wielding my cue, the strip of green between us.

'What?' He looked puzzled.

'I could do you a favour, y'know. If you really want.'

Mark set his beer glass down on the table beside him. I could see he was sizing me up.

'You mean a foursome with this Sasha and Chloe pair?' he leered, and licked his lips. He perched on the edge of the table, his arms crossed round his cue. I set down my own cue on the table's edge.

'Would you like me to set you up with a girl? I could, you know,' I teased.

There remained a hint of suspicion in his eyes amid the jauntiness. 'Yeah?'

'Of course I could!' I toyed. 'Look, business is gradually building up . . .'

Mark relaxed his arms and leaned back against the table behind him, picked up his beer again and took a gulp.

'So, how about me letting you in on a piece of the action?' I challenged.

Mark's brows creased. 'And there's really enough work for you to share?'

He knew enough about what I got up to then, to remain unconvinced that there was more than barely enough for *me*. He was absolutely right. The girls were still only phoning in dribs and drabs, though the calls were certainly getting more frequent. But even if someone phoned, it didn't mean they'd hire me there and then. Or even that month. So this job, at the moment at least, was as much about my phone manner and hoping that might hook a client. There was a lot of hope in this game.

Yet I had faith and confidence in the market out there, even though I was still finding my feet. I'd upped my game lately by signing up with the agencies and that was already making a difference.

I picked up my cue again and sized up the formation of the balls. I could sense Mark's eyes on me, waiting for a reply. I'd been miles away.

The tip of my cue was millimetres away from the cue ball. I looked up from the table level at Mark. 'I can give you one of the girls. No worries,' I grinned.

'You can?'

He half-smiled, still not totally convinced.

'A one-off, okay?' I nodded.

I drew the cue back, then thrust it against the ball, which shot across the baize, scattering others as it followed its course. I pulled away from the table and watched them spill across the table and slow to a halt. The '12' went in.

I turned back to Mark who was now behind me.

'Anyhow, I had such a blast with those two that I can spare one of my clients,' I joshed. 'After all, I need to recharge my batteries.'

I was grinning from ear to ear just thinking about it. Mark didn't say anything but a slight smile lit up his face.

I turned back towards the pool table. 'I tell you what. The very next call I get, you can have it.'

I said it as nonchalantly as possible without casting a glance at him. I sensed that I'd already got him hooked. It was time to start reeling him in.

'Really?' he replied, now with real glee in his voice. 'You'd do that for me?'

'Uh-huh,' I nodded, and leaned over the pool table again.

'That's great,' he beamed across at me, 'because now I'm going out with Natasha, I'm sorted for sex, thanks 'n' all, mate.' He raised his glass to me, and his eyes were filled with good humour. 'In fact, you can have the room to yourself tonight. I'm going round to hers straight after we've finished here. Nice of you to think of me, though.'

I shook my head and laughed with him.

'You thought I'd fall so easily for *that* now I've got myself a girl? I should whack you round the head with this,' he grinned, giving his cue a Jedi-like swing that was designed to miss me.

I back-ducked like an extra in *The Matrix*. Mark was right again, of course. The escort-life was no place to have a relationship. It wasn't fair on a girlfriend, and it would be bad enough just dating. My session with Sasha and Chloe had certainly left no energy for extra-curricular sex. I just wanted to sleep!

And as regards to the ethics of palming off a client to a mate – even if I'd planned on doing it, which I didn't – well, it was bloody unprofessional and disrespectful for one thing. I couldn't promote myself on a site and then fob a client off with a mate of mine who she'd never even seen. I knew enough via my limited experience to have sussed that when a girl got round to selecting a guy out of the tiny clutch of us, it was as much an emotional choice she was making as a physical one. She wanted that man, and that one only. It wasn't like guys, who might have a preference but, when it boiled down to it, would be happy with any of the girls on the website they used. No, women were different, and wasn't my job, if anything, about honouring that?

We continued our game. I let him win. It was my way of saying, 'No hard feelings, mate.' We finished our drinks and gave each other a slap on the back, and set off home on our different paths.

Adele

Late October

It was as if the tables were turned. Adele was sizing me up from the moment I approached her table at Brown's. I was wearing my best suit as if I was going for an interview. Which I suppose I was.

'Pleased to meet you, I'm Luke,' I said, and shook her hand. And as I did so I clocked her grey Armani suit, silk black shirt and black stilettos that flattered her tan, the chic gold jewellery and her straight blonde jaw-length hair.

'Good to meet you,' she replied.

I pulled out the chair opposite her and sat down, and trusted that she meant what she said and liked what she saw. All I could see in front of me was a handsome, together woman in her thirties, styled by the oodles of cash raked in from the girls she had on her books. Who I hoped I'd be joining very soon, if my luck was in.

I ordered a coffee, and as the waiter left our table Adele jumped right in.

'So, tell me, Luke, why you think Pearl Agency should take you on?'

It was brusque and direct. Which I suppose you had to be in her line of work. And she had a point. I would be the first and only guy on the website, so it would be a new venture for Adele as much as for me.

'You've seen the pictures I mailed you?' I asked, playing for time.

'Yes, I have.' Adele nodded from across the table while she scrutinised me. 'There's a photographer we use for the girls,' she disclosed. 'It means that all our photos have a consistent style. If we take you on, we can arrange for you to have a session with him.'

I took the very fact that she mentioned the snapper as a positive sign.

The waiter delivered my coffee, and I was very aware that I hadn't yet answered Adele's initial question. I decided to dive in and address the reservations I suspected she already had.

'I know that you don't yet promote any men on the site. So a solo image of myself among your female employees might appear strange to some clients.'

She looked straight at me as I spoke, not blinking.

'But,' I continued, 'I also am aware that clients sometimes want to hire a couple. My presence on the site respects that option.'

I took another gulp of coffee so I could collect my thoughts. I was desperately winging it.

My appearance on the website would be a gamble for Pearl Agency nevertheless, I recognised that. A picture of a guy such as me on the site made it very upfront what was being offered and what those girls and I got up to. It was, after all, how I'd heard of Pearl in the first place.

I'd met Marie a couple of weeks ago at Brian's. She'd been Girl No. 4 for that evening, I think, and after shagging her she suggested that I join the Pearl stable for any couples work that might crop up. She told me that she regularly got called out to partner some guy she didn't know and who might even be gay, but she liked me and she couldn't see why Adele wouldn't want to take me on instead of having to fish around other agencies for spare men.

A split-second image of Marie, her huge tits trying to force themselves through her purple silk camisole as she lay beneath me, flitted through my head. I looked across at Adele to steady my nerves and saw how I might have the same effect for women out there. Or at least I hoped I would. The difference was, though, that male clients weren't likely to want their own fantasies of the girls on the Pearl homepage interrupted by my grinning mug.

I wasn't about to flag up that possibility to Adele anytime soon. I set my coffee cup down. The clink of it in its saucer seemed to signal that it was Adele's turn to speak.

'Your image would widen what we have to offer,' she agreed, and I breathed out again. I hadn't even realised that I'd been holding my breath. 'It means that not only can a man calling ask for one girl or more, but he can call out a couple too. That'll be new. And of course it means too that we might also attract any passing women clients, which I understand is more your line?'

I nodded with a grin. 'Oh, definitely.'

Adele took a sip of coffee, eyeing me up as she did.

'Tell me, how are you with gay clients?' she queried, almost leering towards me over her cup at the thought of an untried market. I could practically see the pound signs in her eyes.

I shook my head. 'Nope.'

'"Nope"?' she sneered.

I knew I had to explain myself.

'I don't have a problem with gay men. But I'm not about to do any escort work with them, if that's what you mean. That's not *my* market.'

Adele sat back in her chair and set her cup back in its saucer. She didn't reply. I wondered whether I'd blown my chances out of the water completely.

Surely not. A minute ago she was flagging up the hetero work.

'Maybe a gay man on our books will be our next line,' she

mused. For a split second I was sure my fears had been realised. And then Adele offered me her hand over the table.

'Luke, welcome to the Pearl Agency,' she said as we shook on it.

'Thank you very much,' I smiled. 'I look forward to working with you.'

'We will take thirty per cent commission, which includes us taking care of the admin side of your call-outs,' she explained.

'I understand.'

This was new territory for the both of us. Pearl were to take me under their wing – and with luck the extra work for me would cancel out the commission rate.

As I got up to go, I took one last look at Adele, the *real* face of Pearl Agency.

Admit it, Luke, she wouldn't have bothered to meet you if she didn't think you or your proposal had potential.

'Goodbye,' I said. 'I look forward to my first client.'

'Goodbye, Luke.'

It was a question of trusting that the other party was up to the job. I knew I was.

Adele had let Terry, the photographer, know I was on my way to his studio in Battersea. The shoot was as much a whole new ball game for him as it was for me. He was used to taking pictures of 'birds', as he called them in his husky London accent. Terry was in his fifties and looked as if he'd indulged in the good living that his trade in pictures of barely clothed girls had bought him over the decades.

I stood among the tripods at the back of the white room and felt awkward as he shifted furniture and drapes around. Having my photo taken by the art student had been fine, since neither of us were entirely sure of what we were doing. We both relaxed into the session knowing we were helping the other out. I was now entering a completely different league.

Adele had advised me to wear a suit today, so I wore my black one. I'd bought it and the dark grey one I'd worn at the interview with Adele from my local Oxfam store a couple of weeks ago in an attempt to go upmarket. It was a new phase of my new career. A realisation that if I was in any way serious about the escort work then I needed to make more of an effort to look the part. A good but cheap suit papered over the cracks. It looked smart without a great deal of effort, and I could dress it up or down with a T-shirt or white shirt as appropriate.

'Right, Luke. If you could come over here,' Terry beckoned.

I joined him in front of a gold brocade curtain. 'I'm not a model,' I blurted out. 'I don't know how to stand.'

Terry raised his eyebrows and chuckled, and I found myself grinning back.

'Don't worry,' he reassured, patting me on the shoulder in a fatherly fashion. 'We're going to have fun with this, okay? I'll tell you what to do, and how to pose, and before you know it you'll have forgotten there's even a camera pointing at you.'

I wasn't sure if I wanted to forget the camera. In what other situation would I find myself standing with one hand in my pocket, barefoot, shirtless beneath my jacket, with a look on my face 'like you're pleased that you've just given her one', as Terry had suggested. He shot me lounging back on a cream settee as if I was ready and waiting for the girls queuing up. And hanging from the doorframe with nothing but a towel knotted as tight as I could around my hips, battling the law of gravity.

'That's it, Luke, you've got to tempt them but leave the rest to their imagination!' threw out Terry, without looking up from his camera.

It was only the thought of the potential clients these pictures might attract that kept me from bolting out of there. It wasn't Terry, nor the set-up of the studio that got to me. They were all that I had imagined. But there was something that definitely got under my skin about being put on the spot like this and laying myself bare even while I was semi-clad. When I was with a client, I was playing a role of sorts, and it was between me and her. But there was no hiding from Terry's camera. It saw right through me. Exactly what I was doing.

'Now, Luke, if you could get your kecks back on, we'll get a few snaps of you out on the balcony while the sun's still out.'

I looked out on the deep green tops of the trees of Battersea Park, a whole world away from the hustle and bustle of the West End. A late afternoon breeze tickled my skin.

'Very *au naturel*, eh? That's *my* outback, mate,' he smiled with warmth. 'Y'know, they used to have fairy lights running between them, and a walkway. Magical. The rest of London was black and white back then . . .'

I wasn't quite sure what he was getting at. London had always been a Technicolor world for me. Lights and action. That was what had drawn me here. It wasn't the whole story. I'd found *that* out. But it was never monochrome, that's for sure.

Terry coughed to bring both of us back to the job in hand.

'Right, son, if you could turn towards me.' He gripped a leg of the tripod and peered over the top of his camera. 'It goes like this, Luke. You've got London as your backdrop, all right?'

I nodded and awaited further instructions. Terry bent down to look through his viewfinder.

'Now, I'd like you just to think about those hordes of *gorgeous* birds out there lining up for you to work your way through.'

I did. The camera whirred.

Taking precautions

In the heat of the moment, it's very tempting and far too easy not to bother with contraception. You fear it'll ruin the moment; that the passion you both have will quickly fizzle out. But protection isn't just about not getting pregnant. Using condoms prevents the spread of sexually transmitted diseases (STDs) too, that if left untreated can ruin your *whole* life, not just the sex bit . . . Because of my work, I get tested once a month. If you have any worries, visit your doctor or local sexual health clinic for a check-up.

- Be prepared. Guys should always carry condoms if sex seems on the agenda. Wise girls do so too. Take responsibility for your own protection.
- Choosing the right size of condom is important. If in doubt, use Regular. But there is so much variety – size, flavour, strength –- that if either of you have a preference, let your partner know. My favourite is Extra Sensitive.
- Instead of taking time out for the guy to sheath himself, include it in the foreplay so that both of you are involved. The key is for him to be fully aroused, so hot him up via touch and mutual masturbation first. Remove the condom from its wrapper and ensure it's the right way round. And with one hand halfway up the length of his penis, use the other hand to place the condom at its head. Squeeze the condom tip to rid it of any air, and roll the rest down the shaft. Practise on a banana or courgette to hone your skills!
- Though by the time the condom's on, the guy is so ready for action that he's not too bothered about how it got there. Which is all the more reason for a girl to make sure it's properly fitted . . .

Cyan

Late October

Hotel corridors all look the same. Door upon door going on forever, identical with their faceless brass handles. Except for the numbers, of course. But there's a different story behind every one of them. I realised that the first time I'd been called out to one. I had no idea what to expect, so my mind chose to fill in the gaps. I was trying to picture her. Trying to picture I don't know who. Not that it bothered me too much what any of the girls looked like. A woman's body was a woman's body as far as I was concerned. It was their personalities that differed, and so that was my inroad to feeling comfortable with any of them. Every client seemed to have hang-ups of some sort or other about their looks, even the most beautiful ones. So, at the end of the day, it was confidence that proved the great leveller in the sexing-up stakes. *Any* girl who accepted her imperfections and knew what she wanted from me was everything a hot-blooded guy could ask for.

One after another blank door rushed past me as I headed quickly down the heavy-duty carpet of the fifth floor looking for my client's room like I knew where I was going. Because I had to appear to anyone I might meet as if I knew exactly what I was doing. Escorts can't afford to dither or look out of place.

Presumably the hotel staff from the top downwards knew this

sort of thing went on. Only neither they nor I could make it too obvious. So I dressed smart-casual like a hotel guest to blend in. And there was to be No Loitering. Except it was hard not to look conspicuous and raise suspicions when you were trying to find the room number. But if they noticed me this time, it would make it easier for them to notice me another time if ever I got asked back by this client, or anyone else.

I halted outside 553, and took a deep breath before I knocked. The agency hadn't told me the girl's name, but they did say that there was a good chance I'd know who she was. And I'd certainly have heard of her father. Though they weren't saying who he was either.

The point in telling me was so I acted nonplussed, like I didn't recognise her when she opened the door. Which I didn't anyhow.

For a split second she looked as if she'd forgotten she'd even called for me. And then her eyes lit up.

'Luke? Do come in,' she beckoned in a mid-Atlantic twang.

I walked right on in. And stopped dead. The room looked like a bomb had hit it. There were clothes and shoes strewn around, and they seemed to cover every surface.

'Please sit down,' she said, and directed me to the bed. Which was fortunate since there wasn't any space anywhere else. I shifted some of the mess out of the way to make room.

I watched the girl busy herself like she had something else on her mind. Which left me wondering what to do with myself. And while I waited in silence, I tried to work out whether I could work out who she was. I knew I had sort of seen her face before somewhere.

'Oh, I'm Cyan, by the way,' she finally murmured with her back to me, as she peered at herself close-up in the dressing-table mirror. The table was covered in bottles and potions and makeup and whatever.

Cyan? That rang a bell.

And then the penny dropped. I could see her reflection over

her shoulder. The familiar eyes, the pouting mouth. Her face had graced many a tabloid page over the past few years. I hoped the light-bulb going off in my head didn't show on my face if she was watching me watching her in the mirror.

Cyan's father had been big in the Eighties. I mean, *major,* but only for a couple of years. One step up from a One Hit Wonder. And she was still living off his tired fame. But somehow it was working for her. With no visible means of support, she was staying at one of London's top hotels and hiring me for a couple of hours. Presumably the royalties hadn't yet dried up.

I shifted a little on the bed so I could get a better look at Cyan in the mirror. She was in her mid-twenties, with not much flesh on her. She could've done with a decent meal. And she was sort of pretty under all the stuff she'd done to her hair and her heavy makeup.

Cyan finished doing her eyes, straightened herself and turned towards me, and I stopped gawping. I leaned back on my hands on the bed and straightened out my legs and crossed them at the ankle to give her the impression I was relaxed about whatever she decided to do. Yet sitting in the middle of the room I couldn't help but watch her flit about like she couldn't settle – and try to work out what I was doing here.

Cyan stopped in her tracks and stared at me as if she'd only just realised I was still there. She looked puzzled.

'Luke, it's Luke, isn't it?'

'Yes, it is,' I reminded her. 'Are you in London for long?'

She didn't answer but instead headed over to the minibar and pulled open the door.

'You'd like something?' she offered. 'You can come and choose whatever you want.'

'Thanks, Cyan, I will,' I replied, pulling myself to my feet.

It was important to engage with her, I decided, even though she seemed well and truly out of it. So that in those moments when she was back on Planet Earth, neither she nor I would be caught off-guard.

I joined Cyan beside the minibar. She held the door open though she didn't really need to. It was if she was trying to find something to occupy herself with between all her flapping about. Like she could still hear that voice that's inside you when you're drunk, telling you to act as normal as possible. Until you have another drink and silence it for the night.

I bent down to take a closer look at what was on offer, and I ended up picking a Bud. I was surprised when Cyan passed me a glass. I usually drank out of the bottle, yet there was something touching in Cyan even thinking of a glass for me in the state she was in. I looked up at her from behind the bar's door.

'Thanks.' I nodded at her and smiled, de-capping the bottle and decanting the Bud into the glass. I edged the empty bottle onto the top of the minibar above my head, and raised my filled glass to Cyan.

'Can I get you something?' I offered, my hand running over the bottles on the inside of the door.

Cyan held up a glass and shook her head. The tumbler was full with a clear liquid that I suspected wasn't water.

I took a gulp of the beer and stood up and shut the bar door. The beer bottle was pushed up against a crumpled sheet of tin foil.

They don't wrap chocolate in foil any more.

I acted nonchalant, though my mind was whirring. I didn't do drugs, never wanted to touch them. It was a scene I'd always managed to avoid, through chance more than anything. Back home my mates and I had been mostly into sports and keeping ourselves fit, so doing drugs hadn't really figured.

I went and sat back down on the bed again. Cyan was alternately drinking and wavering, looking lost by the minibar now, watching me, though looking as if she wasn't quite sure what she'd got me here for.

Presumably she'd called the agency when she'd been in better shape earlier in the evening. But whatever she'd been drinking since then meant that she'd all but forgotten why I was there.

Or maybe this was how she liked her sex. Drunken and fumbling in the half-light. It wouldn't have been the first time I'd found myself in that situation, one or both of us out of it back in Aus. Though money wasn't in the frame then.

I took another swig from the bottle and watched the girl struggle around the room. It didn't help that she was in stilettos and a tight cocktail dress that didn't leave a great deal of room for manoeuvre. Even less if the wearer was drunk.

'Hang on!' Cyan suddenly blurted, and woozily waved her hand at me. She zigzagged towards the bathroom and careered unsteadily into the doorframe, and then disappeared from view. The door slammed behind her. I heard the metallic grating of the lock, and what sounded like her bumping into the sink. I winced.

When it went quiet I relaxed a little. Cyan was in the bathroom doing whatever, while I was sat here twiddling my thumbs. For a split second it crossed my mind to leave there and then. But I needed the cash.

I got up and wandered over to the minibar again and had another look at the silver foil. There wasn't any other drugs paraphernalia as far as I could see. Maybe I was reading her wrong. But I didn't think so.

If Cyan was doing drugs as well as drink, then there was all the more reason to get the hell out of there. I didn't want to get caught up in some hotel or police raid that might come a pop star's daughter's way. Not if I could help it.

I padded around the room, casting an unfocused eye over the chaos, not wanting to check it too closely. I didn't want to be caught snooping either, but remaining on the bed like I hadn't moved at all seemed just as false. I went and perched on the dressing-table stool and stared at myself in the mirror.

I couldn't and shouldn't forget I was now on the Pearl Agency's books. They, after all, were the high end of the business. That was why Cyan had called them in the first place. It was the agency the high-rollers used. If I did a runner now, Cyan would surely tell Pearl of my escape. It wouldn't look good at all.

I picked up one of Cyan's bottles of gloop, half-read the label, and then set it down again. I traced a finger through a tray of different-coloured powders, inspected it, and then wiped it away on my trousers. I swivelled on the seat so I was facing the room, and stood up and wandered back towards the bed. Full circle.

I scanned the room again. Nothing seemed to have been properly unpacked and put away. The wardrobe door was wide open and if any clothes remained on coat-hangers they were hanging on for dear life. The rest sat in a pile below, having settled where they were flung by the looks of it. An open suitcase was on the floor by the window, also full of crumpled clothes.

Like you'd expect a pop star's daughter's room to be.

It struck me that I'd heard no sound coming from the bathroom for a while. For how long? However slow she was taking things, I would still be getting paid for my time. Though that didn't mean there weren't other things I'd rather be doing on a night like this. This kind of work could sure do hell to your personal life if you didn't watch it, I could see that. Already I couldn't just go out for a drink or to a club with my mates when I felt like it, or a kick-around in the local park like I used to. Arranging anything far in advance was virtually out of the question since I never knew when I might get a call-out. Even letting Mum know when I'd next phone her. I no longer gave her a date. I just called. Because when I got a booking, I went, because that was my job, whoever or whatever might turn up.

A night in with Cyan. What do I hear bid?

And that was another thing. I had to make the most of my clients since I was barely getting it any other way these days. I had the occasional one-night stand, that was true, but that was all I allowed myself. However, even if my mates scored of a night and I went home empty-handed, it didn't really bother me. After all, there'd be a girl coming round the corner shortly who was happy to pay.

Sometimes I got bored of having to put on an upbeat mood and happy face for work, especially on a cold wet night when I'd rather be at home in front of the box. A long-term girlfriend would end up only getting my low moods, like those people who dated comedians and found themselves paired up with sad gits. Sharing me with other women wouldn't be fair on her either. And I certainly wouldn't want to lead some weird double life that I couldn't be honest about. I was already having to be careful who I told about my work. When I'd worked at the pub, I'd never let on to my fellow bar staff what I got up to on my days off. The lot at the café still didn't know either. And as far as back home was concerned, it was a world away. What my Mum didn't know, she wouldn't worry about.

The bathroom door was jerked open with a shudder, and Cyan marched out, too bright-eyed and bushy-tailed for her own good. I sat straight up, on my guard.

'Luke, Luke,' she repeated, with her full focus on me. 'Luke,' she repeated again, 'I'm so glad that you came.'

She stressed her words like she was trying somehow to make up for her earlier absent-mindedness.

'My pleasure, Cyan.'

Cyan made straight for her dressing table and leaned against its edge with a stilettoed foot sticking out behind her like a stork, and fumbled about in her makeup bag. The next thing I knew, she'd tottered over to the minibar and flattened out the foil sheet on the one clean surface in the whole damn room, and was laying out a line of coke, gesturing to me with her hand to join her.

'No thanks, Cyan,' I muttered, feeling uncomfortable. 'But don't mind me,' I countered. *One* of us had to keep their wits about them, and it sure wasn't going to be her.

I watched Cyan bow her head over the coke and vacuum up a line. She sniffed a couple of loud sniffs, and her hand went to her nose to wipe away the excess. I imagined the coke mixing with all the other stuff she'd done tonight – the alcohol and whatever had kick-started her in the bathroom.

God, this was getting too much.

I jerked to my feet.

'I've got to go to the loo,' I blurted out, just to get out of there. Just for a few minutes. I was starting to feel bloody out of it myself.

I shut the bathroom door with force behind me, made sure it was locked, and breathed a sigh of relief. And then looked around the room.

It looked like a bomb had hit it. A much bigger fucking bomb than the one that had landed in her bedroom. The place was a bloody drug den. There were no two ways about it. It was a hell-hole. I felt dirty just looking at it all. I didn't want to touch a single surface. There were syringes, *used* ones too. With Cyan or whoever's blood on it. *Fuck.*

It was all doing my head in. But I didn't know where to go. Out of the frying pan and into the shitting fire, whichever side of the door you were on. I kept my wits about me *now*. I made damn sure that I wasn't in the needle's line of fire. I touched nothing and watched every step I took to the basin. I hit the taps with my elbows and let the water run over my hands and washed my face, avoiding the soap. I let the water on my skin dry itself, and rubbed my damp hands on my trousers, not daring to use the towels.

Even though I had my shoes on, I tiptoed my way back through the debris to the door. I didn't want to risk taking anything with me. Even the air felt contaminated.

I closed the door on it, although the scene on the other side wasn't any better. Not that I'd expected it to be. I stood on the edge of the room, biting my lip, saying nothing.

Cyan was *way* out of it. She had pulled herself up the bed and was now slouched against the headboard. One arm was splayed out and I could see the needle marks, the other was limp in her lap alongside a syringe. Her eyes had rolled back in her head like she was trying to view the underside of her brain.

There wasn't going to be much else happening tonight, I knew that.

'Cyan,' I said in a strong, clear voice that I somehow trusted might get through her muffled skull. 'I'm going to go now. I'm taking my fee from your bag . . .'

I squatted down beside the dressing-table stool and up-ended Cyan's bag. I took care to touch only her money and pulled the notes out of her purse with the tips of my fingers and counted it out loud. It wasn't the full rate for my time but it was enough. It at least made me feel I was being upfront with her, though I suspected that I was the only person in the room who had the faintest idea I was even there.

I slipped the evening's money into my wallet, took one last glance at the comatose girl on the bed, slipped out of the room, and headed away as fast as I could – not looking back – down the corridor and out of there.

Stagz

Hallowe'en approaching

To be honest, I got a real buzz checking out my entry on the Pearl Agency's homepage. Scrolling down the hot shots of all the top-class gorgeous girls on their books, and in the middle of them was a pic of little ol' me, the only guy, just asking for a speech bubble saying 'I can't believe my fucking luck'.

I'd made damn sure my face was plastered *everywhere*. Google 'London escorts' and my details could be found at more or less any of the agencies you happened to log on to. I tried not to think too much about the possibility that someone I knew might spot me on the web, but then again, checking out male escorts wasn't exactly what my mates were into. And since I wanted to be successful, I had to risk it anyhow. It showed I was damn *serious*.

Which was more than could be said about most of the other guys in the business. You could tell by the photos they used. Grainy ones downloaded from their mobiles. Or they'd got a mate to take a snap of them sitting looking awkward on the sofa in the corner of their lounge room. Which meant they were amateurs, like me and my mates had been back when we were doing exactly the same thing.

Terry had definitely helped me up my game. I'd taken the opportunity to buy my own set of pictures from his shoot for use outside Pearl, and they seemed to be doing their job. Because I'd very quickly picked up on one of the most basic laws of business: that you had to be prepared to spend money to make money. The photos weren't cheap but they were damn good ones. I trusted that the girls out there could tell too.

As it turned out, the boys could as well. And that wasn't something I'd bargained for.

Bob's warm baritone voice was friendly and welcoming.

'Luke, I'm from Stagz, the gay site, and we've seen how you stand out on the other sites, and we want to make you an offer.'

I'd taken a walk through Green Park after seeing Jenny as a short cut between Piccadilly and the Mall, down to the Thames. I was in the mood for looking at some of the sights on the tourist trail for a change, like the sentries outside St James's Palace and the view of the London Eye from across the river. It was well into autumn but hot for England, everywhere looked green, and for a change I wore only a T-shirt and jeans. I slowed and listened, intrigued, though wary too. Advertising my wares on a gay site had certainly never been part of my game plan.

'We're getting women calling us,' Bob continued, 'and they want a straight guy.'

I made for the nearest bench. 'Well, you've come to the right place!'

I lounged back on the seat and watched a young woman on the grass opposite bring her buggy to a halt and unstrap her toddler. The boy struggled onto his feet, and promptly tumbled over and began to bawl. The woman rushed to soothe him. I put a finger in one ear and crouched lower to listen clearly.

'As you're no doubt aware, our boys aim mostly at the gay market.' Bob's tone had turned serious. 'We've no one on our books like yourself, who's there for the girls.'

I almost whacked my mobile against my head.

God, why hadn't I thought of that?

Because what Bob was telling me made an awful lot of sense.

If there were so few male escorts aiming at women – and I knew that to be true – then where else would many of the girls start their search but on the gay sites? And it was probably more likely they'd go down that route than search for me on the predominantly female sites. I'd been promoting myself in the wrong place!

The young woman was now sitting on the grass beside the buggy, and the boy was bouncing on her lap and chuckling with happiness. I wondered whether such an image would ever be a part of my own future. If I ever did settle down with Ms Right at some point in the future, I knew for certain that she wouldn't be hearing about what I was getting up to *now*. I didn't want to think too much about *that*. It was easier to look at the woman with the toddler in front of me and wonder whether she'd ever thought of phoning for a guy like me. Or ever would, come to that.

Bob brought me back to my senses. I homed in on the voice coming from my phone.

'Luke, you've gone quiet. I haven't said the wrong thing?' Bob sounded unnerved, like he might lose his latest find, but being a good businessman, turned the situation round sharpish. 'Because I'm sure we could find someone else . . .'

'I'm sorry. I was just thinking things over. Your offer sounds very promising,' I countered, trying to sound cool.

'We think so,' agreed Bob. 'So, because this is a new venture for both us *and* you, we'd like to take you on our books for six months. See how it goes. And then you pay the standard fee from there.'

From what Bob said I couldn't see how I could lose. The trial would either work or it wouldn't, but there was no harm in giving it a go.

'I see, I see,' I said to stall him and let him know I was still engaged.

I could see the advantages of being on the Stagz site spreading out before me. I would be the needle in the haystack for all those poor, yearning girls out there in the ether.

I stretched out on the bench, leaning back, one hand with the mobile still to my ear. I looked up at the clear blue sky through my Ray-Bans. The sun felt pleasant on my skin.

When I next spoke I gave myself the air of a fellow professional in the field.

'So, after six months, both of us will be able to tell whether or not this is working,' I said.

'That's right,' replied Bob. He lightened his tone, like he knew he might be skating on *very* thin ice. Though he was gentle with it. 'Have you had a look at the Stagz site, Luke?'

'No, can't say I have, Bob,' I replied, matter-of-factly.

Why on earth would I?

'I suggest you take a look. Not that I expect you to see anything you're after,' he mused, 'but so you get an idea of the format. And then you can mail us some photos and text and we'll go from there.'

'Sounds good, Bob. I'll be in touch.' I couldn't believe how straightforward this all was.

Bob signed off and I flipped the phone shut. I sat for I don't know how long, but the shadows on the grass were longer and the woman and the child had left, and the hairs on my wrists were raised a little. Across the way, a group of teenagers just out of school were kicking a ball around. I eventually got up and started the journey home with my spirits raised. Things felt at last that they were in the right gear.

I checked the web as soon as I got home. There was page after page of naked toned men. Sometimes they even bothered showing their faces.

Fuck! Ass and cock, the lot of it!

Which wasn't exactly what I was offering.

Not until I knew a girl's name, anyway.

The pictures I had spread across the web were ones designed *not* to scare the girls away. I had that sussed, that you had to do the slow reveal. So I introduced myself with a clothed hint of a friendly dating experience and on the next pages did a gradual striptease photo-by-photo down to the towel. They had to imagine the rest.

Bob was true to his word. Once I'd emailed him the stuff, my Stagz page was up and running within days. As it turned out, I needn't have kept an eye on it. I knew the site was 'on air' because my phone just didn't stop ringing. All day.

The first time, I was making myself a sandwich for lunch. I'd wiped my hands on my jeans and pulled my mobile out of my pocket. I hadn't recognised the number, which wasn't unusual. It just meant that I knew to go into escort mode and put the caller at ease straight away. I'd never bothered getting myself a second mobile for work, since I never saw myself as living a double life. I just had to be careful if I took a business call when mates who didn't know what I was up to were around.

I didn't get a chance to even say 'hello'.

'Luke! I saw your page on the Stagz site . . .'

My hackles rose. It was a man's voice. But then again, maybe I was jumping to conclusions. He could be hetero like Brian, wanting me to test-drive his harem.

'My name's Marty,' he continued without taking a breath. 'I wondered if you could come round?'

I shifted a slice of cheese around on the plate with my index finger in an ever-decreasing circle. I was none the wiser as to what he wanted me for. Or maybe I simply didn't want to think too deeply about it.

'Marty, good to hear from you,' I lied. 'As you'll have seen on the site, I'm only offering my services to women . . .'

'Oh, but Luke, surely you could make an exception?' he purred.

My finger stopped dead on the plate and ground the cheddar into it.

'I'm so sorry to disappoint you, but I can't. I hope you understand.'

How could you be so naive? Who did you think would call you if you advertised on a site called Stagz? God, I'm going to have to make things SO clear.

I piled the pieces of cheese onto a slice of bread, added a few pieces of cucumber and put the other slice of bread on top. I placed my whole hand over the sandwich and flattened it down, then drew the bread knife with a sharp flourish diagonally from one corner to the other. *Exactly* how I liked it.

I had the sandwich halfway to my mouth when my phone rang again.

Bloody hell. Give us a break.

I did a mental toss-up of taking a quick bite of sandwich, but my hunger would have to wait.

'Hello, Luke, I'm Richard,' came a rich baritone down the line.

I held my breath and stared down at my sandwich.

'I'm not phoning for me,' he explained.

Ah, a couple.

An image of a nubile young woman and her older partner watching the two of us getting it on flickered through my mind.

'No, it's a present for my boyfriend.'

The image dissolved and I was abruptly back in the real world.

It wasn't even as if I had anything against gay guys. It's simply that I was avowedly straight. I was very aware that there were other guys out there who were prepared to swing whatever way the job demanded, which was surely why Stagz had called me up in the first place? Because the girls who were calling weren't that hot on hiring a bisexual.

I managed to give Richard the slip, and returned to eating my lunch, although I had lost my appetite. I finished up my meal and ran the plate and cutlery under the hot tap. I had the tea towel over my arm and was putting the plate back in the cupboard under the sink when my phone rang again.

I gritted my teeth, mentally counted to a quick ten to calm myself down, stood up and whipped my mobile from my pocket.

I didn't even bother to check who was calling. It'd be another gay bloke.

Right first time.

'Luke, Charlie here. I saw your entry on the Stagz site,' he chirruped.

'Nice of you to call, Charlie,' I said.

'Would it be possible to book an hour with you for later this week?' There was shyness in his voice like it was his first time.

What he needed, surely, was a nice, kind gay man to bite off his escort cherry. There was *no way* I could, or would, help him out.

'I'm sorry, but my service is for women only. You might not have noticed, but my picture was in the section aimed at *women*? I'm sorry I can't help.'

The call ended, and though I'd remained calm throughout, inside I had been – and was still – fuming. *God, there are hundreds and hundreds of gay guys on Stagz, so why in hell's name phone the lone straight one?*

Because I'd fulfil a fantasy, that was why. Having a straight guy would be a gas for a lot of gay guys out there.

I had no desire to have sex with a man, yet if I convinced myself that I would only be doing it for the money – and I accepted that a straight bloke might convince himself of that – then I feared how I might feel looking back in five years' time when I planned to be well out of this game. There was selling yourself, and there was selling yourself.

I needed to go for a walk. My head was throbbing and I hoped some fresh air might clear my mind a bit. I'd go for a circular tour that took in the local shops and pick up a paper and a Coke or something en route.

I'd just got out of my front garden and closed the gate behind me when my phone went off again. For a split second I considered ignoring it and just not answering. But it kept on ringing, and I felt obliged to answer.

There was no escaping these guys for now, not merely because of the sheer number of them calling me, but also because I *had* to pick up or I risked missing a call from any woman who might be trying to connect with me. And given it could be her male partner phoning for her, it meant I *had* to listen to the whole of a conversation to know what the caller was *really* getting at.

I took a deep breath. 'Hi, Luke here.'

I turned left down the street, my head down.

'Hello, Luke.'

It was a woman's voice. At last. I felt myself relax.

'My name's Christopher, I'm interested in seeing you.'

Fuck!

I felt myself redden, and stared down at my feet again. I set off walking again but it felt like I was wading through treacle.

'If you read my page, I make it clear that I only cater for women. I'm sorry I can't help you, Christopher.'

I spoke like I was talking to someone who didn't speak English. Slow and clear and to the point, so there was no chance of any misunderstanding. Then I ended the call.

I took a few heavy steps forward. I was worried that I shouldn't have been so damn blunt. *Suppose he reports back to the site?*

Surely they'd understand. How did they expect a straight guy they'd specifically signed up for the girls to respond to the gay blokes?

I hurried on to the shops as if just by quickening my pace I'd somehow miss any more calls. It worked for a little while. I was in the newsagent's reading the tabloid headlines when someone called again. I chose to ignore it.

I picked up a copy of the *Daily Mirror* and walked down the aisle to the counter. On my right the whole aisle was given over to confectionery. I still didn't get the Brits' thing about sweets.

My phone rang again. I didn't answer it. It rang again.

One thing I now knew for sure: I was going to have to have a real hard look at my web page to see if there was any way I could shake the guys off my trail.

If it was going to be like this for the next six months then I would definitely have to consider if I really wanted to be on the Stagz site. Because even if the reason I was there was to catch any girls who might stray that way, I had to weigh up whether it was worth it.

Once outside the shop, I trawled through the call register on my mobile and returned the calls.

The first number dialled up another gay man. My patience was definitely now running on empty. It really did feel as if I'd somehow found myself in an alternative universe where the men were all gay. I cast an eye over the guys coming out of the shop and others walking down the street. *Maybe it's just the Brits. Maybe they're ALL gay!*

I shook my head a couple of times, half to get *that* thought out of my mind, half to get it back on an even keel so I could act a bit more professional towards whoever might call. Even if I didn't want to cater for the boys, it was only right that I remained polite *whoever* happened to call me. After all, if they thought I looked like the sort of guy they were after, who was I to complain?

Yet while I might have enjoyed the gays' unspoken flattery, and let's be honest, a part of me did, even though my patience was wearing damn thin, it didn't mean I wasn't on edge the whole day. I wanted my business back to how it was before, when it was only girls' voices I had to listen to.

Why can't the girls be so bloody keen?

I redialled the second number I'd ignored in the shop. A woman's voice answered, sounding ten times more sweet than it would normally have done.

'Hello, Luke, I'm so glad to have found you!' she exclaimed, which mirrored what I felt on hearing the soft tones of a woman.

'I'm Angie, by the way,' she added.

I was back on solid ground.

'Angie, it's lovely to hear from you,' I replied, almost singing with relief. We arranged to meet the following week.

Hallelujah!

The third call I'd received, however, was from another man.

The calls from men just kept on coming throughout the rest of the day. It must have been a couple of hours after I spoke to Angie that they'd reached double figures. I felt like I was being hunted down. By the end of the day I'd logged around thirty calls from guys.

It's a shame I don't swing both ways. I'd be rolling in it!

It had taken *months* to hear from as many women.

Janice

I was starting to realise that I stuck out like a sore thumb on the Stagz website. My picture was *so* different to the others that I couldn't help fearing that it might be giving the impression that I didn't know what I was doing. Even though I was after a different market than these gay guys, it still *looked* like I'd literally turned up at the party in the wrong clothes.

'But that's what gets you noticed, Luke,' reassured Janice after I told her my fears as we nestled together beneath her Egyptian cotton sheets after our bout of fevered lovemaking. 'It's pretty sharp of you, you know.'

I turned my head to look at her. 'You think so?'

'Of course!' she said with glee. 'You scan down the picture index and it's *Naked Man, Naked Man, Naked Man – oh, this guy's fully dressed.*'

'But *that's* my point,' I frowned at her.

Janice was in her mid-forties and stylish, and she flipped between regarding me as a lover, and five minutes later as the son she'd never had. She was in television, though she only told me that on our second date. I hadn't recognised her the first time. I'm not sure if she appreciated that or not.

My arm was round Janice's shoulder, and her head rested against my chest.

'The thing is, you're non-threatening and women like that.' She smiled up at me, then sensed my confusion. 'It's important to think how women think. You're already halfway there. You're appealing to women because you don't look intimidating,' she explained. 'To put it bluntly, you haven't put a picture of your cock on the website.'

That was true. The Stagz site was *so* bottom-line gay.

'My picture's all right, then. Even wearing clothes?'

'It makes you look like you're serious about what you're doing. It's not all out on the table,' she said, stroking my chest and tweaking my left nipple. 'Your picture comes as quite a relief, I can tell you. It made *me* notice you. And you're also cute, of course, which helps,' she grinned up at me.

'Oh, I knew *that*,' I smirked back, and she gave me a playful flick of her index finger against my cheek. Then she pulled away from me and got out of bed. I sat up with a start.

'What?'

'I'm just getting some paper. I'll show you something.'

She wrapped her dressing gown around her and padded across the room to her dressing table, where she pulled out a blank sheet of cream paper from the middle drawer and placed it on the table. She selected a pen from a pot by the mirror.

'Let's take a look at you.'

Janice was bent over the paper, her hand clasping the pen just above the page as if she was waiting for inspiration.

'You're going to draw me?' I frowned at her from the bed. 'What is this, bloody *Titanic*?'

'In so many words,' she nodded, and began scribbling. I craned my neck, but from where I was sitting I couldn't see.

'The photo's doing its job, agreed? Potential clients like to see a happy, smiling face like yours.'

I nodded but she didn't look up. Instead she pulled the stool from beneath the table and sat down. She bent low over the page, her right elbow across the bottom of the page and her left hand scrawling away.

'So the next step is to get your text right.'

She turned to me this time.

'You're saying that what I've written isn't up to scratch?' I gave her a wounded look that was only half-joking.

'It's *all right*, Luke,' she reassured me. 'Certainly better than a lot of the men on the site.'

Which wasn't saying a great deal. Some of them didn't give much more away than the size of the bloke's dick. Or they were so banal: '*Available now. Ring me for a good time.*' The sort of thing a female escort might reel in a man with, but that wouldn't work the other way round. Women were after more than just the physical. At least I knew *that*.

'I'm a writer, Luke,' Janice stressed, looking straight at me. 'Let me rewrite your text for you, and I guarantee I'll triple the amount of work you'll get.'

'You can do that?'

My hands, still under the bedclothes, smoothed out the sheet on each side of me in little circles.

'I'm also a woman too, in case you'd forgotten. I know what we want to hear – and it's a damn sight different to how a man's brain thinks.'

She seemed to know what she was talking about.

'Yeah, that makes sense.'

I pulled back the covers, flipped my legs over the edge of the bed and leaned back on my arms, watching her.

'And you have to remember,' Janice continued, 'that this whole male escort game is a big risk for any woman to get involved with, I can assure you.'

She turned to look at me to emphasise the point she was making. That in spite of all her professional confidence, even admitting to herself that she wanted to hire a man for sex and then going from that point to actually tracking one down had been no easier for her.

I sensed that I needed to remember that, to honour it.

'I have friends who are happy to go on holiday on the other side of the world to treat themselves to a man, but who would never dare to hire an escort on home soil.' She turned back to her sheet of paper and continued jotting down notes as she spoke. 'Through your profile, you can let women know that you are there for them,' she explained. 'That all their bravery has been rewarded.'

Janice was a godsend. She was on my side. But on theirs too.

I had no reason to believe that Janice didn't know what she was doing. She was a well-respected TV presenter, for one thing. She hadn't got there by not knowing how to get a message across. Her expertise and know-how could make all the difference.

'So I have to make it as easy as possible, and make sure women feel secure when they see my web page? To make sure *I* get plenty of work. A reciprocal relationship.'

I liked how that sounded.

'That's exactly right,' she agreed.

I picked up my trousers from the floor and pulled them on before joining Janice at the table. As I read over her shoulder, I massaged the other.

'Oh, that's lovely,' she purred, and carried on with her writing.

I wondered if this was what Janice *really* enjoyed. Doing the thing she was good at while a young buck treated her to a decent bit of TLC. She'd told me once how she'd put her all into getting this far in her career – and when she'd at last found time to think about a relationship, all the guys her age had settled down and had families.

'*I will make you feel completely safe. My pleasure is to pleasure others,*' I read out loud. *Shit!*

Janice stopped writing and looked up at me with a big smile across her face.

'Oh yes, Luke. You're good at the physical side of this game, you know. You just need a bit of help getting the word around.'

Janice shifted sideways along the stool, and patted the space beside her. 'Join me.'

Her hand reached out and stroked its way down my arm. So I sat down and cuddled up next to her. The silk of her dressing gown felt delicious against my skin. I wrapped an arm around her waist and she nestled into me.

'See.'

Her finger traced a list of phrases that ran the length of the A4 sheet. '*Very attentive and caring.*' '*I provide a wonderful and satisfying experience.*' I imagined women reading it, and found myself blushing. She made me sound like a real professional. And like I was talking right to them.

'Thanks,' I said, not really knowing at that moment what else I could say.

Janice folded the sheet of paper in half and then in half again, and held it up, offering it to me. But when I moved to take it from her, she swiped her hand away from me, reaching up as far as she could. And when I held her tighter and went to grab at the paper again, she pulled away and put the list in the opposite hip pocket of her gown and patted it.

What's she playing at?

I reached across to Janice, laughing. She gripped my forearm.

'No, Luke.' There was a stern edge to her voice. She was serious. 'I need to tidy it up. You want it to be the best it can be, don't you?' Her voice was gentler now. 'I'll email it to you when I've finished it.'

Her hold relaxed. 'How many guys advertise on the Stagz site? Thousands?'

I shrugged. I looked down at the stool and pawed at the silk of her dressing gown draped over it. I pictured the pages and pages of boys that any potential client had to go through if they were trawling the site randomly. The guys all sort of blurred into each other.

'I suppose it must be. There's not as many aiming at the women, though.'

At least the Stagz administrators gave those catering for the girls a separate section on the site, so women could head straight for us once they'd logged in. Not that it didn't cut out the gay clients. I was still fending the gay men off, but thankfully not to the same degree these days.

Janice pushed her fingers through my cropped hair. I looked back up at her. She looked her age, but in a good way. She was handsome rather than pretty, with defined features that gave her authority. She kept herself toned and supple through yoga – which meant the sex was athletic too.

My hand crept up the silk and settled on her thigh, and I stroked it through the smooth material. She said nothing for a little while and I carried on, my eyes on hers, and she began talking again.

'You've already cut down the competition significantly just because of the picture you use. It's not difficult for women to home in on you. With the right message they'll be eating out of your hand.'

'Hope so!' I grinned, pressing my thumb a little deeper into her flesh.

I was listening to Janice, but the truth was, she could have said anything. I was impressed with the way she had been able to keep on talking while I was touching her. I didn't know if I could have done that.

Multi-tasking. A woman's gift.

I shifted my hand further up her leg, and felt Janice tense with pleasure.

'With this, instead of competing with other guys out there looking for female clients, you'll cut it down to the top ten, top five of them.'

She'd clearly given the whole idea an awful lot of thought. I stopped for a second.

'Just because of the right wording?'

My hand slipped beneath the silk and then between her legs so I was able to massage the inside of both thighs simultaneously. I noted her mouth quiver a little as if she was trying to swallow all the pleasure back and focus *hard* on what she was saying.

'The right picture and the right message,' she breathed out deeply. 'They need to match each other. Your picture shows you as cute and professional and non-threatening . . .'

A smile crept up her face, and I cocked my head back at her and smirked, intensifying my hand's motion.

'Well, *yeah*.'

She looked away from me for a couple of seconds and tried not to laugh.

'The text should give the same impression,' she managed to say, still not looking back at me.

Both of us were sitting side by side, and now I faced the mirror too. I could see her eyes reflected back at me in the glass, but they were peering at a spot above both our heads. She spoke in one tone.

'And that'll narrow things down to anyone reading it so they'll know that they definitely want to hire you.'

It took all her effort to try to forget that my fingers were tempting her pussy with a little light flick every so often. That it was more important for her to get her message across to me. Very giving of her, if I thought about it. Because what Janice was telling me made *so* much sense. It would never have crossed my mind unless she had pointed it out. I had only been using instinct to get me this far. Flying by the seat of my pants.

The clock on the bedroom wall told me it was almost time to go.

'Janice,' I spoke softly, and ran my middle finger along her clit so her head jerked back and she let out a small guttural yelp, 'I've got to leave.'

I pulled myself away from her and stood up sharply, and she did the same. Janice looked me in the eye, and I could tell she wanted me to stay. Then she sighed and gave me a big bear hug.

'It's a good job I met you, Luke.'

'Ditto,' I agreed, and looking down at her in my arms, then winked. I pulled myself out of the hug, and left her to finish herself off.

Two days later there was a message from Janice in my Stagz inbox.

'Try this!' it read.

I chewed on my top lip for a little while before I chose to open the attachment and read any further. I'd certainly liked what I'd seen Janice write back in her room, but it didn't stop me from being apprehensive about what she might have added. Would I recognise myself?

I took a deep breath, tapped the appropriate keys and the page opened up for me.

Here goes.

<u>Completely straight male escort available for women and couples.</u>
Hello, my name's Luke, and I am a very attentive and caring 23-year-old Australian guy who loves the company of women.

I am extremely friendly and very easy to get along with, and will put you completely at your ease. I provide a wonderful and satisfying experience whatever your needs and desires might be. I take great pleasure in bringing pleasure to others.

If you've always dreamed of fulfilling a fantasy or longed for a new experience, then I am the man for you. I guarantee to put a smile on your face.

Perhaps this is the first time you have contacted an escort and you feel a bit nervous? With me, you will have nothing to worry about. I will treat you the way you should be treated. I will make you feel completely safe and special.

I am the perfect companion if you are after something a little more formal, and am well spoken and intelligent with a good sense of humour. I also have massage accreditations and experience, so if you are just in need of a relaxing evening in which to unwind, I am the man for you.

I also guarantee to be extremely well-presented with personal hygiene always a priority.

Please give me a call and you will not regret it.

Luke xxx

When I came up for air at the end of the message, I felt like phoning myself for a session.

Bloody hell, Janice.

She'd transformed me into every woman's dream!

It wasn't that I didn't recognise myself. It was just that Janice had given my website twitterings a burnished sheen. She'd written what I'd really liked to have said if I'd known to even say it. She was like one of those archaeologists who clear away all the dust and shit to reveal the real picture beneath. It had taken the off-chance of me meeting her to do that. I *knew* just how lucky I was.

I immediately hit reply and fired off a 'thank you', and straight afterwards cut and pasted the block of text onto my Stagz webpage. I imagined the hordes of women who, once finding my page, wouldn't want to leave without getting in touch.

Gotcha!

Exploring each other

If there's one thing I've learned from escorting, it's to take more time with everything. Sex doesn't have to be just about sharing your bits. Each of you has a whole body to explore. This can act as foreplay, revving you up in preparation, but there's no reason why getting to know each other like this can't be an end in itself. Most women need time to get themselves fully into sex mode. The build-up and anticipation has turned out to be just as sexy and exciting for me. Since a lot of guys would rather cut out the foreplay, a man who values what most women want will make a real impression!

- Take turns to massage each other. This can be both a relaxing start to the evening and a sensual experience for the two of you.
- Let your mouth do the talking. Silently. Cover your partner in kisses, and/or lick, suckle, and nibble them.
- Let your fingers do the walking. Alternate between gentle touching with the fingertips or whole hand stroking.
- Begin at the crown of their head and work your way all the way down. Compliment your partner's positive attributes as you go, to help build their body confidence.
- Home in on the non-genital parts of your partner's body that get *you* going. The nape of their neck, their belly, their ear lobes, wrists, nipples . . .
- Instead, tease your partner's favourite erogenous zones.
- Take it *very* slowly, so by the time you get to penetrative sex the two of you have already reached boiling point.

117

Mae

Christmastime

It was the evening of Christmas Eve, and I was stuck in London for the duration of the break because there wasn't any transport until Boxing Day. Mark had been invited to spend Christmas with Natasha's family in Leeds, and no one else in the house would be sticking around either. Even the tinsel in the shops and the lights blinking in the windows of people's houses couldn't really shake off the cold and damp and the dark, although I had to admire this lot for trying. Every type of building was covered in some sort of glittery festive cheer. Even cranes!

But Christmas for me was supposed to be blazing sunshine and everyone outdoors, having barbies. I was homesick, I suppose, and then my mobile rang and my spirits soared to hear another Aussie voice on the end of the phone.

'Hi Luke, my name's Mae. How'd you like to celebrate Christmas Day with me?' she asked.

I was looking at the TV screen but not registering what I was watching. All I could see was a way out from spending tomorrow by myself. How could I resist?

Mae was on her own in Knightsbridge and needing company for Christmas. She arranged for a cab to pick me up tomorrow afternoon and we'd go out for dinner at the Carlton Tower round the corner from where she lived, and I'd stay the night too. *Merry Christmas, Luke!*

I went back to watching the telly, cheerful now. I turned the sound back up, though I wasn't really listening. I was miles away. Just the sound of Mae's accent had taken me to the other side of the world. Everyone there would be spending tomorrow morning opening presents at Mum's before doing the rounds of the other relatives for lunch and dinner. It would undoubtedly be the same as all the other years – too many family arguments and crap presents – though it would have been nice to catch up with everyone. In the absence of *that*, it seemed somehow special that Mae had happened to call. Of all the people who could have called to ask me over, *she* had. I was going to spend Christmas Day with someone from *home* after all. And so would she. Even though we'd never met before, there was that connection. Plus there'd be some sexual adventure thrown into the mix.

Christmas magic. Or something like that.

On Christmas Day I drew back the living-room curtains to check for the cab. The afternoon light had begun to fade. I shivered and closed the curtains again, and checked my watch. I had on my best suit and my thick winter coat was slung over my arm.

And then I realised that I hadn't got anything to give Mae. I couldn't turn up empty-handed. Not on Christmas Day.

Shit, shit, shit.

If I'd had my wits about me last night I could have at least zipped out for something from the local petrol station. But I hadn't.

I scanned the room, looking for something I might give her. On the coffee table was a wrapped bottle of what looked like brandy or something from Mark that I hadn't yet got round to opening. These days I barely saw him, he spent so much time round at Natasha's. His gift seemed to be saying that he hadn't *quite* dropped his mates for a girl.

There was a handwritten label tied round the bottle's neck. I pulled it off, dug out a Christmas card and signed it for Mae.

Sorted.

The cab journey to Mae's was weird. We were in the capital of England but the streets were almost empty, like in some science-fiction film. Pictures on Christmas cards here were of robins and snow and stuff like that, but London remained dull and grey except for the decorations and lights. The cab driver told me that he didn't mind working today because he'd checked the *Radio Times* and there was nothing decent on the box.

I wished him 'Merry Christmas' as I got out and then headed towards Mae's swish Knightsbridge apartment block. The ground floor was white-washed whereas the other floors were brick. I pressed the buzzer.

'Hey, Luke, let yourself in. I'm on the third floor.'

Even through the crackle, her accent took me back down south. I knocked when I reached her door, and a moment later a girl opened it with a sunshine smile on her face, and it was like Sasha and Chloe all over again. Except she was way better than the both of them. She was an absolute beaut – the 'ten' I'd been looking for. I smiled at the thought that I'd crossed the planet to meet a girl from home.

She beckoned me in. The flat was expensive-looking but stark, though I couldn't help noticing the Christmas tree in the corner of the room with tinsel wrapped round it and a handful of baubles hanging from the ends of the branches.

'Nice tree!'

She gave me a mix of a smile and a frown, and turned her head to look at it.

'Hmm, I'm not sure. I could've done a bit more, but, y'know, it seemed a bit funny making all that effort . . .'

I liked it that other people bothered even just a little. It *did* brighten up the city, even though their efforts couldn't quite keep all the winter gloom away. And I liked it that Mae had bothered too, even though she was in another country. All the more so since no one in my house had got their act together to decorate the place. It was as if each one of us was waiting for someone else to set the ball rolling, but nobody could be bothered.

'Well, Mae, I have to say that you've done a better job than me.'

As well as the tree, she'd laid out red squat candles in glass star-shaped holders at each end of her mantelpiece, alongside foil-covered crackers waiting to be pulled. But my focus was mostly on Mae, who shone in the middle of it all.

Who needs lights and glitter with her around?

Mae had tousled long blonde hair, and she was tall and buxom. What I'd call Pamela Anderson pretty.

'I'm so *glad t*o meet another Aussie,' she beamed.

'Well, me too, Mae,' I grinned. 'Especially today.'

I pulled off my coat and scarf and she took them and hung them up. She turned back to face me and I took her gift and card from the bag and held them out to her.

'Merry Christmas, Mae. Just a little something.'

Mae looked surprised, as if a present was the last thing she was expecting.

'Oh, Luke, thank you, but you know you shouldn't have.'

I cocked my head to one side. 'But I wanted to,' then, sussing that she could quite clearly see what it was, suggested, 'we can toast each other. And the day!'

For a split second I worried that I might have made Mae feel bad for not having anything to give to me. But then again, I was on her time and it was my job to make the girl feel as special as I possibly could.

Mae set down the bottle and then drew out the card from the envelope and read my rushed greeting. She looked up at me with a bashful smile.

'Why, thank you, Luke,' she said, and set it down among a clutch of others arranged on a little round table at one end of her sofa.

I joined her. Mae turned to face me and reached out a hand to touch my arm, and I took a further step towards her so that same arm was now around her waist and drew her towards me. We kissed.

She pulled away seconds later.

'Now, your present. I haven't a *clue* what it could be,' she teased.

'I hope you like it,' I said.

She picked it up from where she'd left it lying on the sofa and started peeling off the wrapping. She uncurled it to halfway down, and held it in both hands so she could take a good look at the Courvoisier label.

I sent Mark a mental thanks for getting me out of a hole, and wished him a Merry Christmas.

Mae pulled off the remainder of the paper.

'You sit down and make yourself comfortable, and I'll go and get some glasses,' she said, and left the room.

I hovered in the middle of the room for a moment and then went and sank into the sofa. I looked around the room but my eyes were continually drawn to the Christmas tree and the tinsel and the little lights that twinkled among the green branches. I realised it was a real one; there were needles on the carpet.

And I suddenly *got* what the Brits were getting at. It was as if the glitter and stuff was some sort of desperate wishful thinking against the dark and the freezing cold. I shivered with the thought of it.

Well, it's certainly not working for me.

'You cold?'

Mae had returned from the kitchen with the brandy in a couple of crystal tumblers. She handed me one and I cupped my hands around it. She shifted towards the fireplace. There was some sort of trendy gas fire thing in the middle of it.

'I can turn up the heating if you like.'

122

She fiddled with a switch at the side of the fire and the flames crept up a little. You could tell they were fake because they didn't change their shape or size beyond that. I wondered what you'd see in them if you kept on looking.

But I had better things to keep my eye on.

I looked back up at Mae, who was leaning against the mantelpiece looking stunning. I mentally backtracked to what she'd last said.

'No worries,' I said, raising my glass. 'I was just thinking about what the Brits have to put up with in winter.'

'I *know*.' Mae grimaced. 'Makes you glad you're an Aussie, doesn't it?' She was trying to be upbeat, but I detected a slight far-from-home sadness in the way she said it.

'You got yourself a real pine tree . . .'

'Just like the English do. It sheds needles like anything though.' The sides of her mouth dropped down. 'But I couldn't see the point of one you have to store away year after year . . .' she half-mumbled to herself, like she was thinking about something else.

'Come and join me, Mae,' I beckoned.

Mae blinked herself out of her daydream and smiled. I budged up to make room for her and she sat down beside me. A moment later she shifted right up so our legs were touching.

'What brought you to England?' I asked, and took a sip of brandy.

The words sounded corny, even as I said them, but it was the question that had to be asked. It still seemed so weird, both of us so far from home but finding ourselves sharing the same sofa on Christmas Day.

Mae pointed to a large black and white photo on the wall. I'd noticed it out of the corner of my eye when I'd arrived but hadn't registered what it was of. She had edged the frame in gold tinsel. I now realised it was a striking headshot of Mae.

I turned to the girl beside me, and moved to stand up. I wanted to take a closer look at her picture.

'Can I?'

'Yeah,' she nodded. 'Go ahead.'

I crossed the room while Mae sipped her brandy and watched me. Close up it was an impressive portrait. Although Terry knew what he was doing, and his pictures were quality, Mae's was premier league.

I took a step back and Mae was suddenly right there behind me. She tucked her thumb into the waistband of my trousers, and I in turn tucked my arm around her neat waist. The two of us stood looking at her picture.

'I'm a model. You know *Vogue* magazine? I've done stuff for them,' she explained, but not in a boastful way – she made it sound as if it was the most natural thing in the world.

'*Shit*. You have?!'

I turned my head to look at her, and she returned a light smile and nodded. I could see why it might seem run-of-the-mill. To *her*.

I looked at the picture again and then back to her to compare the two. The real-life version, not so sharply lit, was touched by softness.

'Do you have a portfolio? I'd love to see it!' I blurted out.

I felt Mae stiffen for a moment.

Social faux pas alert.

'I'm sorry. I didn't mean to sound like a magazine editor,' I corrected myself. 'I bet *everyone* asks to see your photos,' I back-pedalled.

'Wait a second,' she replied, and ushered me back to the sofa while she headed for the bookcase next to the fireplace and, perching on tiptoe, pulled an unmarked album off the top shelf. It was bound in green vinyl and looked heavy by the way she gripped it to her, one hand beneath so she wouldn't drop it.

I began to rise to my feet. 'Let me help you with that.'

'No, Luke.' She shook her head and lugged the portfolio towards me and set it down on my lap.

She was used to looking after herself, I realised.

'There.' She said it like a personal triumph. I looked up at her.

'Take a look,' she instructed, 'and I can fix you a refill. Another brandy?'

'That'd be nice, thanks.'

I'd never really drunk brandy before – beer was my poison – but I liked the warm glow it gave me. And anyhow, we'd be going out to dinner soon, and it took the chill off the thought of going back outside into the cold.

'No problem,' she said. She took my tumbler and I watched her twist round on her heels, her silk and chiffon shift dress fluttering around her bare tanned legs as she did, and then she headed out to the kitchen again.

I shifted my gaze to the album sitting on my lap. I flicked through it in one swift move. Like a time-lapse film I watched Mae evolve from a pretty child to the full-bodied and gorgeous creature I saw before me today. She grew more and more beautiful with the years. I closed the volume again, and waited.

Mae returned, and I watched her graceful stride from the door straight to the sofa.

'Yeah, you're right,' she agreed, confusing me as she handed me my glass. 'People only ever want to see my pictures,' she teased, and nudged me with her elbow.

I hope to see a damn lot more than your pictures, love.

'Shall we?' Mae asked. She didn't wait for an answer but her fingers slipped around the edge of the album cover, and as I drew my hand away she pulled the book open.

She turned the pages, recalling when the photos were taken, and her life story poured out of her. How she'd started off in the children's section of catalogues back home, moved to Sydney and then worked her way out of the country. I set down my glass by my feet and listened, picturing her journey. We pored over the photos, our heads touching. We were very different, it struck me, but on the other hand we weren't that different at all.

Same small-town escape.

Mae closed the album and my hand instinctively reached for hers resting on the book, and I squeezed it gently. She turned and looked me in the eyes, and without saying anything drew her hand and the album away from me and set it down on the floor. She snuggled up to me again and I put my arm around her shoulders and rested my chin on her head. We sat there, saying nothing but just enjoying each other's company. It felt so intimate.

I'd been told by some of my clients that they felt like they'd known me for years. I knew I had that knack of making them feel relaxed in my company. They told me so much about themselves that I might as well have known them for years. But tonight the tables were turned. The feeling with this girl was mutual. We might as well have been boyfriend and girlfriend.

I could see myself walking down the street with this one.

Although, listening to myself, I knew that that was more wishful thinking than anything. As an escort, it was important to remain professional and not step over the line. Things would surely become way too complicated if I were ever to try to take my relationships with clients any further. That's not to say that there weren't ones I'd grown close to, enjoying the level of trust that grew between us. But it came with a mutual respect for the boundaries of my work. It had to. They were paying me for my time with them. And I needed to remember that at all cost.

After a few minutes' silence, Mae pulled her head away and gazed back at me. I gave her a quizzical look in return.

'Do you ever think of returning home, Luke?'

I shook my head. It wasn't something that much crossed my mind.

'Maybe if things don't work out over here, y'know,' I shrugged.

'I live out of a suitcase,' she sighed, her crossed hands gripping my wrist as if to anchor her down to something. 'It's like living in a hotel sometimes.'

I looked around the room at the tree and the decorations. The windows were shielded by long, warm-looking deep green curtains, and the room was carpeted and comfortable,

It doesn't look like a hotel from where I'm sitting.

And then I tried to imagine the room without the Christmas cheer. And *then* I realised what she was talking about. I reached out my hand to stroke Mae's thigh. Yes, there was the obligatory sofa, telly and coffee table, but there was no lived-in feel about it all. The photos on the wall and her album were the only things that made it Mae's.

I shot a glance at the girl sitting next to me, still clinging on to me, before being drawn back to looking at the tree. If that temporary tree was revealing something about Mae's life, it was also telling me something I didn't want to be reminded of about my own. My life wasn't rooted either, and the glitter and shine of being paid for sex were just fragile add-ons.

'I tell you what, why don't we go out for dinner? Now.' I spoke with a voice that sounded a degree too highly-pitched to me. I was trying to lighten the mood, but in truth I just wanted to get out of there.

Mae looked at me, a frown spoiling her beauty. 'It's early, Luke.'

I sensed her disappointment, like I was cutting things short. Which I suppose I was. I gave myself a mental telling off.

It's not about you, remember? Get into gear. Make it her special day.

I nodded back at Mae, and slipped the arm that was on her thigh around her waist so she turned back towards me. 'You're right. I was getting ahead of myself. Looking forward to Christmas dinner, y'know,' I shrugged, and hoped it appeared casual and throw-away.

But it was actually true. If it hadn't been for her, Christmas would have been an absolute wash-out. I had no idea what I would have done instead.

Watched the telly that the taxi driver found too boring to watch, I guess.

Mae pulled me to her and I could feel her breasts through my shirt. I took a deep breath, and with the rise of my chest I felt her hard nipples up against me. We both gripped the other tighter. I burrowed into the nook between Mae's neck and shoulder, one hand cradling her head, lost in her golden hair. I kissed a trail up her neck, and Mae's face turned towards me. Our mouths met. She was sunshine, summer and long sandy beaches all wrapped together.

With my other hand around Mae's waist, I laid her down on the sofa so we were stretched out side by side, still kissing. My hand slipped down to Mae's legs and then up again beneath her dress, but my thumb merely brushed between her thighs.

For now.

We remained fully dressed, although it wasn't as if that would be much of a barrier anyhow. Mae's thighs tensed around mine, and she had undone a couple of my shirt buttons and her hand was pawing my chest.

'Not all now,' I whispered in her ear as she bent her head so her tongue could reach inside my shirt.

'Umm,' she sighed back.

Because we had the whole evening and Christmas night together, I wanted to build up to it. And allow her to enjoy the anticipation now and through the meal.

Just give her enough so that she can't bear to wait for the rest of it!

Mae turned her face up to mine and we were kissing again. I teased her lips open with my tongue, so her own tongue flicked to greet mine.

I broke away from her, but Mae's lips searched for me as she kept her eyes closed. And then I transferred my kisses to the top of her thigh. Her whole body rippled in pleasure and she let out a gasp.

I gave the tips of her toes a little kiss and a flicker of my tongue, and pulled sharply away from Mae, sitting up at the other end of the sofa.

'Time to go and eat, Mae.'

Mae bolted upright, and her eyes opened heavy with lust. She looked confused. I leaned back towards her and ran my hand down her slender, tanned arm.

'It's Christmas. Let's have dinner,' I whispered. 'And then I swear I'll give you your *proper* present.'

'Can't wait,' she murmured.

I swear she quivered in anticipation.

I buttoned up my jacket and Mae straightened her dress, stood up, and went to collect our coats. We walked round to the Carlton, me wrapped in my overcoat with one hand in my pocket to keep out the cold, the other holding Mae's. She was wearing a big black trench coat that looked like she'd stepped out of *The Matrix*. She wore the collar up like she meant business, but her blonde hair and her feminine grace as she strode beside me in her long black boots made her seem all the more vulnerable. The air in front of us misted up with our breath.

The hotel was a welcome sight. The orange-yellow light of its interior that shone through the glass front was a warming contrast to the bitterness of the cold outside. The door was held open for us and I followed Mae through. It felt odd, though. There was a Christmas greeting from every member of staff we met, but it couldn't quite disguise the reality that anyone eating here was somehow missing friends and family.

Mae and I headed for the ground-floor restaurant. We faced each other over the table.

She really is a dream come true.

129

I held her hands between mine. I could feel the crackle of excitement between us.

'We don't need to see the menu, do we? You'd like the full works?' she asked.

'Turkey and Christmas pudding, the lot of it!'

Just saying it made me salivate. Mae laughed at my clear delight. Her eyes met mine and they were sunny with laughter too. And deep, deep blue. I wondered for a split second what she ate. *If she ate.*

No, she looked too damn glowing. Elle Macpherson hot.

'I'll have what you're having,' she agreed.

The conversation as well as the food and drink flowed. The two of us had plenty to talk about over our meal: where each of us had come from, what we were doing now and where we hoped we were heading. Just being with Mae shook away the chill of the London evening we'd braved to be here. Mae was seated opposite me in a rose red armchair but it was this girl's own glow that warmed me. I trusted that I had the same effect on her.

'That was certainly unlike an Aussie celebration!' Mae beamed, pushing away her plate and leaning back in her leather chair with contentment. I loved it that she tucked into her food like she hadn't eaten for years. So many girls didn't and it was deeply unsexy. Like all guys wanted to shag a skeleton. Count me out!

The half-eaten mince pie signalled her defeat. I took a sip of port and nodded in agreement.

'That was delicious. It was a good idea to come here,' I agreed, and my ears picked up the piano tinkling in the background.

That was one of the perks of this job. Not only were my clients paying but they also showed me some pretty fine places. I just had to never forget that not only was I on their time and money, but also their lifestyle too. I looked around at the restaurant and the other well-off guests treating themselves. Like Mae. This wasn't a place I'd have chosen or afforded to go to if I wasn't with *her*.

If an escort forgets that this isn't their life, they're stuffed.

Sharing a room with Mark and meeting up with our mates for a drink or a kick-around in the park helped keep my feet firmly on the ground. Not that crossing the bridge between my clients' life and that of the guys was always simple. I'd open one side of our wardrobe of a morning to a row of increasingly sharp suits and Boss shirts, while Mark's side was more Haute Primark. The kitchen was the same. Anything *I* wanted to eat. Versus Lidl. I'd been doing escort work for just over four months now. I'd made enough of a success of it to see that it was time to say goodbye to the café and pub jobs at last, and think about moving out of the house so I had more room too.

'Thank *you*,' Mae stressed, nursing her glass.

I raised an eyebrow, not altogether sure what she was getting at. For one thing, as far as I was concerned, the night had hardly started. Mae reached out a hand across the table and stroked mine as I fiddled with the stem of my glass.

'I mean it, Luke. You've made this meal really special. I dread to think what I would have done had I not found you.'

'I've enjoyed myself too,' I replied, trying to lift the mood.

She really *was* a girl alone in the city as far as I could see. It made me think about her family back home, and I wanted them to know that she had Aussie company today.

'You called your family today?'

She brightened. 'Well, of course! Why, didn't you?' she teased.

I smiled back, nodding, and my hand smoothed out a stretch of damask tablecloth. If there was one ritual an expat had to undertake at Christmas, it was phoning home to let your folks know you were okay. Mind you, whatever might be going on, it wasn't as if you wouldn't put on your brightest smile for them. Mae wouldn't let on to her family that she was alone, and I wouldn't tell mine what I was getting up to. *No way.*

I brought my focus back to Mae.

'Miles away?' she asked with gentleness.

'Yes.' I gave her a light smile. 'Sorry.'

Both of us had been drawn to think of home, then brought back with a pleasurable bump to this Christmas luxury right here, and the company of someone who knew just where we were coming from.

Mae called the waiter over to pay the bill and I noted the gold Amex she drew out of her leather purse. I took in the waiter as he waited for Mae to key in her pin number, and wondered what he made of us. The slightly older woman and the younger man, and her paying. I looked across at Mae, who smiled at me as she handed back the waiter's gizmo.

Whatever he reckons our relationship is, I'm the jammy one. Merry Christmas, everyone!

I helped Mae on with her coat and put my own on, took her arm in mine and we headed back out into the night. She shivered as the cold air hit us, and if she was acting up it certainly worked, since I pulled her closer to me and held her like she was my skating partner, and we braced ourselves and marched back to her flat.

'Let me take your coat, Luke,' she said straight away, and began to undo hers. It was *her* place but I'd decided to turn the tables as soon as we got through the door.

'Uh-uh.' I shook my head. 'It's Christmas night, remember, and I'm your personal Santa. Leave it all up to me.'

I shifted closer to her and reached for her lapels from behind, drawing her coat off her shoulders and folding it over my arm.

'I wouldn't mind a coat like that. It kicks ass, doesn't it?' I put it on its hanger and hung it up. I took off my own coat and watched Mae as I did.

'I'll get you one if you like,' she said.

I stopped, just as I'd tucked one end of a hanger into an arm of my coat.

'You would?' I asked, taken aback.

She nodded.

132

'That's very kind of you.'

I held back a couple of moments from looking at Mae again because I wasn't sure what to say. Clients often did me a favour by giving me a present, the same as I would do them a favour if I knew I could help them out. It was the same as a friend would do, was the way I saw it. The only trouble was that in these rich girls' worlds, what might be a 'little something' to them was hard for me to return in any kind of equal measure. All I could do then was to accept any present offered me in the generous spirit that it was intended. I spun round to face Mae with a big smile on my face.

'Thank you, that's kind of you,' I repeated. I held my arms out wide. 'Now, come here you!'

And she did. She flung a royal blue cashmere throw over the sofa, and we slowly undressed each other in the light of the fake fire, the mantelpiece candles and the lights from the tree. And when we made love on the cashmere's softness, the baubles tinkled against each other among the branches. I don't know if it was because it was Christmas, or that we felt like the last people on the planet, but there was something unspoken between us, something that flowed, the sex and the two of us. Like it hadn't with any other of my clients. Afterwards, we lay there in the half-light, and I stroked her hair and she held on to me with her head on my chest, both of us rising and falling with the other.

I stretched my leg over the side of the sofa, and sat up in slow motion so as not to alarm Mae. She looked up at me with a look that asked where I thought I was going. I pulled myself away from her and stood up.

'To the bathroom,' I whispered, as I drew a handful of condoms from my trouser pocket in preparation.

I turned to view Mae lying there before me, pulled the dishevelled throw off the back of the sofa and draped it over her so only her head was still showing.

'And you're coming with me!' I laughed, at the same time as I lifted her and the blanket up off the sofa.

'Luke!' she half-admonished, thrashing her feet to and fro, though it came wrapped in enough delight to tell me she was as excited as I was about what would happen next.

I'd already sampled the bathroom's delights before we'd left for dinner. It was half taken up by a shower. There were floor-to-ceiling marine-blue tiles around the entire room, and a wall that curved outwards like a sideways wave separated the shower half from the rest.

Mae said nothing until I had set her down on the tiled floor, still holding on through the blanket. I peeled it off her and let it drop to the floor. She stood before me, wearing a great big smile on her face and nothing else, ready and waiting for whatever I was going to come up with next.

'Do your stuff, Luke,' she grinned, and gave me a *very* knowing look as I ripped open a condom packet.

I took a step back to savour her beauty.

'Wow, Mae,' I couldn't help exclaiming.

Like people who wanted to see her pictures, over the years she must have got used to people being in awe of her looks. It was up to me to let her know I appreciated the same.

She gave me a knowing look beneath her long, dark lashes and took a step towards me so she was right up against me. The wicked glint in her eyes coincided with her hand slipping down between the two of us. Mae licked her lips. I readied myself and slipped the condom into her grasping hand. I knew *exactly* where she was going with this. Her hand ran up the length of my fast-hardening dick, then closed around it.

Aw, man.

My head jutted back and slapped against the wall behind me.

'Ow, fuck!' I shouted.

I found myself looking down at the back of Mae's blonde head as she was now on her knees, and her arms were tight

134

around my legs ready for some real action. She looked up at me and concern flickered across her face.

'That must have hurt. You sure you don't want to sit down?'

I was rubbing the back of my head and it still stung a bit, but I wasn't about to let her stop what she was doing. She was down there on her knees on the brink of putting that hot model mouth of hers around my stiffening cock.

'Just you carry on,' I winced. 'Don't you worry about any stars I might be seeing either now or in the next few minutes.'

She got the message. I gripped on to the towel rail with one hand, the other hand pushing down on her head, and she let me have it right there, her tongue savouring every sweet inch of my dick. I kept my head far away from the wall tiles this time.

It might have been the bang on the head, or just the sheer momentum the two of us had started back in Mae's living room, back at the moment I entered her flat to be honest, but I forgot about the time, forgot about the money. With Mae it didn't mean anything.

Mae was back on her feet again. She took my hand and, mesmerised, I followed her into the shower. She turned it on and within seconds we were gliding against each other under the hot streams. My fingers scuttled blindly among the expensive gels and shampoos that crowded the shower ledge, and gripped the nearest bottle. I took Mae's hand and poured whatever it was into her open palm. She looked up at me with her large sea-blue eyes, and without saying a word began to coat my body in the golden elixir with the stroke of a stable-hand wiping down a horse.

Fuck, she's making me horny.

I bit my lip to concentrate as I spilled some gel into my own palm. Then did to her what she was doing to me.

The water flooded over us. And when the soap was washed away, we stood beneath the shower head's hot fierceness and let it drench us. Mae had thrown her head right back and the water sheared down onto her face and over her cheeks and chin, down her swanlike neck and over the edge of her delicious tits.

I slipped one arm round the back of her and lifted her up against the wall, and as she leaned her head against my shoulder I stroked the back of her neck, while with my other hand I re-armoured myself and fucked her through the curtain of water. Her head dug hard against my collarbone, and my hand was now splayed flat and pushing against the tiled wall as the rest of me plunged into her, and her arms gripped round my back and squeezed the life-breath out of me.

The shower had been turned off and the room was quiet now, except for our breathing and the dribble of the water away down the plughole. I pulled a huge soft towel off its rung and wrapped it around Mae's shoulders and began to rub her down.

'Give it to me!' she cried, and snatched it out of my hands before I could stop her.

I lunged to grab it back and she slipped beyond my reach, laughing and waving her conquest at me. '*This* is how you do it,' she stressed, bringing herself back to me and winding the towel round the two of us.

We were cocooned together in its drying fluffiness, the sheer closeness of our bodies and our skin touching keeping us warm. Mae looked up at me out of the towel. 'My bedroom. Now.'

'Yes, ma'am,' I agreed, and pulled the towel tighter around us.

We tiptoed so we wouldn't fall over on the way to her room. She pushed open the door and we all but fell onto her bed. We lay there for a couple of seconds looking at each other, both with big smiles, then both of us laughing full on as we wriggled out of the towel. Mae threw it across the room so it landed on the floor by the door.

It was only then that I had my first real chance to look around. Mae's huge bed was like a scarlet island in the midst of a tasteful cream sea. The soft down-filled quilted bedspread we'd sunk into, the matching pillowcases and the dark wood frame of the bed beneath, were like a flash of succulent richness fighting the flat's otherwise blandness.

Up above us, the ceiling, like the skirting boards and window ledges, was pure white, but the lampshades and curtains and other stuff she'd picked out in dark reds and purples like berries. At our feet was a grey fur cover that looked like it had come from a wolf. It was as if Mae had made a point of doing as much as she could within her landlord's constraints to colour the room as her boudoir, her refuge.

'God, Mae, this is amazing!'

She stroked my arm as we lay side by side, snuggled in the bedspread. I readied myself again and closed in on her. As far as I was concerned, this was the perfect place to make love again.

So we did.

'A very Merry Christmas, Mae,' I whispered afterwards, and nibbled her earlobe as she chuckled.

She turned to face me. 'And a Merry Christmas to you too!' she grinned, and we kissed each other and sank further into the down.

Later, gone midnight, we unfurled together beneath the bed's covers. Mae's head rested on my shoulder and she gazed up at me. Her long, smooth legs were entwined in mine.

'It's been one of the best Christmases ever,' she sighed with pleasure.

'It has,' I agreed, taking in her blonde beauty and her golden-ness in the middle of this jewel-twinkled room.

I'm a very lucky guy.

For this Christmas night at least, I'd found in Mae a place of both excitement and refuge. The world outside, and my mates and their jobs that were furthering their careers in a way that mine just couldn't, circled around me, but the ache I sometimes felt was silenced for now. It was as if the two of us, so used to making fleeting connections with other people through our work, could at last truly relax in each other. Our lips met again and we nestled further under the quilt.

Mae shuffled a little with sleepiness and muttered a muffled 'Good night, Luke,' and grew quiet. I bent my head down and gave the top of her head through her hair a gentle kiss.

''Night, Mae,' I whispered.

I lay there and looked up at the bright white ceiling. I was ready for sleep too. In a few hours I'd be heading home in the back of a black taxi through the chilly grey London streets. The fairytale of Christmas and my time with Mae would be over. I took a deep breath and snuggled closer to Mae for the rest of the night.

Shelley

New Year's Eve

I could hardly make out what Mark was trying to tell me. We were with the rest of the guys, all squashed up against each other in the crowd at our local's New Year's Eve bash. He had pushed himself from behind Rob and for a few seconds just stared at me and didn't even attempt to speak through the thumping bass. I wasn't sure what to say either. I watched him draw his bottom teeth over his top lip as he sized me up.

We hadn't seen each other for the best part of a month. Mark had effectively moved out to live with Natasha without telling me. Except he hadn't. His stuff was still taking up half my room and at least he was still paying his share of the rent for it. But both of us knew without saying anything that it was only a matter of time before he decided to leave for good.

Which would mean a decision for me too. I could find a replacement roommate, or move out and try to find somewhere even cheaper. Or use part of the money from the escort work so I could have the whole room to myself. Whichever decision I made meant more stress. We needed to talk, if only I could pin him down.

Mark's lips were moving but I couldn't read them through the wall of noise. And then he squeezed his hand through the crush and it closed around an imaginary pint that he lifted towards his mouth with a raised eyebrow.

The universal sign of peace.

I smiled back and gave him a nod.

He got the message. He shifted towards me. His other hand held on to a good-looking girl around the same age as us.

'Natasha, this is Luke.'

'Hello, Luke,' she smiled. 'Pleased to meet you. I've heard a lot about you.'

I smiled back and shook her hand, and tried not to think too much about what Mark might have told her. Rob hovered behind her with a wolfish glint in his eye that was directed at me. I returned it with a hard glare.

'It's nice at last to meet Mark's *mates.*' She said it like she was trying on an Australian accent. 'Rob was just telling me that he's leaving for Europe next week. Do you have plans to go travelling too?'

'Not really. I'm enjoying just getting to know London.'

Which was certainly one of the benefits of my work. I got to experience some of the best hotels and restaurants the city had to offer, but I was also developing a real sense of its layout from the Zone 1 and 2 wealth to its semi-detached suburbs far out beyond the Circle Line.

'I feel I've already got to know London,' boasted Rob. 'I can't wait to visit Paris. And Amsterdam. Prague's meant to be worth seeing too.'

'Honey, you've been to Prague, haven't you?' Mark prompted Natasha.

'You have?' Rob turned towards Natasha. 'What's it like?'

'I loved it,' she said, giving Rob her full attention as Mark and I made our way to the bar.

David, a mate of Mark's who went way back with him, had phoned me earlier in the evening and told me to 'just be there' tonight. It was New Year's Eve. What else was I going to do?

I suppose I'd expected Mark to be there. *Of course I had*. With Natasha, presumably, so I could see him more likely choosing to spend the night wrapped up in her rather than talking about his tenancy with me. Not that that was my idea of fun either, but that would be the elephant-shaped Issue between us that would make spending a decent New Year's Eve together difficult.

Mark was neck and neck with me now as we leaned over the bar and tried to get the barman's attention. It was mad on my side and utter chaos on his. I observed Mark as he stretched out his hand with a tenner clasped in it and shook it like that might do the trick. He caught me watching him.

'What?' he frowned.

I smirked back and indicated his waving hand with a nod of my head. He recognised the absurdity that what he was doing might make a blind bit of difference at getting us our pints.

'Yeah, well,' he chuckled.

The barman, I noted, was serving the other end of the bar, and had hands stretched out to him like he was the lead singer at a gig. I could see we were going to be standing here an age.

'That's a nice girl you've got yourself,' I said to Mark.

His whole face lit up. 'You bet,' he beamed.

I could see just by Mark's glow that Natasha did him the world of good. For a split second I envied him his connection with her and the TLC she gave him while he was so far away from home. But the following second reality kicked in. I knew that my lifestyle just wouldn't be fair on a girlfriend. There was too much of dropping everything – *literally* – whenever the phone rang for me to be able to make a go of any kind of a relationship while I remained an escort. Part of me couldn't help thinking wistfully of Mae. I wondered if I would give up that world if she asked me to.

Mark hadn't worked out that I wasn't in the market, though, it seemed.

'Luke, two doors down to your right,' he hissed. 'The blonde with her mate.'

It was like he was back to his old self, before he met Natasha. I laughed. 'Mark, you can't be doing *that*!'

'Not for me, dummy. For *you*.'

I didn't know if it was for symmetry's sake so we could go out as two couples, or if he thought I needed someone to come home to, or maybe even hoped that me having a girlfriend might make me think again about how I was making my living. Whatever, he still had one eye looking out for his mate. That was good of him, so I decided to take up his challenge and shifted so I could give the girl a good look.

She was a couple of years younger than me, and looked up for it. And her mate wasn't bad either. Which meant I had the choice of either of them.

I turned back to Mark.

'You game?' he queried.

'Yup,' I nodded, and left him standing there waiting to be served. I shifted behind the guy standing next to me and sidled up to the two girls. I sized them up for a second from behind. Two dyed blondes slightly shorter than me. Then I went in for the kill.

'Girls, have you been waiting long?' I said it in my friendliest tones.

The pair of them turned and I could see them sizing *me* up now. The one I was after eyed me all the way down to my feet and made a split-second halt at my crotch on her way back up again. She looked at her friend and something passed between them but I couldn't tell what. Neither of them said anything.

'Hi, I'm Luke,' I smiled, 'and you are?'

'Shelley,' the first blonde said, giving little away.

I made a point of looking directly at her friend.

'Karyn,' said her mate, who sounded in that one word like she

was used to being second-in-line to the prettier one and sometimes not even being noticed at all.

'Well, Shelley and Karyn, what can I get you?' I asked, slipping
beside them so I was square with the bar again.

'A couple of red wines,' Shelley requested, looking at Karyn
as she said it.

It was my turn to edge over the bar and grab the barman's
attention. Mark was at my left arm with our two pints in front
of him.

'So how's it going, Mr Expert Escort?' he teased, out of the
girls' earshot.

'In the right direction, I think you'll find,' I grinned.

'He's coming back this way now,' he said, and jutted his head
towards the barman. 'Wave your cash,' he smirked. 'I want to watch
this, you know. The master at work. And then I'll get back to Tash.'

The barman lined up the drinks on the mat in front of me
and I passed the wines to Shelley and Karyn.

'There you go, girls. We'll find some space somewhere so we
can talk.'

'Thank you,' the girls chorused together.

I turned to pick up my own lager and took a sip to stop it
from spilling. And when I turned back to the girls they'd
already gone on their way, pushing through the crowd to
beyond the mêlée merged round the bar, where we could all
take a breather and hear each other talk. Mark followed
behind me.

I pushed through the crush, losing sight of them. I kept my
head down and kept on going, before I broke out into a bit of
space and Mark all but barged into me, because the girls were
now nowhere to be seen.

'Where the fuck . . .?'

I scoured the other drinkers for the two of them. It was no
use looking for a pair of blondes in this place. I'd be checking
out girls all night and way into next year.

'They done a runner?' When Mark caught my eye I saw a mischievous glint right there in the middle of his. 'What happened to your knack, Luke?' The sides of his mouth crept upwards and he was tilting his head back and roaring with laughter. And I was too.

The truth was, since I had so much success on the escort front, whether I scored on an ordinary night out with my mates was hardly here nor there. My work actually took the pressure off to pull any chick I happened to fancy, though clearly Mark was still under the impression that the complete opposite was true: that I was a guaranteed womaniser at work, so surely that carried into my social life too. He thought it hilarious that Mr Score-Plenty had fallen at the first hurdle with Shelley. Whereas I couldn't really have given a toss.

Shelley and her mate Karyn didn't know it but they'd managed to crack any ice that might have been growing between my and Mark's friendship. Our laughter had brought us back to an even keel. I mentally wished the two of them a *Happy New Year* and took a gulp of my pint.

We saw the New Year in at the pub and decided to carry on celebrating back at David's place. Various Aussies were crowded onto the sofa and assorted chairs around the coffee table in David's living room, and what had started raucous had now grown subdued with the beer and the approaching morning.

'Luke, you didn't manage to score tonight?' Mark piped up, the sparkle still in his eye as he looked straight at me. His arm was around Natasha and she nestled against his chest, dozing.

I shrugged my shoulders with a smile.

'You didn't? You losing your touch?' quizzed Simon, who was sharing an armchair with his girlfriend Jane.

Jane didn't say anything as she drank from her can of Bud, but she looked concerned. Like she thought I *should* be with

144

someone. Even though it wasn't exactly part of my plan for the coming year.

'Well, y'know . . .' I shrugged again.

Not that I was about to make any actual New Year's resolutions. To be honest, my plans for the future were pretty vague. I knew that I didn't see escort work as a career, but I also wasn't sure what other direction to take just yet. All I could do was trust that sometime, somewhere along the line, the right door would open to make things clear. In the meantime I was squirrelling away a lot of the money I made from escorting. Because when I eventually returned to Australia I'd have no proper work experience to back me up. I'd effectively be having to start from scratch. *Again.*

It was that fear that kept me going. I had no other choice but to be as successful a gigolo as was possible.

A couple of the others had turned to peer at me like they were curious as to what Mark and Simon were getting at. Because if it was a talking point that I'd missed out tonight, then it stood to reason that me and my sex life must be something else.

'Hey, it's no big deal. Some you win, some you lose,' I threw out.

'Yeah, right,' teased Mark.

My mates were making more of this evening's failure than I wanted to. There was also a guy called Steve, who I'd only met once before, and he was frowning at me because it was plain that he just didn't get it. I took a noncommittal swig from my can.

And that was the trouble. My closest mates like Mark and Simon knew just what I got up to of a night, but not everyone else here did. And because I had no idea how they'd take it I didn't want them to know. So, the more the guys went on about my strange and sudden lack of pulling power tonight, the more they drew everyone else's attention to what I might be about. And, sooner or later, one of them was bound to ask too many questions.

I got to my feet. 'I need a slash.' *Anything to stop the topic dead in its tracks.*

Mark knew exactly what I was doing. I climbed over his feet and avoided his stare as I sidled past the coffee table to get to the end of the sofa.

Just as I'd manoeuvred past, my mobile went off.

'S'cuse me, folks,' I apologised, as I pulled it from my jeans and made my way to the hall door.

Mark tipped his head to one side and raised a knowing eyebrow. He was right, of course.

Bastard!

A woman's voice I didn't recognise brought me to a halt. I went into professional mode without skipping a beat.

'Yes, this is Luke. How might I help you?'

'It's a brand new year and I just thought "I know how I'd like to celebrate it"! Could you come over now?'

There was alcohol and plain high spirits mixed together in how this girl spoke. I looked back at the group around the coffee table. Any party mood there'd once been had all but petered out. Nobody seemed to be up for anything much more than sleep.

I turned my attention back to the girl down the phone. *She's right. It IS a brand new year.*

'I'd be happy to visit. Sorry, I didn't catch your name?'

I looked up as I spoke. Mark had craned his neck round so he was watching me over the back of the sofa. I eyed him but kept my mind on the job.

'Michelle,' she said.

'Well, Michelle, if you can give me your address I'll be over as soon as possible,' I breezed.

I flicked shut my mobile and placed it back in my jeans. Mark didn't say anything, but our eyes met and he gave me a slight smile.

'Look, I've got to go, folks,' I announced. I wasn't about to start explaining myself now. Or anytime soon, come to that. I turned on my heel, grabbed my coat and let myself out the front door. As I shut it behind me, there came a loud guffaw, and a 'He's got his mojo back after all!' It sounded like Mark.

Sasha

The door was pulled open a moment after I'd rung the bell, and before me was Sasha, looking stunning in a silver-grey satin slip dress. We lunged at each other almost before I'd stepped over the threshold.

'Luke!' She said it huskily when we came up for air, with a broad smile that hit me right in the groin.

'Sash,' I breathed out, almost in unison, though I couldn't help smiling too, and hoped I hadn't broken the mood as I thought of what I knew lay ahead. For me as much as her. Sasha was one seriously good lay.

Our arms wrapped around each other and we were locked together, snogging our hearts out. Joined at the lips, we tugged and ripped at each other's clothing.

We had to pull apart to make any headway. There was hot lust in her eyes and I could feel it burning out of mine. I grabbed at the straps of her dress to pull them down.

Sasha untangled herself from my arms. 'Let me!' she yelped, and crossed her arms and pulled the skirt of the rumpled dress inside-out up her body. Suddenly, she was naked, bronzed and entirely hairless beneath.

My arms snaked around that golden torso, pulling her towards me, and I cloaked my face in the folds of her dress that entwined

148

her breasts and her neck while she struggled her way out of it, her elbows jutting skyward.

She worked more quickly and tried to get her clothes out of the way. I grabbed her crossed hands and jerked them upwards, my palms stretching along her smooth arms and forcing them straight above her head. With her wrists held together in my right hand's tight grip, with my left I pulled the dress over her shoulders and up over her head. And then I let that hand fall to fondle her tits, and her lips were forced against mine and we had fallen together, keeping the other one up.

I let go of Sasha's wrists and she pulled her dress the final few inches off her arms and let it drop to the floor in a heap. Her hands almost immediately went to my shirt and clawed at the buttons, dragging it open. I had to let go of her to let her draw the shirtsleeves down my arms so she could swipe it off and toss it aside. I kicked off my shoes not bothering where they might land. My hand delved into my pocket and my fingers pincered a couple of condoms and retrieved them from the tight space, just as I almost lost my balance completely as Sasha pulled my jeans off one leg. I had to cling to her shoulders to let her yank the other leg free. There was no stopping her. Because we were in the mood for hard, hard fucking.

And this was a race against the clock. Because Sasha had phoned me this morning to tell me she had a literal window of opportunity today between her cleaner leaving just before lunch and the workmen arriving this afternoon. It would be tight but possible to squeeze in a session. *That* was the thrill of the chase. An hour's worth of sex squeezed into minutes with that suggestion of being found out adding to the passion. The two of us tied together at the lips and the hips and the groin, sinking into each other. Our mouths open, loins burning, fired up.

We stumbled together down the hall and fell up the stairs. My arm was wound around her shoulders and Sasha clung to my waist, while our legs were tangled together like we were a pair of drunks. When we got to the half-landing we were both panting heavily, but I still managed to sweep Sasha up so her arms were around my neck, her legs round me too, and I backed her into the wall and, armouring myself, daggered into her right there. Her hands were tight on my back, her nails digging into me, and she bit hard into my shoulder, giving as good as she got.

When it was over I didn't set her down, but with my hands cradling her ass and her head burrowing into my shoulder, I climbed up the remainder of the stairs, half-blinded by her lush body blocking my view, and almost made it, tripping across the landing. I hovered there, not sure which way to go. All I could make out were a jumble of closed doors.

'Turn left, turn left,' Sasha was repeating, though she couldn't see where she was heading. She had to direct me because we hadn't made it this far last time.

I forced both of us through the bedroom door and quickly to the double bed so I didn't drop her, and then we fell together and the two of us sank into the bed's softness. Without catching my breath I pulled myself together, and with Sasha egging me on, I gave it to her again.

I felt like I was grinding her into the bed with the sheer force of it. My head was down like a Pamplona bull and her hands gripped high up my wrists so she felt the full shunting energy of it, and it was as if we were panting our lives away. I could hear my blood pumping in my head, and our heavy breathing matching each other's rhythm. Sasha arched forward, clamping my torso in her arms and biting my shoulder as the passion heated up. She began to reach the boil. It started with a low moan of pleasure like a hint of distant thunder over the far hills, and then she gasped with the heightened shock of it, and the pitch turned higher and faster, and I sensed the thrill in my own voice mounting in my throat.

'Lu-ke,' she let out once, and caught her breath again. And then she repeated herself, letting my name out in a sigh like compressed air from a tyre, and then again and again.

My own voice joined the fray. Our bodies chafed and hit a thrusting rhythm, getting harder together, quickening like wheels forcing a train to the top of a hill. Sasha's tits grew firm against my hard chest, like my dick hard in her hole, my tongue taut in her sweet mouth. Both of us were panting and shouting, sharing the same breath. I was boring into her, and she was taking it, opening to me. And then came the shouts and her plentiful screams, and then we were careering together down the other side so the words and the passion tripped over themselves and lost all meaning. We pulled ourselves together and caught our breath, and gave each other another longing look. And fucked again.

I had to go. An hour is a short time in the world of escorting. You see, you conquer, you come. Then take the money and run.

I pulled myself away from Sasha. There was limited time for any pleasantries bar a last-minute snog. I stepped back from the bed. My feet sank into the deep pile. I bowed to her spread-eagled on the bed, and shut the door behind me.

The trail of clothes I could see as I looked down from the top of the stairs was as good as a ball of string leading me back to the front door. Sasha's dress lay in a huddle on the bottom stair. *Hansel and Gretel. The porn version.*

I trotted down the steps and once back in the hall set about picking up our clothes. I heard myself whistling under my breath as I pulled on my jeans, picked up my white shirt halfway down the hall and pulled it on, stuffing it beneath my waistband, and found myself in the hallway looking for my shoes. One had somehow miraculously found itself on the doormat. I looked around for the other. It was on its side by the door leading to Sasha's sitting room,

I picked up Sasha's dress and folded it, placing it beside her strappy sandles on the doormat. A silver envelope with my name on was taped next to the spy-hole in the middle of the front door. I ripped it away, took one last look up the stairs, and let myself out.

Mutual masturbation

Move from all-over touching to mutual masturbation, but remember that lubrication is the key to smoothing the way to satisfaction and avoiding soreness as you heat each other up.

- Women would generally rather a guy get her in the mood before hand-diving straight in. Her breasts are a good place to start for both of you.
- Don't ram your fingers in her hole. Slowly ease in your index and forefinger and bend them slightly to form a gentle hook to give her more pleasure. At the same time, let your thumb lightly play over her clit.
- The clitoris is the only organ throughout the entire human body which has no purpose other than pleasure. Which doesn't mean it doesn't need to be handled with care. Guys, don't treat it like a lift button. For many women, its tip is *way* too sensitive. You'll give a girl far more enjoyment if you gently edge up to it and around and around it.
- The head of a guy's dick is the equivalent of the clitoris, so while a girl shouldn't completely ignore it when giving a hand-job, it shouldn't be her only focus. Some guys like the entire length worked on and a little ball play thrown in. Ask your partner what he prefers, though and take account of his body language and what he's enjoying throughout too. I prefer a woman to gradually build up into the action rather than opt for a fast hand-job straight away. Guys *do* agree that a girl shouldn't go for tight squeezing nor painful hammer-and-tongs wrist action.

> - At the end of the day, a girl can NEVER give as good a hand-job as a guy can give himself. But please do at least offer!

Fiona and Martin

I walked into the bar of the Heathrow Hilton and tried to give the impression that I knew who I was looking for. It was more or less empty, except for a couple of middle-aged suits at one table and a few other people surrounded by suitcases at others, presumably about to check out.

She was the only one on her own, wearing a black dress, as her husband had said she would be, and sitting in the corner with a drink. I made a beeline for her as if we'd known each other for years.

'Fiona? Pleased to meet you. I'm Luke.'

She looked up at me with a confused frown.

'No, I'm not. I'm afraid you've got the wrong person.'

Shit.

Exit stage left with my tail between my legs.

Start again. I got myself a drink from the bar and found myself a seat where I had a good view of all the comings and goings, and sat and waited.

Ten minutes later, a blonde-haired girl, real pretty and round about my own age, walked through the door and straight up to the bar. Too straight, in fact – it was as if she was trying *not* to appear nervous. She waited for the barman to serve her, and as she did she gave a cursory glance across the room. While he

155

poured her drink, she looked around more intently, like she was looking for someone.

I took my cue, and walked over to greet her.

'Fiona?'

'Yes,' she nodded, with relief in her eyes.

'Hello, I'm Luke. Martin told me I'd find you here. Pleased to meet you,' I smiled. 'Do join me.'

I let her have my seat so that she would see her husband when he arrived. He had been in some business meeting and was driving back to the airport.

'So, you've been doing some sightseeing while Martin's been at work?'

Fiona gave me an awkward smile that told me it wasn't my place to ask. 'He shouldn't be long now,' she said.

I had to be careful working with couples. It was twice as easy to say or do the wrong thing. And if you happened to offend one of them, you were making both of them feel uncomfortable. Martin wasn't here yet, but that didn't mean I didn't have to remain mindful of him.

When I'd first started as an escort, working with partners had barely crossed my mind. Sasha and Chloe were the fantasy, but in actual fact the twosomes that called me were more likely to be heterosexual couples. I'd treat the wife and the guy would get off on watching us. It was quite a tightrope to walk between pleasuring her to his delight without it flipping over into jealousy. I knew I must never forget the third person in the room.

When Martin did turn up, you'd have thought that they hadn't seen each other for years.

'Darling!' Martin exclaimed as he burst through the swing doors, turning the head of everyone else in the bar. He all but marched towards Fiona as she stood up to greet him, and then he took her in his arms and they kissed. Hard.

Don't mind me.

Once they'd uncoupled, Martin drew up a stool and edged himself right up against his wife. He must have been at least ten years older than her, turning craggy and greying round the temples. He'd managed to avoid acquiring any middle-aged spread, though, and looked in good shape. Martin and Fiona's clasped hands rested on the table, and they kept giving each other looks of love like newlyweds. I wondered how I was going to fit in to all this.

'When I heard that we were meeting at the airport, I presumed you were flying in on a business trip? Are you stationed abroad?'

They looked at each other.

'It's not quite as simple as that,' coughed Martin. 'Shall we go up to the room?'

We finished our drinks and left the bar.

These two were *so* hot for each other that we almost didn't make the hotel room. Even while the lift doors were closing they were tightly embraced and on the brink of dry-humping each other when a briefcase was swung through the gap between the doors so that they opened again and another passenger embarked. Martin and Fiona went back to standing side by side and holding hands. No one's eyes met.

We reached the third floor and all four of us disembarked. Letting Mr Briefcase through, I followed Martin and Fiona down the hotel corridor, though I felt that I almost might as well not have been there. She was wrapped round him like a raincoat. Yet for some reason they'd invited me along for the ride too.

But mine was not to reason why. I'd learned that long ago.

We finally reached their room. Martin unlocked the door and swung it open.

'Ta da!'

'We'd better make this clear,' Fiona giggled, taking hold of the Do Not Disturb sign and making sure it was switched to the outside door knob.

Martin had clearly pulled out all the stops for Fiona. The curtains were closed and the lights dimmed, and once my eyes had adjusted I was able to make out vases full of flowers, bottles of champagne and bowls of strawberries dotted around the room, in the middle of which was a kingsize double bed.

Fiona stepped into the room and swung herself right round to face us. 'Come here, you two,' she exclaimed, grabbing a hand each and dragging us towards her. Martin kicked the door shut behind him.

The two of us stood and watched as Fiona handed us a glass of champagne each, took a sip from her own, and then began to strip, wending her way between us as she did. I knew by now to follow the husband's lead until I was given any indication that things could be taken into my own hands. But this evening Fiona made it very clear that although Martin had arranged everything, it was very much *her* fantasy and that she was the one in control.

'Luke,' she said, taking my glass from me and setting it down on a windowsill, and then she took me by the hand and led me to the bed.

Martin took a step back and sat down to observe me with his wife. Fiona began to peel off my clothes and I followed suit, until we were lying together on the bed, exploring each other's bodies. If we'd continued, we'd have got to sex. But we didn't. She slipped out of my embrace and off the bed to Martin, and it was my turn to watch her seduce and undress her husband.

She's bringing us both to the boil.

As she straddled Martin, I stretched across and selected a strawberry from the bowl on the bedside table. I lay on my side, up on one elbow, and rested my head on my hand and watched this couple enjoying each other as I bit into the fruit. Fiona was splayed over Martin with her legs between his and her head upturned so that their lips met. Their hands slid all over each other, and every now and again one of them would give me a side glance to make sure I was watching.

And then Fiona stood up, slipped out from her husband's arms and returned to me, all the while her eyes on Martin. Even though I was well and truly in the picture, this was between them. That's what you never had to forget when you played the escort game with couples. You might be right there in the room having sex with the most beautiful girl, but it was only because her partner had allowed it. It was all about *their* relationship and had nothing whatsoever to do with you. Even if the sex was damn hot and you'd even forgotten that there was another guy in the room, you had to remember that on another level you weren't there at all.

Fiona had already revved me up, and I would have loved to have gone at it full throttle, competing in my mind with the thrust of the planes roaring overhead, sinking deep into the bed. But it was mid-afternoon in an anonymous hotel room with paper-thin walls, and the only option was to go at it real gentle and slow so that nobody would guess what was going on in here.

So I went easy on Fiona. Giving her pleasure was going to be all mine too.

There was a knock on the door. I stilled myself for a split second.

Hotel staff.

And then returned to caressing Fiona and vice versa.

The knock came again, more earnest and sharp. And then a double one.

Fiona pulled herself away from me. 'Martin!' she hissed.

He was wide-eyed in return, his hands gripping the arms of the chair as if he wasn't sure whether to jump up and answer it or not.

'We're asleep,' Martin called out.

Fiona and I held on to each other as well as our breath.

'Can you come back later?' Martin called again, his whole body tense.

There was silence, and I relaxed and returned my attention to Fiona. I kissed her lightly on the neck, and her head leaned backwards into the moment.

'Martin, I know you're in there,' came a defiant woman's voice from outside.

Fiona scrambled from under me like a teenager not wanting to be caught by her parents and flung herself towards Martin. He had turned white as if he had seen a ghost.

'Richard's out here as well,' the voice came again, and this time it was Fiona's turn to look aghast.

'We know you're both in there.'

I lay on my front on the bed, my chin on my knuckles, and watched both of them. They were deep in animated whispers I couldn't quite catch, and every so often one of them shot a fearful glance at the closed door.

'You'd better fill me in on what's going on *real* quick.'

My words cut the tension. Both of them stared at me like they were so caught up in what was going on outside that they'd forgotten I was even there.

'Luke,' instructed Martin, 'get your clothes back on and help us clear up.'

'What's going on?' Both Martin and Fiona were dressing *really* quickly, so I followed suit.

'We met at work,' Martin explained in a loud whisper as he collected the champagne bottles. 'Those are our partners outside.'

He looked around the room, and then grabbed a corner of the mattress, lifted it up and squeezed each of the bottles beneath.

God, I'm appearing in a bedroom farce. How the fuck did I get myself caught up in this?

Fiona had busied herself arranging the vases. She took a bite out of a strawberry.

'There's no way we can eat all of these in one go,' Fiona said.

She offered me the bowl and I took one and enjoyed its sweet succulence.

'The loo, Fiona,' urged Martin, as he shifted the armchair back into its original position.

'Fiona!'

It was a man's voice this time. Presumably 'Richard'. Fiona jumped and sped up as if to quell her fear.

I looked around the room for my own belongings. I was fully dressed, but there were also the tools of my trade to take care of. The condoms and their wrappers. My hands full with the evidence, I almost barged into Fiona on my way through the bathroom door. She poured the strawberries into the toilet bowl and I threw in my own rubbish. I pulled the flush and we watched it all disappear down the pan.

Back in the bedroom, Martin was smartening himself up like he was getting ready for a military inspection.

'What can we do, Luke?' he pleaded, as if it was my job to have the answers to the shit *he'd* got himself in. 'How can we get out of this?'

We? How am I going to get out of this, let alone you two?

I surveyed the room. Everything was now present and correct, all the romance tidied away. Fiona, on the brink of tears, stood beside her lover and gripped his hand.

It was a sorry state of affairs whichever way you looked at it. Whichever side of the door you were on. And I was caught bang in the middle of it.

I marched over to the bedroom door.

'Who is this?' I called to the other side.

'Martin and Fiona, come out!' the woman's voice demanded.

I looked over at Martin, who had his arm around his girlfriend's waist, and gave him a quizzical look.

'Carol,' he whispered loudly back.

I nodded.

161

Carol and Richard, Martin and Fiona. Like some Sixties sex comedy.

'There's no one here of that name. You must have got the wrong room, I'm afraid.'

Surely my Aussie accent would put them off the scent. 'Look, can you go away, please. I'm trying to rest.'

There was silence.

Is that it? Have they gone?

'Luke, we know that's you in there as well.'

I froze. *How the fuck!?*

I looked over at the couple holding tight to each other.

'Luke,' she repeated my name, 'just tell the two of them to come out so we can work this whole thing out.'

I was half-tempted to sell Fiona and Martin to the highest bidder. I threw a glare at Martin.

'No, Luke, it wasn't me. I don't know how they've got your name,' Martin hissed across the room. He and Fiona had planted themselves as far away from the door as possible.

I returned my attention to the couple on the other side of the door. I opened the spy-hole and peered through. There was a large eye peering right back. I dodged towards the doorpost, hoping I'd moved beyond their field of vision, and beckoned Fiona and Martin to do likewise.

'Look, go away. I don't know what you're talking about,' I stressed to the wood panel in front of me.

The minutes ticked away and no words were heard on either side of the doorway. I checked my watch. It was now a quarter of an hour since Carol and Richard had last spoken to me. Were they biding their time too on the other side? I looked over at the lovers and signalled them to keep dead quiet. I stepped up again to the eyehole and peered through. This time I had a clear view of the hotel corridor. Nobody was in sight. I pulled away from the door, leaned against the wall and breathed out.

'It's okay. It looks as if they've gone.'

At that very moment, the phone rang. Fiona shivered, and Martin tightened his arm around her, but he made no effort to pick it up. The money he would be paying me for this session included admin services rendered too, then. He needed someone else to take over just now.

'Hello, who is this?'

'Luke, we know all about you.' Carol didn't need to identify herself.

'You know nothing about me,' I countered. 'Just leave me alone.'

I looked over at Martin and Fiona and gave them a 'Don't worry, I've got things handled' smile. At the same moment I couldn't help wondering how my name had leaked out.

If Martin's saying he had nothing to do with it, then how?

'I've seen the emails going back and forth between you and my husband, Luke. And your webpage. I even know what you look like. If you want something done, you can always find some-body you can pay to do it, can't you, Luke?'

So, Carol had hired a private investigator. She'd been keeping track of her husband for quite a while, it seemed. I suddenly remembered the chap barging into the lift at the last second and getting off at our floor. Mr Briefcase. Had he had anything to do with all this? Was it *him*? Or maybe I'd just watched too many spy movies.

And anyhow, what was I supposed to say in reply? If Carol knew about me, then she knew about me, and that was all there was to it. I came off the phone and sat on the corner of the bed, collecting my thoughts and Martin and Fiona's limited options. I spoke to them in a quiet, matter-of-fact tone.

'They know everything about you. And me, I'm afraid.'

'There must be something we can do,' stressed Martin, in a way that was half-asking me to come up with the goods and half-telling his girlfriend that *he* had everything under control so she had nothing to fear.

'Look, my advice to you is to go out there and face the music,' I told them.

Fiona looked at Martin and Martin just looked deflated.

'Or . . .'

'Yes?' Martin raised his eyebrows at me.

'Or, you walk out of this room and into the elevator and get out of here. Quick smart.'

'Oh.'

It wasn't much of an alternative, I knew.

'I'm sorry.' I said it quietly, and I meant it. I looked at the two of them standing there and wondered what must be going through their heads. Trapped in a room and tracked down by their spouses. As it was, I felt bad enough just being cornered with them.

I had an idea.

'Look, Martin, you knew your wife had suspicions, didn't you?'

'Ye-es?' he replied, and frowned as if he wondered where I was going with this.

'Well, what if you tell Carol and Richard that you hired me for that very reason?'

Martin, nor Fiona come to that, didn't look convinced.

I gave it another go out of sheer desperation.

'What I mean is that you turn the tables on them. I'm here to *prove* that nothing's going on between you two, so there's no need for *them* to have you followed or to keep pestering you.'

Martin pursed his lips and shook his head. 'No, it wouldn't work. The emails for one thing. Our names, where we'd meet, what I wanted you for. *Everything* was in them.'

Shit.

Fiona said nothing but looked on the brink of tears. She was the junior in this relationship and clearly in the office too. Letting Martin take control was presumably the package she'd bought into.

'I don't feel ready to leave just yet, Martin,' she plucked up the courage to say in a tiny voice.

'I know, love. No one's leaving here until we know exactly what we're doing. Would you like to sit down? You'd like a glass of water?'

She nodded. He led her by the arm to the armchair he'd first watched the two of us from. All that now seemed a world away.

Martin had squatted down beside the chair so that he was at eye level with Fiona. He cocked his head at me.

'Would you be so kind as to get Fiona some tap water?'

'Sure.'

I went into the bathroom and found an upturned tumbler on the basin shelf and filled it. By the time I was back in the bedroom, Martin had Fiona's hand in his over the arm of the chair and was encouraging her to make a move. I handed him the glass, and noted his trembling hands even as he was determined to put on a brave face.

'Look, we love each other, darling. We can't be apart. Let's just go for it,' pleaded Martin.

'But Richard and Carol. They know everything. They're bound to be waiting for us downstairs when we try to leave. I don't know . . .' Fiona's voice trailed off.

'But what do we care? It doesn't bother me one iota what kind of trouble we might get caught up in, just as long as you stay with me. That's all that matters to me, I swear.'

Martin was trying to be 'the Man' about this fiasco, but I could tell by the way he gripped Fiona's hand with such tightness that he was almost as petrified as she was.

I could tell too that both of them needed a helping hand. Otherwise we'd never leave this place. I coughed to get their attention but also to shake them both out of the mutual fear they had of literally facing their demons.

They looked across the room at me.

'I'll lead the way out of here. All you've got to do is follow right behind and keep your eyes solely on me. Nobody's going to stop us, you hear?'

It wasn't as if I knew who or what we might be confronted with on our way out of the hotel, but it was important to give Fiona and Martin the impression that I was in control. The coast sounded as if it was clear, anyhow. We hadn't heard anything from the other two for the best part of an hour. I went to the door and placed my hand around the handle and turned towards the lovers.

'You've got everything?'

They stood up together. 'Yes,' they nodded in unison.

I let them pass me through the door and shut it behind me. The Do Not Disturb sign was on the floor.

And that was it. We left the Heathrow Hilton with haste, Fiona's heels padding along the carpet and then clattering behind me as we hit the polished tile flooring. I looked straight forward and just kept on going and trusted that they would keep up.

It was a relief to get out into the open air and the sunshine. I shielded my eyes from the glare and halted.

'Where to now?'

Both of them looked terrified, as if they were expecting a police searchlight to pick them out any minute. Fiona held her boyfriend's hand and looked to and fro.

'My car's over there,' she whispered, pointing to the far end of the car park.

Martin turned to me. 'Thanks, Luke, for all you've done.'

'Sure,' I said, 'and I want to make sure things are okay.'

It wasn't the session I was expecting, but hey.

Just as we were about to step off the pavement in front of the hotel entrance to cut across the tarmac, a sleek Mondeo drew up and braked hard beside us. The driver, it turned out, was making a point. She didn't say anything but glared at Martin and Fiona through the windscreen. Martin turned ashen, then looked down at his shoes and kept on walking. His grip on Fiona's hand tightened.

'She's my sister-in-law,' he hissed.

Shit.

But she didn't get out of the car. Or shout at us. All she could do was stare her displeasure and watch us reach Fiona's car.

Fiona got into the driver's seat and gave me a farewell wave from behind the side window. I nodded back, and followed Martin round to the passenger side.

'We're going to collect my stuff, and then go over to Fiona's and pick up hers,' he explained as he counted out my fee.

We said our farewells, and he got into the car and I watched them drive out of there.

Back to face your spouses. God, I don't envy you one bit.

I was in my local supermarket the following week when there was a call from Martin on my mobile. I parked my trolley by the ready-meals cabinet and put on my cheeriest voice.

'Martin, how are you? And Fiona?'

'We're . . . fine,' he replied, clearly not intending to give me the whole story. 'Luke, all the fuss we got you involved in. We're very sorry. We had no idea that things would turn out like that.'

I pictured the strawberries being flushed down the loo.

I shifted the trolley so it couldn't budge, and turned and leaned against its handle so I could give Martin my full attention.

'It's such a shame that things couldn't have been different,' he continued.

I gazed down at my feet and the tiled flooring that seemed to stretch forever.

In my mind's eye I saw the two of them running round the hotel room like headless chickens.

There was silence on the other end of the phone, so I waited. I looked over at the freezer cabinet across the aisle. It was piled high with boxes of pizza. I let all the colours of the wrappers meld into each other.

Martin still hadn't spoken, but I could sense that he hadn't finished what he wanted to say. I fiddled with the coin-deposit chain attached to the trolley handle, ready for Martin to speak again. There was an awkward cough at his end. My body tensed, wondering what he wanted to say. And then the thought struck me.

He wants another bloody favour, doesn't he?

I gripped the trolley handle with both hands, and rested my wrists and elbows along it too. And waited.

A heavy sigh came down the phone.

'Luke, the thing is, what happened the other day. It forced the issue. Fiona and I have decided we really want to be together, but there's stuff that has to be sorted out with our partners. You understand?'

I wasn't sure I did. I let him talk on.

'It's just . . . if you should ever hear from a lawyer, whatever they might say I said or did, you'll back me up, won't you?'

I ran my finger round the trolley's wire mesh edge. *What have I got myself mixed up in? What have they got me mixed up in?*

'All right, Martin,' I sighed. 'You know where to find me.'

All part of the service.

Giselle and friends

I'd expected the door to be opened by Robert, the older guy who'd called me to Paddington for himself and his wife. But a pretty girl of about twenty ushered me in, and I could tell by the tight designer jeans, her spotless hair and makeup, that she was there for the exact same reason as me.

'Come in,' she smiled. 'I'm Giselle, by the way.'

Ah, she's playing 'the wife'. Fair enough.

'Luke. Pleased to meet you,' I replied, half-craning my neck round the door, expecting to see Robert. But the flat was empty except for the two of us.

Giselle glided over to the drinks cabinet and I stood beside her and watched as she fixed me a vodka and tonic and passed me my glass. I turned it round in my hand, puzzled.

Where's Robert then?

'Your partner's not here?'

Giselle stopped in her tracks and cocked her head at me.

'What partner?' she frowned.

I felt like the rug was being gradually pulled from under my feet.

'Robert. The guy I spoke to on the phone? The guy who asked me here.'

This wasn't the set-up I had in my head. I tried to rewind

169

back to our talk on the phone to what he'd actually said. Or maybe I'd misunderstood what he was asking for, and that he just wanted me as a treat for his girl?

Giselle beckoned me towards the sofa and we sat down. She had on a miniskirt that looked like a kilt, except it was a silvery grey and made of lighter material. Her strapless top was a darker grey and her cleavage peeped out over the top of it. Over that she wore a short black military jacket complete with epaulettes and gold buttons running all the way up, the sort of thing Madonna used to wear. Her long stockinged legs arched out over the geometric-patterned rug.

'How long do you want me to stay for, Luke?'

I noticed that Giselle hadn't answered my question, but since the goalposts seemed to have shifted, I knew I needed to get to grips with the new game sharpish. And it had to be said, I liked the look of the pitch. I shifted closer to her.

'That's really up to you. How long would you like *me* to stay for?' I added a drop of seductiveness into the mix.

For a split second Giselle looked confused, but levelled herself almost immediately. She pursed her lips.

'Well, my fee is two hundred pounds for the first hour, and one hundred and fifty for every hour after that.'

It was my turn to be in shock. The set-up was getting more bewildering by the second, but I wasn't about to let Giselle see my confusion.

Play it cool, Luke.

'Well, that's funny.' I looked straight at her, half-grinning, 'because that's the same rate as mine.'

Giselle didn't see the funny side. 'No,' she stressed, like she was damned sure she was going to get things her way. 'You're here now. You've got to pay for the first hour.'

Can't she see the joke too? What the fuck is this all about?

'No I don't. You've got to pay for *yours*,' I volleyed.

But we'd reached a stalemate, and she was glaring at me. The atmosphere had turned ugly. I suddenly realised she was dead serious.

'Look, Giselle, there's clearly been some misunderstanding. I'll go.'

I stood up. She got to her feet a second later as if she wanted to confront me, but she remained where she was and said nothing.

As I was about to open the front door to let myself out, the bell went. I stopped dead, and looked at Giselle. She reached straight past me without saying a word, gripped the handle and opened the door. There were two short, stocky men standing there, shoulder-to-shoulder.

'Has he paid yet?' one growled at her.

I looked from them to Giselle, and then back at them, and edged up against the doorpost.

What is this?

They'd got the wrong man, surely. It was Robert they were after. Wasn't it? Or was I *exactly* where Robert and these three wanted me to be because I'd walked right into their trap? I didn't want to think too much about the possibility of *that*.

'Look, guys.' I held up both hands, elbows bent so not quite in surrender but certainly wanting things to slow down. 'I'm here for the same reason as Giselle,' I stuttered.

'No, you've got to pay for your first hour,' stated the one who hadn't yet spoken.

So, they were on the same page as Giselle after all. I'd been set up. I'd walked right into it. But I had to admire how they'd synchronised getting to the other side of the door at the moment I planned to leave.

The arseholes stared hard at me and I looked at them right back. I never carried money on me on a job anyhow, but if these two were going to try and find out, it wasn't as if I couldn't handle them if I had to. One on one. I knew that they could only hurt me as much as I could hurt them. I'd been in worse situations back in my home town in Australia, growing up. Unless they were carrying weapons, that was. That would be an entirely different story altogether.

If Robert had set all this up in the first place, as I presumed he had, the fact there were three guys involved made the deal all the more serious. I thought of all the other escort boys who must have been set up in just the same way. Called out and then forced to pay under threat of violence.

The poor saps. And I'm just another one of them.

You could have cut the atmosphere in the room like a knife. All that was needed was something to snap. Giselle only had to let out a shriek or a whimper. I might move too quickly and set a whole load of hassle in motion. I had no idea what these guys had in mind except that they wanted me to hand over any money I had. And I suspected that they'd be quite happy to give me a good kicking.

It hit me then between the eyes.

Fuck, Luke, what are you doing even hanging around?

I had everything to lose and nothing to gain by remaining even one more minute in that room. And since there was a gap between me and these guys at the door that they hadn't even got their act together to close, I slipped right on through, and just kept on walking down the hall, straight out of there.

I was still feeling distinctly unnerved by the whole thing when I got a call from Robert on my way home.

'Where *are* you, Luke?'

I came to a halt in the middle of the street.

Like I'm going to give him any idea of THAT.

'What are you talking about? I turned up and found myself stitched up,' I spat down the mobile. My whole body was curled in on itself, head down, listening to what Robert had to say for himself. There was a pause at the other end.

'You've got me wrong, Luke. That's the girl in the downstairs flat you're talking about. You went to the wrong address.'

What the . . .?

Had I made a mistake? I was thoroughly confused.

'Luke, come back,' Robert demanded.

I thought for a second. Nope, I knew I didn't trust him. There was no way I was going to go anywhere near those goons. I had been lucky. *This* time. I'd found myself in a situation that could have got *so* much nastier.

'No, Robert. And don't ever call me again.'

I hung up, and put Robert's number in my 'Don't Answer' file, along with all the other creeps, wankers and timewasters. As I put the phone into the pocket of my trousers I noticed that my hand was still shaking.

Mae again

Walking up to the door of Mae's Knightsbridge apartment block, I couldn't help thinking back to Christmas Day and the last time I was here. I found myself shivering, but at the same time I felt a warm glow at the thought of what a great time it had turned out to be for two Aussies with nothing better to do that day.

Mae had called me out for just an hour tonight. I buzzed her flat and thought of her golden model looks. An hour wouldn't be enough.

Not that I'm complaining. Any time in her company is something!

Mae's voice came over the intercom. 'Luke!' was all she had to say. She sounded joyous.

The door unlocked and I headed up to her flat in the lift. I stepped out on her landing and there she was before me, hovering at her open front door in a black floor-length Chinese silk dressing gown.

Ready and waiting.

Mae's whole face lit up as soon as she saw me. 'Luke!' she exclaimed again. I gave her a big bear hug. For the moment neither of us needed to say anything else.

She ushered me into her flat and I held back to let her pass over the threshold. This was one of the little things I now knew

174

to do. Hold a door open for my client. Stand between her and the traffic when we walked down the street. Whether or not she even noticed.

I passed into the sitting room. The Christmas tree, of course, had been thrown out. There was a large empty space where it had stood. The tinsel and candles that had added a bit of sparkle and colour back in December were also gone. It looked bare now.

I took off my coat and handed it to Mae, and as I did I stole a glance at her monochrome portrait on the wall.

Even she looks a bit under the weather.

'Please sit down,' she said. 'I've still got some of that cognac left if you'd like some?'

I settled myself down into the sofa and looked up at her leaning against the kitchen doorpost. 'Thanks, Mae. That'd be lovely.'

She disappeared from view as she fixed our drinks, and I surveyed the room like last time and gave myself a pep talk.

Of course it's going to look a bit flat after last time. It ain't Christmas any more! And hadn't I realised back then anyhow that Mae was the most glittering thing in the place?

Mae came back into the room with a smile and a glass of brandy in each hand, her pretty bare feet making their way straight for me. I rose from my seat and reached out my hands to her.

'Let me take those for you while you come and sit down.'

She gave me the glasses and cuddled up beside me and I handed her back her drink.

'Cheers.' We spoke in unison and each took a sip of our drink.

Mae's head rested against my shoulder and I rested my head against hers. It felt good to be back together again. Neither of us said anything for a couple of minutes, and then she spoke like a sigh.

'Sometimes doing the shows, I can barely remember what city

I'm in,' she murmured without raising her head, though she held on to me a little tighter. I took my cue from her and kept still. It felt right. Cosy.

'As long as you remember which designer you're appearing for, that's all that matters,' she continued in the same quiet tone.

'Mae,' I breathed her name like you might make a candle flame flicker, 'tonight *I'm* here beside you.'

This time I drew my head away from hers and bent my neck so I could see her eyes. I reached out and ran my finger along her jaw line to underneath her chin. She turned her head so she was now facing me, as I knew she would, and I gently raised her chin up so her lips met mine.

Mae pulled away from me and shook her head. 'Hang on a minute.'

I looked up at her, confused about what was going on. She left the room and returned minutes later with a tin box. She set it down on the side table at her end of the sofa and removed the lid, then set out the gear. I watched but said nothing.

Mae settled herself back down on the sofa next to me and leaned over the arm of the chair with a rolled note to her nose. She sniffed up a line of coke and then turned to me and offered me the note. I shook my head sadly.

'No thanks,' I said, hoping Mae could see that I wasn't judging her or anything, though what she was up to gave me a jolt. I got offered Class A drugs three or four times a week. For free! It was part and parcel of the high-roller lifestyle a lot of my clients lived. But I could see the downside too. It would be way too easy to get addicted. I didn't want to risk it.

Mae jumped up and twisted her body towards me, then held out her hand and grabbed mine. Her dressing gown had loosened and I caught a glimpse of her naked body through the gap. The roped tie tantalised as it swung between her legs and I yearned to reach out and pull it undone, but Mae yanked me to my feet before I even got the chance.

'Come with me,' she leered.

God, you've changed your tune. The sweet angel I'd spent the night with at Christmas was a world away. In her place was a woman possessed.

Together we floundered through her bedroom door, pulled off our clothes like the race against time it was, and lunged ourselves onto her scarlet bed. We fell down laughing.

'Come here, you,' I guffawed, pulling her to me and rifling my hands through her hair. A second later we were enveloped in each other.

'Nope, you're coming with *me*,' she jabbered, drawing me tight to her. She wanted the upper hand. I got the message. I chose to give it to her as much as I knew she wanted me to and went in for the kill.

It was hard to tell where I ended and Mae began. She was as hard as me. We pummelled against each other in unison, and didn't want to stop. The tension built, yet when we reached the point just before each of us shattered into a million pieces, I took a deep breath and against all my instincts and my body's high-pitched desire, pulled away.

'No! No!' Mae screeched, until a blink of an eye later I brushed the back of my hand against her inside thigh and began the fall back into her scarlet eiderdown and the steep climb to the granite-metal heights all over again.

I was closing in on her clit with my fingers when Mae rose up and gripped my wrist and forced me onto my back before lunging onto me. She gave it to me every which way. Sex with Mae this time was as fast and loose as the coke she'd done.

When we eventually broke apart, we lay there on our backs side by side on the bed, both breathing hard. As we came back down to earth I stared at the white emptiness of the ceiling overhead. I turned to face Mae. She was still on her back, miles away. For a few seconds I chose to just watch this Aussie sister, her chest rising and falling. She was still a girl all alone in the big city. One thing hadn't changed since Christmas, then.

177

I stroked Mae's bare shoulder with my finger and raised myself onto my elbow to look at her face. She bit her lip and managed a smile back.

'You'll come visit me some other time?' She forced the words out through the fag-end of her cocaine high.

'If you want me to, Mae, it'd be a pleasure,' I nodded.

Mae rolled herself off the bed and onto her feet and picked up her dressing gown. I watched her as she knotted her belt and then dismounted the bed myself and put on my clothes. She waited while I did and then I followed her out of the room and back into the living room. I finished off the dregs of my brandy as she counted out my fee, and even before I'd made my way out of the flat, Mae had got back on the sofa and was bent over its arm, busy vacuuming up another line.

Giving a blow-job

Nobody gives girls lessons in blow-jobs. It's a combination of trial and error plus what she enjoys while she's giving him one – and hoping he's getting off on it too. The trouble is, that it's a rare man who's going to admit that she's not quite hitting the spot.

- The most crucial point to remember is to keep your teeth and nails, in fact anything that might scrape or cut his penis, as far from the action as possible. Placing your lips around the tip and your hands around its base is a good way to start.
- It's not *blowing*. It's sucking, like a lollipop.
- Flicker your tongue lightly around the head, and lick the length of his cock hard. Variety adds spice, but always remain aware of his excitement levels.
- A girl giving me eye contact at the same time is a real turn-on.
- Use your hands plus lubrication to provide added satisfaction. When your jaw's beginning to ache, masturbation keeps the momentum going while you take a breather.
- Guys, take account of your partner's pleasure while she's pleasuring you. Don't force yourself so far in that she's gagging for breath. Or just gagging.
- Don't assume that blow-jobs are top of her 'To Do' list. Unless she's taking the initiative, ease her in gently rather than force her head down because it's what *you* want her to do.

Sasha farewell

March

It was nearing the end of another week, and I was down the local with my mates when Sasha phoned. I'd last heard from her about a month ago.

'Excuse us, lads,' I said, and put up my other hand like a traffic cop as I squeezed past them to a quieter corner of the pub. They were used to me escaping to make business calls and said nothing, though a couple of them gave me wolfish grins on my way out. My new BlackBerry all but invited them to. It cried out that my escort work was proving a great success, and that I was dead serious about it too.

'Hi, Luke, would you like to come out tonight? It's sort of my hen night with the girls from the club – I'm getting married at the weekend – but you'd be very welcome,' she garbled.

I paused as if I was catching *her* breath, trying to take it all in. I could hear traffic and female laughter in the background.

'Wow, Sasha, that's kind of you to ask.' I pictured the lot of them tottering on their heels down the street, *Reservoir Dogs* style. The porn version. *What do you call a group of strippers? A Hefner? Heaven, more like.*

'I'd love you to join us,' she declared. 'You wouldn't mind being the only guy?'

Oh, hang on.

I was back meeting Sasha and Chloe for the first time and feeling out of my depth. It would be like that, but multiplied.

'I'm so sorry, Sasha. I just can't make it tonight.' I looked over at the guys yacking away at the other table. 'You and the girls have a great time, okay?'

'We will do. It's a real shame you can't be here.'

'I feel the same. Look, I hope you have a marvellous wedding.'

'Yeah, thanks.'

I slipped the phone back in the pocket of my jeans and walked back to the lads. Simon was building a tower out of beer mats. He'd already got it up to two storeys high and was clearly having trouble building it any higher.

I hadn't been lying to Sasha. It *was* a shame I couldn't be with her and her friends. It was just that I couldn't for the life of me *imagine* what a night out with a group of über-babes might be like. It would be overwhelming, that I didn't doubt. For all the experience I'd been fast gaining since I'd begun this lark, there were still things that could floor me.

But I wasn't about to let the guys know that. They wouldn't understand, anyhow. Who would? A hot-blooded male turning down the chance of a lifetime. I'm not even sure *I* understood.

Simon looked up at me as he placed the horizontal foundation on the top of his balancing tower for the next floor of beer mats, as I slipped back behind the table to my seat.

'Well, stud, what's the lucky lady want you for this time?'

I gave him an inscrutable smile, and the bottom of the tower a sharp flick.

The beep on my mobile went when I was buttering my toast the next morning. I set down the knife and pulled the phone from my jeans. Sasha had sent me a text.

gr8 nt. Dlete my no. I'l dlete yrs. Lvly 2 hv nown u. Gd luc wth evrythg. Sx

I sent one back.

Ditto. Lx

I felt a certain relief. Sasha was glamour and danger wrapped up in one gorgeous package. But I was also sad to see her go. I stood for a moment and let her beautiful image play through my head, then I went and got the jar of marmalade out of the kitchen cupboard.

More Stagz

'It's crunch time, Jenny.'

I stirred the cream into my mug of hot chocolate and watched the colours merge, and then looked across at her and gave her a rueful smile. Jenny sipped at her tea, then set it down, and fiddled with the saucer.

'Oh, I don't know, Luke,' she reassured. 'I'm sure you'll find another Sasha.'

I nodded but said nothing. Jenny was right but she was also wrong. I took a gulp of my drink and savoured its warmth. Sasha was gorgeous for one thing and I'd liked her. But it felt like it was the end of an era too. Sasha was among my first clients, and now she was gone. I wasn't sure what lay ahead.

'And anyhow, you've still got me,' winked Jenny.

I looked at her over the top of my mug and gave a quiet laugh. *Not quite the same.*

And *that* was really what I was worried about. That Sasha's leaving – and, come to think of it, even Jenny, my very first client, sitting across the table – also seemed to underscore that my six-month trial with Stagz was almost up. I looked out of the window at passers-by dodging a light shower, then turned back to Jenny.

'Do you think Stagz will have me?' I asked. I set down my

drink on the table and ran my index finger round and round the inside of the mug handle.

'I'm sure there are plenty of boys who would love to have you, Luke.'

I looked up at Jenny again with a frown. She was peering straight at me with her teacup held in both hands.

'Stagz, the agency, I mean . . .' and even as I said it I could see a little teasing glimmer in Jenny's eyes.

I remembered how shy Jenny had been when we'd first met. But nothing seemed to faze her now, or nothing I could tell her, anyhow.

I stirred my chocolate again, even though I didn't want it any more.

'It's not really if Stagz will have me,' I back-pedalled. 'It's whether I want *them* –' I kept going so Jenny couldn't jump in with more innuendo, 'y'know, whether it's worth my while to pay for the service I've been getting free for the past six months.'

The words hung in the air. Jenny nodded in understanding.

'What do you think, Luke?' she asked. 'What's your gut feeling?'

I looked across at her. Her whole aura was more relaxed these days. And I liked that she was genuinely interested in what I had to say.

I sighed. 'Well, it's more expense for one thing.'

Jenny nodded again, waiting for me to fill the gap. Signing on with any agency didn't come cheap, so the longer I worked as an escort meant it was important to be selective and only remain with those sites that did their job and drew in the clients.

The question was whether Stagz was one of them?

I cocked my head. 'I've certainly done very well out of being there, I know that for sure.'

'From what you've told me, it sounds like you have,' she said, and pushed away her empty cup of tea.

184

I peered down at the thick chocolate dregs at the bottom of my mug and thought back to what a difference being on a gay site had made. Certainly in the early days. It was as if there had been women out there crying out for someone like me. And Janice rewriting my profile had been a real asset too.

'There have certainly been plenty of pluses from being with Stagz,' I confirmed.

'And the minuses?' Jenny quizzed.

'The thing is, suppose I've had the best of it? That the rush of women was because there was barely anyone else like me out there, and although there's always got to be a few new clients out there, there won't be half as many as the lot I've already had?'

I realised I was gabbling now.

Jenny reached across the table and stroked my hand. Her other hand, I noted, was clenched around the money she was about to give me. This week's session was drawing to a close.

'Honey,' she whispered, 'you don't really think that.'

I shook my head with fierceness. No, I didn't, but suppose . . .

However, I didn't want Jenny to leave on a downer. It was my job to keep things bright.

'It's a risk, I suppose, that's what,' I stated. 'But given that I haven't had to pay for my first six months, then effectively I'd only be paying half price for the next lot.'

That was one way of looking at it anyhow, though I'd still be paying out the full price for the next six months.

'And then, once the year is up you'll be better placed to know if you want to continue with them or not.'

A waitress came and cleared our empty cups away. There were just our hands held across the table now. I wondered what the people around thought when they looked at us.

'Yes.'

I knew Jenny had to go. I took my hand away from hers and stood up. She stood up with me, and reached across and gripped my arm and released one scrunched hand and pushed her money into my right palm.

'What I really want to do, you know, is have my own website. Then I wouldn't have all this worry. I'd cut out the middle man. The girls would come straight to me.'

'They'd come running, Luke,' winked Jenny. 'You know that.'

But I wasn't there yet, I knew *that*. It would mean a whole new lot of expense for one thing. Certainly more than signing up for another six months with Stagz, that was for sure. I knew I couldn't set up my own site. Computers had never been my strong point. I wouldn't know the first place to start, which meant hiring someone to set up a website for me. And to maintain it too. Even more expense. And some stranger knowing what I got up to. That would have to wait.

So I had to make the best use of what was already open to me. That was all I could do.

Jenny hugged me farewell for another week and we kissed before walking out into the Piccadilly bustle and going our separate ways.

When I got home, I headed straight to my laptop. I tapped into the Stagz main page, took a deep breath and signed up for another six months.

It was *that* easy. I could only hope it was worth it.

Emma and Louise

Mid April

I suppose I shouldn't have been able to believe my luck. I was sitting across the table from one gorgeous hooker and her just-as-hot mate was standing with her back to me at the sink and I had full view of her tight little ass through her D&G jeans.

I took a gulp from my mug of blackcurrant tea and smiled at Emma as I did.

But it wasn't about sex at all. It was good just to take time out from the game. The three of us.

Emma had called me late last night.

'Hi, Luke, do you remember me? Brian's place. About a month ago.'

How could I forget? Well, that was what I'd made her think, anyhow. Truth was, I got through so many girls as voyeur Brian's sex boy that I had no real hope of remembering any of them. Regardless, I'd scrolled through my mental file but it was no good. So I'd checked her out on the internet instead before I went round to her flat in Notting Hill.

Oh, THAT Emma!

There was a photo of her sizzling in tight denim hotpants with a white shirt knotted at her cute midriff, her delicious tits all but spilling out of it.

Hello, girls!

Emma had set down her mug now and was fiddling with its handle. She still looked gorgeous even in mufti. Her long blonde hair was tied in a loose ponytail so a few fronds of hair spilled over her forehead, and she wore a pink velour tracksuit and full makeup. She looked up with warmth in her eyes and observed Louise hang up the tea towel, pick up her own mug of tea from the draining board and come and join us at the table. Louise was tall and slim in four-inch platforms and with a spiky blonde crop. She was wearing a man's shirt tucked tight into her jeans and open at her neck, around which was a tiny gold chain. Her shirt reminded me of the one Emma had worn in her balcony pics.

'Budge up, love,' said Louise, and Emma shifted along the bench so I was now facing two hot babes.

I looked around the kitchen. The girls had kept it spotless. It looked like it had come out of a Sunday supplement. I thought of my own house-share, where it was an effort to get *anyone* to do the washing-up. I could see a small garden banked by trees and decked with a string of fairy lights through the French windows.

'You've got yourselves a nice place here.'

Emma surveyed the room.

'Thanks, but you know what they say. "You never get a second chance to make a first impression." It's keeping the punters satisfied, y'know.'

Louise butted in. 'Even if they don't even see downstairs, you have to be ready in case.'

'Yeah,' Emma added, and nudged Louise with her elbow. 'Imagine them looking out of the upstairs window and the garden's a real mess!'

I could see what they meant. I pictured my own house and its overgrown garden that nobody had bothered to touch since I'd been in London, and imagined a date looking out of *my* window.

'That'd *really* ruin the moment,' I agreed, setting my mug back down on the table.

The image of Emma on her balcony flickered across my mind. That had been taken at the front of the house, and from where I was sitting I had a clear view out the back.

'I saw your pic, Emma,' I admitted sheepishly, and looked beyond her to the polished chrome that ran along the wall between the kitchen cabinets and the worktop. 'The one on the balcony.'

Louise smiled and turned to look directly at her friend.

'Oh, *that* one,' laughed Emma.

I caught her eyes this time. I liked how they sparkled.

'It was taken here, right?'

'Why, of course,' she grinned.

It was an easy mistake to make. I'd had that myself. Clients who expected to meet me somewhere that looked like my pictures because they hadn't realised that that was the photographer's home, not mine. It might be different for the girls, but I had made damn sure that my escort work was completely separate from the rest of my life. If a client couldn't invite me home or to her hotel for our session, she could always book a room elsewhere. Home was a place where I got away from being an escort, where not even my flatmates knew my business. Since I'd taken over Mark's half of the room, I'd had even more of a space to call my own. But at Emma's and Louise's, everywhere they looked reminded them of what they did.

'It was just that I was worried for the people across the way!'

Emma pouted with playfulness. 'And *what* have they got to get worried about?'

There was a moment's silence. We all *knew* how our game got people rattling their cages.

'Oh, that you might fall off and that they'd have to call the Emergency Services!' I shot out.

The three of us all laughed.

Louise shot a glance at Emma. Emma nodded right back.

'The balcony's in my room, actually,' revealed Louise.

'It is?' I smirked back.

That added a whole new dimension to Emma's pics. *Emma looking ready for action and Louise off camera, revving up!*

'Would you like to see it? Would you like a guided tour?' The two of them turned to each other and nodded conspiratorially and turned back to face me.

I shook my head. 'No thanks, though it's kind of you to offer.'

My fantasies were working overtime but I chose to turn them off.

That's not what I'm here for.

Though I still couldn't help thinking about the rooms above my head as I sipped at my hot blackcurrant and gazed at Emma and Louise.

God, if those walls could talk!

It felt weird chatting with the girls over our cuppas, with the washing-up done and our dead teabags sitting in a saucer in front of us. And this whole other life we were supposed to keep quiet about hanging over us.

God, that'd do my head in.

The challenge was to separate out your life so you were more than *just* an escort. And *that* was why Emma had called me. When you lived under the same roof as your work, the only way to forget you were a hooker was to ask over a fellow hooker so you could talk about other things.

Strange but true.

We all needed a break and this was the time for it. Emma had called me over because she *didn't* want to talk shop for a change. It stood to reason, really, because Emma wasn't the first working girl who'd invited me back to her place. So I'd soon learned that it was a friendship thing. I made a point of treating the girls I hooked up with for work with a respect I'd learned not a lot of the other working guys gave them. Which meant that when the girls were at a loose end and wanting a bit of male TLC or just someone to talk to, more often than not they thought of me as someone who could give it to them. Because I knew that there was more to life than being an escort, and I reflected right back at them what they hoped *someone* would see.

'And what are your plans once you've moved on from here? You're not going to stay in Notting Hill for the rest of your lives?'

What I was saying was that we each had to believe in some life beyond escort work. That *that* wasn't the sum of us.

Emma turned the question back to me.

'Will you be going back to Aus?'

'I suppose I will, eventually. If I can save enough, then that'll give me a bit of a safety net so I won't have to take the first job I'm offered. I could start my own business, y'know.'

Louise shook her head. 'I don't know how you manage to save anything living in London.'

'It's not easy,' I agreed, scratching with a filed-down fingernail at the flower pattern on my mug, 'but it helps knowing that I don't want to be doing this forever. *That* motivates me to put something away.'

Louise flicked a look at Emma beside her. 'I've saved all of a couple of grand.'

Fuck! I was aiming for a minimum of ten times that. I didn't get how she didn't have more; she'd been in this game much longer than I had.

But then I'm not living in some flash pad in Notting Hill . . .

I looked across at Louise and *then* I got it. The regular hairstyling, industrial-strength cosmetics and manicures. The designer gear and the photos to get your face and name around. And presumably the interior design to match. I felt exhausted just thinking about it.

Whereas I just comb my hair, shower 'n' shave, put on some clean clothes and show up!

These days it was true that I spent more on my gear than I

used to, that I'd moved on from Boots own-brand shower gel and my T-shirts were Abercrombie & Fitch. But I aimed on getting the balance right between treating myself and putting something away for the future. I wanted to have something afterwards to show for what I was doing now.

'Emma, what do you want to do after this?'

I feared for her even as I was asking her. But Emma replied with a smile that unnerved me more than what Louise had said.

'I'm good at what I do, Luke. I've plenty of time to work out what I'll be doing after this. But for the moment I'm intent on being among the best.'

I hadn't for a moment doubted what these two could do, either going solo or working as a pair. But I also couldn't help being aware of the money these girls spent on keeping themselves up to scratch. It was a damn sight more than I was paying out for the same reward as far as I could see. And since their line of work never seemed to be short of newer and younger colleagues, I couldn't see it getting any cheaper over the years for them. I could see an ever-heightening slog of a job stretching out into the future if they weren't careful. With neither of them having the wherewithal or any alternative to allow them to get off the conveyor belt.

And the men. I bet the clients don't get better with the years either.

It was as if Emma had heard what I was thinking. She looked me straight in the eye from across the kitchen table.

'Do you ever get any scuzzy women, Luke?'

I shook my head in slow motion as if to emphasise my good fortune.

'Can't say I have. Not one.'

Louise whistled under her breath. 'You haven't? No dried-up old crones?'

I laughed and took a gulp of tea, then set the mug down again.

'*I know*. Every time I go out I keep thinking that my luck's got to be over, but it never is. Touch wood.' I gave my head a light rap of the knuckles.

The two of them looked at each other in surprise.

'Really?' Emma gasped.

'I know,' I shrugged. 'If I think back over all my clients, it's rare to find one who I wouldn't have been happy to pull of an ordinary night out with my mates.'

Just saying it made me realise how fortunate I had been. I raised my mug and shot a mental 'Thanks' to whichever fates arranged such things as they were clearly on my side. I looked across at Emma and Louise. I could tell that they couldn't quite believe my luck either.

And then I felt ill when I considered the type of straight guys who tended to call out for a woman of a night.

God, it is SO different for girls.

Emma had her elbows on the table and her fingers crisscrossed together around her mug. When she spoke again, it was in a small voice and she barely looked up. Her eyes were half-hidden behind her long lashes.

'Would you be happy to pull one of us on an ordinary night out with your mates, Luke?'

Louise was aware of it too. Her hand that had been under the table now rose above it and she gave the arm of her friend – *lover?* – a sweet squeeze of support.

'Of course he would, wouldn't you, Luke?!' she bolstered, with a fixed look towards me.

I smiled with my eyes. If I didn't know these two, if I came across them in my local, I'd be impressed. Their heightened glamour would make them stand out, and if I didn't know what they did for a living, either or both of them could sweep me away. But the trouble was that I *did* know. And I wondered not for the first time what any future girlfriend would think of what I had done for a living.

193

'Both of you are Something Else!' I beamed, and raised my drained mug to the two of them.

Louise's arm was around Emma's shoulder now, and she pulled her friend to her. Emma relaxed a little.

'See?'

I brought my mug to my chest and looked deep down into it and sighed.

'I'm going to have to be going, I'm afraid.'

Emma's eyebrows creased together for a moment. 'So soon?'

I pulled myself up from the bench and took my mug to the sink. 'Stuff to do, y'know . . .' But I couldn't leave them just like that. 'I tell you what, when me and the guys are next out, I'll call you up, and you can join us, okay?'

I meant it. It was the least I could do.

The very least.

<u>Going down on a girl</u>

A guy can do wonders with his tongue, and I've found that using my lips as well – lightly rubbing them up and down – works wonders! But either way, the secret lies in knowing what a woman wants – and how she wants it.

- Don't go straight for the jugular, so to speak. It's called 'going down' because that's good advice to begin elsewhere and ease into her treat. Women on the whole prefer a bit of foreplay to get in the mood, so adapt to suit *her* pace.
- Begin with all-over-body stimulation – light touching, kissing and stroking – to turn her on, then move down between her thighs to tease her clit.
- Because the clit is so sensitive, avoid going full-on. Instead, veer to its side, flicking your tongue lightly beneath and horizontally.
- Allow your fingers to play really, really lightly while you lick, but avoid their penetration. The trick is in *suggestion* to arouse a woman rather than diving straight in.
- Take account of your partner's body language to check she's enjoying what you're up to. That way, you can gauge your technique and decide whether she's happy for you to go full-scale drilling with your tongue or gentle round-the-houses exploring.
- Girls, don't just lie there but let your body express your pleasure. Signal with your hips if you want your guy to go deeper.

Bob and Deborah

Early May

The lights of Paris sparkled up at me beyond the plane window as we touched down. The jolt and then the tarmac smoothness of the runway marked the start of a whole new chapter. I'd arrived.

I suppose crossing the Channel means I can call myself 'international' now.

Bob, a posh-sounding Englishman, had called from France midweek. He and Deborah, his wife, were based in the capital, and he wanted to treat her for the weekend. The flight, my hotel for tonight and tomorrow, everything was on him.

That had been a tricky deal to seal. A whole new ball game. It was one thing to charge my standard rates for a few hours or so. Charging for a weekend away was a balancing act between doing myself justice and getting a fair rate while not sounding *too* overpriced in case it scared off the potential client.

And God knew, I needed the cash.

I was in my suit in Bob's hotel bar the following morning, where the two of us had arranged to meet. I barely had to scan the room before a man marched towards me.

'Luke!' His handshake was as forthright as the way he said my name. 'Pleased to meet you.'

'You must be Bob,' I smiled.

'Do sit down.' He guided me to his table, and in the next breath asked, 'What can I get you?'

I looked up at him. His eyes crinkled; I could see charm amid the brusqueness.

'I'll have an orange juice, please.'

I watched him at the bar. Bob looked in his early forties, and wore a slightly rumpled suit over a lamb's wool sweater and white shirt. Smart casual without even trying.

He returned to the table with a coffee for himself and my drink.

'Thank you.' I half-raised my glass.

'You had a good flight over? Transport links are so good these days that we barely feel we've left Britain.'

I am an International Escort. I am an International Escort.

The small talk was for the benefit of both of us. Bob was sussing out whether or not I was good enough for his wife, while I was foraging for any information that might help me to get and keep him onside and be useful when it came to servicing his other half. I passed his test, it appeared.

'You'll get to meet Deborah this evening,' he explained. 'I'm afraid she's in a business meeting all day.'

I paused for a minute.

Hang on, does she even know about me?

I set down my glass. 'Is this a surprise, Bob? I mean, her mind's not going to be full of facts and figures so she won't be able to relax? Or she'll only be up for an early night?'

Bob watched me. When he next spoke it was in measured tones, as if he had given the whole scenario a great deal of thought.

'Isn't an early night the point of it? No, Luke, in all serious-ness, this is a special occasion for my wife *and* myself. We've been considering it for a while. She knows you're on the cards, Luke, don't you worry.'

I nodded. 'But not until tonight,' I countered.

'That's correct. You and I will meet here again at around seven, and Deborah is due with us a short while later.'

I got up from the table. One of the skills you picked up pretty quickly as an escort was timing and knowing when to leave.

Never overstay your welcome.

It was my turn to offer him my hand. 'It's been a pleasure to meet you, Bob. Until this evening, then.'

'*Au revoir*, Luke,' he replied.

I turned on my heel and walked out of the bar. I now had a whole afternoon to myself to kill in the City of Love.

Paris had done her magic and got under my skin. I wasn't exactly in the mood for *love – Hell, that's not my job –* but the muted spring sunshine and slight chill in the air had freshened me up and there was a lightness in my step. I might have been here on business, but I'd allowed myself to act the tourist for the afternoon. A boat trip along the Seine. Up the Eiffel Tower and down again. I'd enjoyed myself even though I was on my own, but all the while I'd remained aware of the *real* reason I'd crossed the English Channel, and how I couldn't afford to relax *too* much.

Yet there was a headiness about that thought too. My work was proving a success to the extent that people were now calling me from abroad! That was a real step up. And I felt ready for the evening ahead with Bob's wife. It was going to be a *real* pleasure, I was sure.

Bob hailed me with a raised arm as I swept through the door of the hotel's bar just before our agreed meeting time.

'Over here, Luke.'

As I sat down, he got up, both his upturned hands gripping the curved edge of the table as he did.

'What'll it be this time, eh? Something alcoholic, I hope?'

When in France.

'I'll have a red wine, thanks.'

I never drank on the job unless I was asked, and then I always went for something in keeping with the situation and what the client themselves was drinking. It meant I kept my wits about me. Which, along with my body, was the other most important part of my weaponry.

It was funny really, because when Bob had called me the other day, it was the job with his wife that my mind was on. But here I was, drinking and having guy-talk with her husband to pass the time. I did the calculation in my head as I sipped from my glass and looked across at him. My time really would be split in half between him and Deborah. We were even having a meal together.

'So, Luke, once you've met Deborah, she'll go up to the bedroom and we'll follow on a short while later. We wouldn't want to arouse any suspicions with the hotel, would we?'

'No problem at all, Bob.'

I was beginning to wonder whether she was a figment of his imagination, whether he had simply hired me for the company over dinner. It wasn't as if he wasn't a nice enough chap, but it was now over an hour since I'd turned up and Deborah was still nowhere to be seen.

I was going to say something. And then, looking over my shoulder, he said, 'Ah, here's Deborah now.'

I swivelled on my stool to face her. And a moment later feared the shock might show across my face.

There's no way I can go through with it. Oh, God, she's huge.

But it wasn't just her size. There were lumps or mumps or something over every visible part of her body. I swallowed hard.

Swamp Thing. Sex with the Swamp Thing.

I felt ashamed just listening in on my own thoughts.

Don't be so shallow!

But I knew there was no way round it. Bob had flown me from London to Paris, lavished me with a couple of nights in a decent hotel, fed and watered me. And still I didn't want to sleep with his wife.

I'd been lucky up to now. Visions of dream girls like Sasha and Chloe sashayed across my mind. But in front of me now was the prospect of Deborah.

Bob introduced me as she sat down at our table.

'Darling, this is Luke.'

'Hello, Deborah. Pleased to meet you,' I said, though I didn't really mean it. I watched this couple settling themselves around my table. And then it clicked.

He's not having sex with her, either, is he? Which is why they hired me.

Shit.

I wondered how many times poor Deborah must have been dismissed or blanked by men. And Bob had married her when? Before or after she'd ended up looking like this? And if before, was he aware of her condition?

But whatever I was thinking and instinctively feeling about her, I had to try as hard as I could to keep it to myself. I felt sorry for Deborah, but I couldn't let her or her husband see it.

'I'm sorry to have kept you both waiting. I'd hoped my meeting would have finished earlier,' she explained, as she pulled her stool closer to our table and undid her coat.

'It must be irritating work cutting into your weekends like that.' *I should know.*

Deborah was something in French banking. That made her professionally bilingual. She'd made it then, in spite of her skin condition. I had to admire *that*. I wouldn't have had the balls to leave the house.

'Oh, we make the most of being in Paris, don't we, love?' countered Bob, clasping his wife's hand. 'Once work's over for the day, it's over.'

'Definitely,' she stressed.

Bob and Deborah *were* a charming couple. Their conversation ricocheted between them. If he was no longer able to sleep with her, you could tell he still loved her. He wanted to do right by her. Which was why he'd hired me. He wasn't going to leave her with nothing at all. *I was.*

'Well, that's me for the night. I'm going up to my room now and will leave you two boys to it.'

This was the signal I'd been dreading. And I reckoned I'd have at best ten minutes to worm my way out of the situation. If I was in any way able to.

I looked over at Bob, took another sip of my wine and tried to work out what to say. I gulped it down with discomfort as I weighed up the options before me. I either told Bob now, outright, that I didn't want to sleep with his wife. Or I followed him up to her room and went through with it.

Or, I followed him up to her room and told the both of them I couldn't go through with it, and made the shit I was already up to my neck in even worse. The truth of it was that I had no option at all. Honesty was the worst and best policy as far as I could see. And all I wanted to see right now was the tarmac at Heathrow.

I took a deep breath and set down my glass. *This really is do or die. It really is.* So I just said it. I threw my cards on the table and let them fall where they might. 'I'm sorry, Bob, I can't do it.'

I don't know how I expected him to respond. To hit me? To turn white like a ghost?

He did neither. He looked straight across at me and said nothing at all.

It was the silence that frightened me because it gave no hint of what might be next. I couldn't bear the quiet any longer. I couldn't look him in the eye. I dug a fingernail into the table's edge and started sawing.

Why doesn't he say something, goddammit?

So I began talking. Except my fear and embarrassment flooded out of my mouth with the words.

'I'll pay for my own flight back. I'll reimburse you for the room. I won't even stay here tonight,' I garbled. 'I'll be on the next flight home. I'm sorry I've wasted your time . . .'

I wanted to say 'and Deborah's', but couldn't bring myself to utter her name. *She* was the elephant in the middle of the room. It would only make things worse. And make me feel even more of the absolute shit that I already felt myself to be.

No 'feel' about it, Luke. You're a Class A shit.

Bob held his hand up in front of me. 'Stop, Luke,' he sighed. 'I'm the one who's wasted *your* time.'

He spoke in a calm, deep voice as if he was doing everything to maintain control. That he didn't flare up as I expected threw me. That he was apologising, when *I* was the one who wanted to cut and run, stopped me in my tracks. I noted that I'd dug a clear dip in the tabletop. I frowned at him, confused, but he only went on talking.

'It's about trust and honesty, isn't it? That's the bottom line,' he stated.

I was about to answer – he was describing my work exactly. But just in time I realised that he was directing it more to himself than across the table at me. He was lost in his own little world. Or already upstairs in the bedroom with his wife. Who was still waiting.

God, has she any inkling what's keeping us?

'Luke, I phoned you last week and asked you to Paris for the weekend. Everything paid for. And all you had to do was spend some time with Deborah . . .'

My fingertips were clipped over the ridge of the table. I felt like asking Bob to punch me, there and then. He had every right to knock me flat.

'But I never mentioned anything of what you might expect. I kept it from you.'

He'd turned the tables and was blaming himself. I listened, fascinated.

'What would anyone imagine, offered an all-expenses trip to

Paris? Especially in your game. The city at its best, eh? I'm sorry I couldn't give you that.'

'It's not all about . . .'

'No, Luke. I offer you my apologies. I had a duty to tell you what was what.'

Bob pulled out his wallet and counted out my fee. I said nothing, but picked up the wad, folded it, and placed it in the inside breast pocket of my suit.

'Goodbye, Luke.'

He shook my hand. I remained at my table to finish off my drink and watched him head for the lift to his wife, ready and waiting in a room somewhere above us.

Out with Mae

Heads turned when Mae walked through the door of the bar, and I knew then that I'd made the right decision to invite her out, if only for my ego's sake.

She stood there in all her six-foot polished glory like some proud Amazon and surveyed the room, looking for *me*. I glanced at the guys I was with and they had stopped dead in their tracks as if time had stood still. Even the girls looked as if they couldn't believe their eyes.

I had to give it to Mae. She sure looked the part, and some. Her blonde mane was pinned up, but a couple of tresses had been allowed to hang loose, which made a guy want to release the rest of it. Her black *Matrix* coat hung open, revealing a duck-egg-blue halter-neck dress belted at the waist, and she was wearing four-inch strappy gold shoes.

Fuck me, girl.

If there was a momentary shyness in Mae's eyes as she hung back in the doorway, she shielded it well when she caught sight of me, and a broad grin spread across her beautiful face. She headed swiftly across the carpet towards me, and while it might have been Rob's birthday I sure as hell felt that *I* had something to celebrate.

We hugged and kissed our hellos, and I couldn't help but be

aware of my mates looking on, wondering where I'd found *her*.
I pulled away but left my hand still grazing her upper arm.

'Mae, let me introduce my friends.'

Rob, I noted, was first in the queue. I'd already explained to
Mae why my mates and I had decided to meet in Leicester Square.
It was Rob's birthday and the first time for the lot of us to catch
up since he had returned from his walkabout through Europe.
Mae had phoned for a chat earlier in the evening, so I'd invited
her along.

'The birthday boy himself!'

'Happy birthday, Rob. Pleased to meet you.'

A look of surprised welcome crossed his face at the sound of
her Aussie accent. She reached forward to hug him, and over her
shoulder he gave me a raised eyebrow of approval. I grinned and
mouthed 'My pleasure!'

Mae pulled back and gripped both Rob's biceps and looked
straight at him. 'Can I get you a drink? I'm afraid I didn't get
you a present or anything but would you like something from
home?'

'You bet! I'll let you choose.'

A sly smile crept up her face and she turned on her sharp
heels. The tails of her coat flapped back against his legs as she
strode across the floor to the bar. The lot of us watched her go.

'Fuck, Luke,' breathed out Rob, still gawping. 'That girl sure
speaks my language!'

I slapped him on the back. 'She's with me, mate, but happy
birthday all the same.'

'So, where the hell did you find *her*?' quizzed Rob.

'Y'know how we expats somehow dig out each other,' I
shrugged.

'And I bet you've been digging *her* out. Fner fner,' he added,
which I suppose I'd walked straight into.

It was his birthday. I didn't say anything and let his words fall
to the floor.

'So, how *did* you two meet?' Mark piped up.

I gave him a 'let it lie' stare. He knew exactly how, but not everyone round here needed to.

At that precise moment, Mae returned with her hands full with two pints, and the three of us looking on fell silent at her beauty before us. Mae handed Rob a Fosters.

'Well, everybody,' she said, raising her glass, 'here's to Rob on his birthday.'

We all followed suit and then knocked back some of our drink. Mae took a gulp of hers and waited for the rest of us to catch her up.

'It's a long time since I've bought a pint,' she admitted. 'I'd almost forgotten what to do.'

I liked how she was with me. Wouldn't any guy? But I liked it too how she didn't hang back from talking with my mates rather than hiding behind her hot looks.

'Back home, *of course!*' she made it clear though I couldn't help thinking of how long since she'd lived in Aus, 'but when I'm out at the clubs for some promo or other . . .'

'Mae's a model, for magazines and fashion shows,' I interrupted, and just as quickly shut my mouth again.

The guys were putty in her hands and hung on her every word.

'Yeah, because of my work,' she smiled at me, making a concession for what I had said, 'the Cristal's practically on tap the entire evening. I only have to stretch out my empty glass and I get a magic refill!'

Simon pressed forward. 'Happy to oblige, though Cristal's a bit out of our league, I'm afraid,' he offered, looking around and shrugging as he did.

'No worries.' Mae smiled and took a swig of her pint. 'This makes a nice change.'

I gave her a double-take. *It does?*

She could tell what I was thinking. She nodded.

'Oh yeah,' she smiled. 'You have to remember I'm always working on those nights. I have to be on my best behaviour,' she winked.

Rob butted in like a bull in a china shop. 'Do you know Elle Macpherson?'

She gave a light laugh. 'Our paths have crossed,' she admitted with a smile.

'What about Naomi Campbell, Kate Moss, Linda Evangelista . . .' he rattled on.

'*Linda Evangelista?*' David spluttered. 'God, you're so *Eighties*, Rob. And you were barely born then!'

I turned to Mae, who was calm amid this boyish maelstrom.

'I wouldn't worry about him,' I laughed. 'He's just reeling names off the front of his older sister's fashion mags before he was old enough for porn!'

And then I realised what I'd just said.

Shit, shit, shit.

'I didn't mean . . .' I stuttered.

'Oh, come on, Luke,' she said, crossing her arms in mock haughtiness. 'We know *exactly* why you straight guys look at fashion magazines. It's the same reason you buy Kylie CDs. To flick your way through the pics . . .'

'Ah,' sighed Simon, raising his glass, 'the service you Sheilas do for the world!'

Mae shook her head but she was smiling too. It was water off a duck's back. Any girl who looked *that* hot could afford to let that sort of bloke-talk pass her by, because at the end of the day, whatever anyone said, she still ended up looking hot. But I liked how Mae fitted in with me and my mates. For all her stunning looks, she was a regular girl from back home. I hovered beside her and drank in the knockabout banter she got going with the guys.

When Simon went to get in the next round and there was a lull in the conversation, I ran my finger down her arm.

'I'm glad you came tonight, Mae. It's been great having you here.'

She turned to look straight at me with her full attention. 'It was nice of you to invite me,' she said. 'I'd have been stuck at home otherwise.' She took a sip of her beer. 'Your mates are a nice bunch.'

I tried to see the guys from her perspective. As soon as she'd arrived and they'd got over their shock at her sheer Wow factor, the lads had been good enough to give her the space to settle well into our groove.

'Yeah,' I nodded, 'they are.'

I'd had a long lie-in and was easing into the afternoon by checking my emails. There was one from Mae.

'Hi, Luke, thanks so much for last night,' it began.
My pleasure, hon.
'I had a lovely time and it was great fun meeting your mates. It's one of the best nights out I've had for a while. Just to let you know I got home safely. Mae xx
'PS: If you're ever thinking of going there again, I'd love to join you!'

I sat back and stared at the screen.
God, she's serious.
It had been Rob's birthday but that was just an excuse for an ordinary night out with the lads in the West End.
Nothing special at all.
But presumably, for Mae it had been a rare enough event among all those high-end parties and opening nights with the stars, where her job was to ratchet up the beauty quotient. And she'd proved last night how she was good fun to hang out with, although she was otherwise way out of my league.
Yeah, I nodded to myself, *the next time we do that, you're coming with us, girl.*

Back home

I was lying on my back and the sun was streaming through my bedroom window, and everything was where it was when I'd left Australia just over a year ago. I was glad to be home. After the crush at Heathrow and the long flight here, it was just good to relax in a quiet, familiar place.

I crawled out of bed and went to the window. I half-expected to see the terraced rooftops I was used to viewing from my London house, but I could see the edge of town and, beyond, the dried-out Western Australian plains. London was crammed full of homes and people. This place went on for as far as the eye could see.

I went and had a shower, the cool water washing off the night's clamminess. I threw on a T-shirt and pulled on my jeans and barefooted it downstairs to the kitchen for something to eat.

My mum was doing the ironing in the lounge room and humming as she did. She gave me a broad smile as I came through the door and smoothed out a shirtsleeve with her hand before running the iron over it.

'You had a good night's sleep?'

I ran my finger along the curve at the end of the board and nodded. 'Yes, thanks. I'm not sure if I'm yet over the jetlag though.'

'You take it easy.'

She up-ended the iron on its board, and turned in the direction of the kitchen. 'I'll put some eggs on for you. You sit down.'

I laid my hand on her arm. 'Thanks, Mum, but you don't need to. Let me do that.'

'But you've had a long journey,' she pleaded.

'I know, Mum, but y'know . . .'

She cocked her head – 'You're sure?' – and picked up the iron and went back to the shirt.

Mum was only being kind, I knew that. But the truth was, I needed to get myself back into the groove of this place, and making myself breakfast the way I liked it and at my own speed seemed a good enough way to get going.

I walked into the kitchen and its neat freshness hit me. It was as if nothing had moved since I was last here. 'A place for everything and everything in its place,' as Mum would say. I breathed it all in.

Yup, it's good to be home.

I leaned against the kitchen doorframe with my mug of tea in one hand, and bit into my slice of crisp toast and watched my mum, her head and shoulders bent forward over the ironing board and her arm gliding in a smooth rhythm to and fro. She sensed me standing there, stopped her work and turned right round to look at me, as if to get as good a view of her faraway son as she could.

'It's lovely to have you back,' she smiled.

'It's nice being back,' I agreed.

She didn't have to say it, but I knew that although she was happy for me to see the world and come home again, she would just as much have liked me never to have left here in the first place.

I took a gulp of my tea, and then stopped and held my mug up to her. 'Can I get you one?'

She glanced at the ironing and then back at me. 'Yes, that'd be nice. And then come and join me,' she said, as she shifted the pile of ironed clothes and patted the sofa beside her as she sat down.

I put the kettle on and wondered about what I was going to do now that I'd got myself here. I'd missed something of Aus while I was living in London, certainly, but now I was back everything seemed a bit vague.

I poured the tea and took the mugs out to the living room and handed one to Mum and sat down beside her. She swivelled towards me so her knees almost touched mine, but drew her head back so she could observe me in all my glory.

'My, how you've grown!'

'Aw, Mum!'

She nudged me with her elbow. 'I was only joking. Isn't that what mums are supposed to say to their children after they've not seen them for a while?' she teased.

'Nope. That's *aunts*,' I winked.

She took my hand and squeezed it, then released it.

'I'm glad you've come home.'

She said it quietly and I knew she meant it heart and soul.

We both drank some of our tea.

'So,' she brightened, 'now that you're here, what are you going to do with yourself? It's for how long?'

'Three weeks. Take it easy, I suppose. See how Matt and Dan are getting on, y'know.'

'You know Chris got married?'

Chris had been in my year at school and lived at the end of our street. He wasn't one of the guys I went round with, but I'd sometimes bumped into him when I'd been out for a drink. Round here you'd bump into almost everyone you'd been to school with in the pub sooner or later.

'I'd heard. Another one bites the dust, eh?'

Mum shook her head with a smile. 'You haven't met any nice English girl you want to introduce to your ma?'

I shook my head too. 'Nope. Sorry, Mum,' I grinned.

I drank some more of my tea so I didn't have to say any more. I could think of a good number of nice English girls I'd met while I'd been in London. Eastern Europeans, Aussies and Americans too. They ran far and away into three figures. And counting. Not that I could ever tell Mum that. Not that I could ever tell anyone back here. That was the glitch in my life story that I didn't want to think too much about. The gap between what people expected me to be back here and who I really was. My escort work wasn't something that bothered me, but I knew it would bother *them*.

Because Chris had done what most guys seemed to do in this town. You left school, then found yourself a job and a serious girlfriend who inevitably became your wife. And that was that.

The last time I checked, Matt, Dan and I were almost the last men standing from my year. I felt more for them because they were here, having to face the pressure. And not only from their mums worrying about them. Round here, *everyone* noticed *everything*.

'Well,' said Mum, draining the last of her tea and moving to stand up again, 'that pile is not going to iron itself.'

'Can I have your mug? I'll wash up.'

I reached out to take it from her. She handed it to me with reluctance.

'You shouldn't be doing that. You've only just got home.'

'I'm happy to. It's no problem,' I replied, and made my way back to the kitchen.

I wondered how often Mum put her feet up. It was odd, because she wasn't much older than some of my clients if I thought about it. Except I rarely did, if I could help it. Age had turned out not to be much of an issue at all for me, but it freaked me out to think of my mum in that context.

'Have you got any plans while you're here?' Mum called from her ironing board.

I could hear the rhythmic thud of the iron as she set it down. I ran the tap and watched the washing-up bowl fill and wiggled my fingers in the water to check its temperature. Mum had already asked that once. It was as if she wanted to see me fitting snugly back into my life here.

'I'm not sure really. See old friends. Mooch around, y'know,' I threw back, though I wasn't certain I could still fit back here.

I looked out of the kitchen window at the back garden as I washed up. Home was the blanched yellow of dried-out grass, whereas England was a rich green. It was what you noticed in central London, especially in the summer. The trees rising above the grey stone buildings.

'You can pick your brother up from school,' said Mum, popping her head round the door. Her arms were laden down with layers of ironed clothes.

'Yeah, I can do that,' I nodded with my back to her.

Jack was the youngest of the lot of us and I'd got a lot to tell him about my travels. I'd got home too late to see him last night and slept through him leaving the house this morning.

I heard Mum walk back across the living room and the door to upstairs close behind her.

If she thinks I've changed since I was last here, then how different is he going to look?

I thought of me, his big brother, drawing up in the car to collect him. It'd be a great way for us to see each other again after such a long time.

As I got ready I knew *exactly* what I was going to do. Mum had given me the idea. I'd pick Jack up from school, as she'd suggested, but first I would take the car for a spin round the old haunts and get my bearings. That would help me work out what I was doing here.

I swung the sunroof back and drove as far to the edge of town as I could go. The sun was hot on my back, which was taking a bit of getting used to. Back in London, everyone was gearing up for what they hoped would be a hot summer. Not that the weather seemed to be cooperating. It never seemed to be able to make its mind up from one day to the next, and anyway, what the Brits meant by hot wasn't a patch on the heat out here.

I brought the car to a halt at the crossroads. I could keep on going right out of here into the distant outback, just straight on until morning, not really thinking about where I was heading but just knowing that home was behind me and drawing further and further away.

I knew I didn't want that. There was a world of difference between here and my life in London, and I couldn't see a way that the gulf between the two of them could ever be bridged. But that didn't mean that there wasn't something of me in both of them, and *that* was the challenge. Although I wasn't altogether sure I knew what to do about it.

For now, though, I was here and my London life was a literal world away. I swung the car to the left so there were buildings to one side of me, the expanse of the desert on the other, and kept on moving round the road that encircled my home town.

I checked my watch. Jack would be coming out of school in half an hour. I pictured the look on his face when he saw me waiting in the parking lot for him. It brought a huge smile to my own face. Yup, he was worth coming halfway round the world for.

I spotted Jack before he saw me and rose to my feet behind the windscreen and waved without thinking.

'Jack!' I shouted across the field of tarmac.

Jack had that lope that teenage boys have, and blond hair longer than mine so it flopped over his eyes. He was walking with two other guys I recognised but whose names I couldn't remember. None of them had changed much since I'd left here, except they were strangely stretched with growth.

He didn't hear the first time I shouted. And then I called again, and Jack's head swivelled round as he scoured the schoolyard trying to see who was calling him.

He stopped in his tracks when he caught sight of me. His eyes widened and a look of glee split across his face, and it was like he'd forgotten he was one of the older boys for a moment because he started running. He didn't stop until he was right by my side and hugging me over the edge of the car door.

'Luke!' he was laughing.

His mates had caught him up.

'This is Luke, my brother,' Jack jabbered. 'He's only just got back from London!'

'We *do* know,' the other two chorused in that Smart Alec way guys have at fifteen.

I reached out my hand to shake theirs. 'We've met before, haven't we, though I'm sorry, I can't remember your names,' I apologised.

'Tom and Adam,' Jack indicated with a flippant thumb, though he didn't give them a second glance. He kept his eyes on me all the while, as if he didn't want me to slip out of his sight.

'Right, lads,' I said, rubbing my palms together and gripping the steering wheel although I was still standing. 'How'd you like me to take you to . . . Hungry Jacks? Is that still there?'

I almost called it Burger King. You crossed the world only to find exactly the same fast food, and same company selling it under a different name.

'Yes please!' The three of them clambered into the back of the car without bothering to open the car doors. I started the car and we set off.

I could see Jack watching me in the rear-view mirror.

God, how he's grown. I heard myself thinking it and thought about Mum. I stopped the car. 'I've got to let Mum know. She'll be wondering what I've done with you.' I pulled my BlackBerry from my pocket and scrolled up her name.

Tom leaned over the back of my seat, his hand reaching out to touch my gadget over my shoulder.

'What's that?'

'It's a BlackBerry. You've never seen one?'

I heard myself say it. *Listen to yourself, Mr Big Shot. Of course he's probably never seen one.* I swivelled in the driver's seat so I had a better view of him and Adam.

'Y'know, a mobile with knobs on. You can send emails and stuff as well.'

He looked impressed, but not quite knowing what to say next then leaned right back in his seat again. Jack shifted to give him room and then lunged up and over the seat in front of him and kicked up his legs and crumpled into the seat beside me. He was roaring with laughter.

'Ja-ack!' I blurted out as I jumped out of the way of his flailing feet. He untangled himself and his head popped up to meet mine and his eyes flashed with humour. He high-fived his friends, and then turned and offered me one and my hand slapped his with a reassuring clap.

On the other end of the phone, Mum had heard the kerfuffle.

'What's going on, Luke? They're not causing trouble?'

'Don't worry, Mum. We're just getting reacquainted, y'know. We'll see you later, okay?'

I turned off the 'Berry and put it back in my pocket, and shook my head at the boys but I was grinning.

'Right, are you upright now? I can't have you mucking about while I'm driving.' I turned on the engine and gave one last look over the three lads. 'Hungry Jacks it is, then.'

The place hadn't changed at all since I was last there. There were big 'Hello!'s and 'Long time no see's from across the counter as I ordered our food. We'd been coming here since Jack was very small. We'd told him back then that it was *his* place and for years he believed it, like that kid in *I Own the Racecourse*. We still kept coming, though Mum preferred that it was seen as a treat. I scanned the room and its primary-colour rows of fixed tables and moulded plastic chairs from my corner vantage point. I pulled a handful of fries from their bag and stuffed them into my mouth. Jack sat opposite me and unwrapped his burger. To one side of us Tom and Adam dug into their own bright red trays of food. On the other side ran a plate-glass window that gave us a view of the car park and the comings and goings into this place. If you sat here long enough you'd see the whole damn town pass through.

Jack took a bite from his Whopper, set it down back in its paper wrapper and wiped his hands on his sleeves. He picked up the small car he'd managed to wangle out of the girl behind the counter and ripped it from its wrapper. It was supposed to come free with a kiddie meal but the boys had used their teenage charm to get her to give them one each. It was some film tie-in, and he ran it back and forth over his palm to grease the wheels and then pushed his tray to one side and tried it across the tabletop. It sped towards me and hit the side of my own tray.

Jack continued to push the car across the ridged plastic right up to the edge of the drinks cup I was holding, and then round the edge of it and straight into my hand.

'Jack,' I frowned, 'don't do that.'

He looked straight at me and said nothing, but the car continued to bump into my flesh with increasing ferocity.

I swiped my hand away. 'Hey, what are you doing?'

He looked at me and laughed, as if what he'd just done meant nothing at all.

Adam took a slurp of his Coke, and fiddled with his own car beside me. 'These toys are so much better than the ones you get at Maccy D's.'

Maccy D's?

He noticed my blankness.

'McDonald's!' He reached across to Jack and tapped him on the arm. 'Your brother doesn't know what Maccy D's is!'

A blush of red flashed across Jack's face.

'Don't they have *those* in London?' crowed Tom.

I looked straight at Jack.

'Oh, you mean McDonald's,' I yawned. 'God, there are so many fast-food joints out there . . . Burger King – which is really Hungry Jacks – KFC . . .' I was beginning to run out of names, 'oh, and Wimpy!'

A laugh bubbled up from Jack's throat. 'Wimpy? What sort of name's *that*?'

I smiled right into my younger brother's eyes. 'That's the *English* burger chain. And get this. They serve it on plates. And use cutlery!'

Jack chuckled. I took a bite out of my own burger. The four of us were quiet for a few minutes as we ate. Jack watched me with a glint in his eyes.

'Luke?' piped up Adam.

'Um?' I turned to him with my mouth full. He was nibbling the tip of a French fry.

'What's London *really* like?'

Jack's and Tom's eyes were on me. Tom was sipping from his straw, and Jack had licked the tip of his index finger and was tapping it over the crumbs and salt at the bottom of the fries' bag and then putting it in his mouth.

I couldn't tell them the whole story. Obviously. I had to quickly find some way of telling them about my London life without telling them very much at all. Like I might write on the back of a postcard.

'Well, there's all the stuff you imagine's going to be there. Y'know, Big Ben and the Houses of Parliament . . .'

'The Tower of London,' butted in Tom. 'Buckingham Palace.'

'Have you seen the Queen?' smirked Jack, though I could tell he was only half-joking.

I shook my head. 'Nah. Though I've seen the red guards outside her place. They have to keep completely still, even the ones on horseback.'

I shot a glance out of the window. *This place is so small-fry.* I frowned.

'It's more than that, y'know. Like Sydney isn't just the Opera House or the harbour, though that's what the tourists like to see.'

Jack cocked his head to one side. 'What's it like *living* there?'

And that was all the stuff I couldn't let on about. I sighed.

'It's *huge*. There are millions of people from practically any country you can name all buzzing around in one city.'

It's a different planet.

I pointed to the view beyond the glass. There was a spacious flatness to the world out there.

'You see that?'

The boys nodded.

'London is everything that isn't.'

Matt slapped me on the back so hard I almost dropped my pint.

'Great to have you back!' he boomed.

'It's nice to be back,' I agreed, as we stood in the backyard of his local.

I'd called Matt after I'd taken Jack and his mates home, when I knew he'd be back from work. We arranged to meet over a drink later in the evening along with Dan.

Though it was so much later in the day, the air was still warm on my skin. I shivered, thinking about how cool England could get. Dan noticed.

'Someone walked over your grave?' He was perched on a low brick wall that edged the pub garden.

'I was just thinking of Britain. It can get bloody cold there!' I explained.

He took a sip of his beer and pursed his lips.

The trouble was that I couldn't get London out of my mind. I wondered what Mark and Simon and the lads might be up to right this minute.

Getting up for work, presumably.

And what they'd be doing when work was over. You could go and drink in your local if you wanted to, or kick a ball round the park with your mates if you felt like it. But there was also everything else that you could be doing too if you were in the right mood. And a lot more that would blow people's minds round here!

It was a shame really, because Dan and Matt were exactly the guys I'd want to tell – wanted to, if I was honest – but it was too much of a gamble. We'd all laugh about it, for sure. Getting paid for sex was a guy's dream anywhere on the planet. But when it sank in, or when I returned to the UK, I wouldn't be able to guarantee that the news wouldn't spread. And somehow make its way back to my family.

Matt shifted from beside me, and Dan's and my gaze followed him as he snuck out of view.

'Where's he going?' I asked, and sat down beside Dan on the wall.

Dan looked deep into his half-empty pint. 'You remember Rachel, Rache Shaw from our class?' He looked sidelong at me.

'Rachel Shaw. The name's familiar.'

Dan stood up. 'Ah, here she is now. Luke, you remember Rache?'

I stood up to join the three of them. Rache, I noted, had her hand in Matt's. I did remember her now. She'd had long, straight light brown hair at school that was now a stylish crop that flattered her eyes and suited her more. I looked from Matt to Rache and back again. They suited each other too, in that way some couples had where you'd never consider they'd be a pair until they were.

Another one bites the dust.

'Yes, I do. Great to see you again, Rache.'

She smiled.

'Matt's been telling me you've been in London. You're enjoying it there?'

'Very much so, thanks. It's pretty different from here, y'know . . . More people and much faster.'

As soon as I said it I hoped I hadn't offended anyone. Dan picked up on it.

'Hope your home town isn't too slow for you now,' he teased.

I shook my head, though I feared he'd hit the nail on the head. This might be my home town, but I was fast realising that I wasn't feeling at home here any more. I didn't know where that left me. I looked Dan in the eyes and chose to be diplomatic.

'I tell you, either side of the planet takes some getting used to once you've been away a while. Even the weather!' I showed him my pallid arms.

'You're vanishing before us, Luke!' he exclaimed in mock horror.

'Is there anyone you're seeing, Dan?' I asked, when Matt and Rachel had gone off to get drinks.

It was a question I didn't really want to ask. Not because I feared any answer, but because the very asking put both of us on the spot and hurried us along to where everyone else expected us to be heading.

'Oh, I keep my options open,' he countered. 'And you? I trust you're making the most of all that London has to offer.'

And some.

I took a sip of my drink, to give the impression I was mulling over my answer. But the truth was, I knew if I told him he simply wouldn't have been able to handle the truth, however much he might at first regard my new life as a real laugh. Round here, even if people like Dan weren't in serious relationships, they were monogamous per each date. Round here, *that* was considered louche.

I returned Dan's gaze with an inscrutable smile and said nothing.

My feet felt back on solid ground once I was in London again, though it was going to take a while for Australia and my home town to seep out of me. I wasn't ready to return there for good just yet, I knew that, but at the same time, having been there and been overwhelmed by the place's slowness, it would take me a little while to gather up the pace so I was up to speed with London living again.

Jenny.

Her name flashed through my mind. Jenny was just the person to help me ease back into things. A return to my weekly half-hour with her would steady me until I *really* got my bearings. There were a couple of other calls awaiting a reply – *clients hopefully* – but first I'd get things sorted with her so I'd feel at least a little way back on an even keel.

I sat on the edge of my bed and rang her number and brought the phone to my ear.

Dead tone. That's odd.

Even though she was on speed dial I still checked the number I was dialling.

Nope, that's hers all right.

I tried it again. I got the same cut-off sound.

I bit my lip and looked at the wall.

Out of order.

That shook me. I hadn't wanted to admit it to either her or myself, but since the very beginning when we'd first met, Jenny had helped ground me. When sometimes the work seemed to be running away from me, casting its spell as if somehow my clients and their desires had control of me instead of the other way round, I only needed to think of Jenny. Jenny might have had her problems, but she made *sense*. I knew our weekly meetings did her some good. And did me some good for knowing that.

I knew of no other way to contact her. I picked at my phone's keypad. That half-hour on Friday afternoons now opened up like a deep, deep hole.

I swallowed hard and tried to put things back into perspective. If Jenny wanted me, she would call me. Surely. Hadn't that been the way we'd first been in touch? It was the client who had to make that move. Everything that came after was my business. And the fact that I couldn't now get through to her reminded me of that. The ball was in *her* court.

If she's going to call, she will.

And I left it at that. It was all I could do.

Penetration

The type of sex you have could range from slow lovemaking to an out-and-out fuck session, and will depend on the mood you're both in. In all cases, it's vital to take account of your partner's needs and desires as much as your own for the sex to be the best it can be.

- Beforehand discuss what your preferences are and what you're both comfortable doing. Communication is key.
- Read your partner's body language to sense what they're after.
- To prolong the pleasure for you both, begin slowly and build your rhythm together. Talk to each other as you do so about how you feel. You'll both know then whether to either continue at a slow pace together or instead gather speed and follow your instincts for hot sex every which way.
- Developing confidence is vital to ensure you get the sex you want. Let him know what you're enjoying and anything new you'd like to try. It's fine too to take charge as long as you remain respectful of the other's desires too. Work as a team; it makes for better sex.
- To prevent a guy ejaculating too soon, don't build up the action too quickly. Masturbate beforehand, change position regularly, take things slowly, and halt the sex at the first sign he's getting close. Or squeeze the head of his cock. He shouldn't try and think of his granny to cool things down, the only image in your head should be the person in front of you. If you've spent a good time on the foreplay, then whether or not the sex is over too soon or not

shouldn't be an issue. Both of you will have had a good time anyhow.

- Just because you've just had whore-level sex, doesn't mean a girl doesn't want decent aftercare. Don't just turn over once you've reached orgasm. Instead, cuddle her and go to sleep together.
- Don't go too far. 'No' means No. Don't force her boundaries.

Sheena

Late June

Sheena was standing where we always met, a hundred yards down the street from the hotel. She was wearing a navy jacket, a calf-length floral print dress and navy court shoes. Her hands were in her pockets and her head turned this way and that so you could tell that her biggest fear was that she'd been stood up. Because Sheena had been stood up her entire life.

She was in her early forties, and lived with her younger sister and her mother. There was no man around, which was where I came in.

I called out to Sheena from across the street, and she turned towards me and her whole demeanour instantly changed. A smile broke across her face and took years off her age. She hovered on the opposite kerb, and waited for me to join her. A couple of cars sped past, and I crossed the road and took her in my arms.

Act the boyfriend.

'Love,' I beamed, and kissed her on the lips.

There was a tightness in her grip, and then she pulled away to look at me.

'Luke, it's so good to see you,' she exclaimed.

'Shall we?' I cocked my head in the direction of our regular rendezvous, and took her hand in mine and squeezed it.

226

'Yes,' she nodded.

To anyone watching us make our way to the guesthouse, we looked like a couple, hand-in-hand, in love, strolling along the street. Only I was young enough to be Sheena's son. And I had my whole life ahead of me, while Sheena, however much she might try to fight it, couldn't quite shake off the air of someone who life was determined to pass by. No, it wasn't going to take much to work out our game.

The receptionist at the guesthouse wasn't letting on she knew, though we'd been coming here once a week for how many months now? I watched her go through the motions as Sheena handed over the cost of the room, acting courteous but all the same showing nothing in her eyes. We'd be out of there in an hour.

Sheena turned towards me with warmth in her eyes.

It doesn't matter a rat's arse what anyone else thinks.

This was Sheena's time, and I was here for her. I took her hand again and led her through the doors to our room. They swung shut and we were on our own again. I grabbed her in a bear hug and kissed her on the neck. She pulled away and giggled, and skipped up a couple of the steps, looking over her shoulder to make sure I was following.

I held back a moment or two, and then caught her up by the time she reached the first landing, stretching out my hand to give her a playful nip on the bum.

'Don't!' she laughed, though I knew by now that she most definitely wanted it. From session one Sheena had told me exactly what she was after, and it was to begin before we even got in the room.

'Come here, you,' I mock growled, and curled my arm around her waist and drew her to me again. We snogged and stumbled together up the remaining stairs and headed down the corridor. All the while I still had hold of her and was necking her even as she was unlocking the door to our room. Once inside we drew apart and she slammed the door shut. That brought both of us to our senses.

I knew exactly what to do next. It was the same every week. She sorted out the cash, and while she was doing that I went into the bathroom and got my act together. When I came out again five minutes later, I wasn't The Boyfriend any more.

'Stand right there,' I barked at her, 'and don't move.'

Sheena stopped dead in her tracks and her whole body stiffened. I marched towards her, placed my hands firmly on her shoulders and ran them down her clothed body, feeling her quiver with the pressure against her flesh. Her mouth opened slightly. I kept mine tight shut and stern. I continued my body search right down to her ankles and back up again.

It was pretty easy to get into character, once I'd put the black balaclava on. Sheena was one of the few who wanted anything extra. That didn't surprise me. After all, it was one thing for a woman to call me up in the first place, let alone specify that she wanted me dressed as anything. Even my regulars were restrained on that score. I wasn't keen to go there anyway. The point about fantasy, surely, was that real life could never live up to it.

No wasting my money on any fireman's gear.

We were both standing facing each other.

'Right, remove your clothes. Now,' I ordered.

I undressed at the same time. Right down to the balaclava. I tried not to think of me butt-naked except for that.

I am a terrorist. I am a terrorist.

Whatever she wanted me to be.

'Get on the bed.'

As Sheena clambered on, I reached to take hold of her, but as much as I was trying to remain dead serious, a guffaw still sprang out of my mouth, and she caught it too so that both of us ended up laughing together on the bed. It was hard to keep a straight face at all, but that was what Sheena was paying me for so I pulled myself together and got back in the zone.

I am a terrorist.

Sheena rolled over on the bed and onto all fours, and buried her head in the pillow. Same as usual. She didn't have to say a word. She wanted me to give it to her doggy fashion.

But that wasn't all.

If only it were.

Afterwards, Sheena wanted the *proof* that I came too. She wanted to put her finger in the condom afterwards and swill it around in my cum. She'd requested *that* from our second session onward.

I sat on the edge of the bed and grabbed my jeans and rifled the pockets for a condom and a little bottle of lube. I set them on my lap and sat back up and turned to look at Sheena, still waiting for me. I reached out a hand and stroked her calf.

'I'm just getting myself ready, Sheen.'

'Uh-huh.'

That was all she said, like the waiting for things to get going was all part of the sex.

I pulled the condom from its wrapper and unrolled it and held it in my left hand. I picked up the lube. It was called Liquid Silk and was white like cum. I poured a small amount into the condom, just enough, and then put it on. I looked at the back of Sheena's head again. She hadn't budged.

She really hasn't a clue.

And then I gave it to her all right. I shifted onto the bed so I was square behind her. I ran my hands up the back of her legs to let her know I was on my way, and then they went up to her hips and onwards beneath until they found her tits for something to hold on to, and at the same time I arched my back and rammed into her.

The sex lasted for about a quarter of an hour, and all the while she never changed her position. Towards the end I did what I always did around that time; I had the best orgasm of my life! My hands had shifted to her ass, and I gave her a playful slap every now and again, the way she liked it. I rocked myself against her and inside her, and I flailed my head around as I did and cried out 'This is the best! Sheena! Yes!'

I toned things down until the sex act was over. Sheena turned over so she was on her back. She brushed her hair out of her face with her hand and watched me remove the condom. There was a light expectant smile across her face. She didn't say anything but edged towards me, and I held it open for her and she dipped her finger in. Her eyes were on mine as she stirred the lube. She really did think that it was all mine. But it was because of that that I faked it.

I wasn't overly attracted to Sheena anyway, but the very fact she insisted that I had an orgasm had created a block in my mind. I didn't have a problem with any of my other clients. Only with Sheena.

It wasn't just that, though. I suppose it was because she wanted me to act as her boyfriend that I feared she might see something else if I came.

I can't be her boyfriend, nor give her any reason to believe I could be.

Sheena stopped stirring and pulled her finger out of the condom and put it in her mouth and sucked on the finger as she drew it out again, then wiped it on her naked thigh. Her eyes hadn't left me all this time.

That was the real difficult thing about this job. You were giving girls exactly what they wanted but you still had to be *so* careful how you played it. You didn't want to give them the wrong idea.

I broke Sheena's gaze and folded the condom over, and the two of us slid off the bed together and headed to the bathroom. While I disposed of the condom she washed her hands at the basin. She turned to me as I joined her, and my hands enveloped hers under the running tap. Her fingers played with mine. There was a girlish smile on her face. She pulled her hands away from mine and we were now at the next stage.

'Let me take that,' whispered Sheena, and took my limp dick in her hands and washed it. The quietness of her voice made it feel like some sort of special ritual. I let her get on with it, and caught myself in the mirror above the basin, the tall terrorist looking back at me, and the shorter, slight woman beside me, her head bent downwards, all her attention drawn to my cock. Making sure it was how she wanted it.

I placed an arm around her shoulder and squeezed her closer to me.

'Come back to bed with me,' I beckoned.

'Yes,' she replied.

I took both her hands between my own and drew her out of the bathroom. We padded across the carpet and lay down beside each other, and I took her in my arms again. We held each other close. Her breasts pressed firmly against my chest and I could feel the steady pummelling of her heart. We snogged. It took all of three minutes.

The same every week.

The time was ticking away. In this line of work I'd come to know *exactly* how long an hour lasted without even needing to check my watch. I peeled myself away from her and she got the hint. She got off the bed with me and each of us got dressed. The mask came off.

We were back in the bedroom together, just the two of us, looking as if we'd just got through the door. I sat at the dressing-table chair that I'd turned to face the middle of the room, and she came and sat on my lap.

'Ah, Luke,' she smiled, stroking the back of my hand. 'I so like coming here with you. I don't know what I'd do if I couldn't get away for this.'

I wondered too. People might laugh at what we got up to.

God, I was one of the first to when I told my mates. But I felt sorry for Sheena too. Stuck at home at her age, with her mum and her sister.

What sort of life would that be? What sort of life would that be if she hadn't found me?

'Well, Sheena,' I teased, 'if you couldn't get away for *this*, I'm sure you'd have tracked down some other young buck on the net who'd come up with the goods.'

She squeezed my shoulders in a ripple of pleasure, and I squeezed her thigh.

'I'm afraid it's that time again, Sheen. We have to go.' I edged forward a little on the seat to encourage her along. It worked.

'I know, I know. I wish we had longer . . .' she sighed, slipping off my lap.

I stood up with her, but said nothing in response to that. I didn't want to get into money talk while she handed me my fee. She could afford some allotted time with me and that was good enough. I wasn't going to treat her any differently because she wasn't one of the big spenders.

I took Sheena's hand again.

'But you'll call me again, next week, yes?' I asked her.

'Yes,' she grinned, and the years fell away from her face.

We took the stairs more calmly this time, hand-in-hand. There wasn't a word between us, though there was definitely a feeling of something shared. Sheena handed back the key at the reception, and the woman behind the desk was as courteous as before, but still her smile didn't quite reach her eyes.

The two of us headed out into the fading daylight, back onto the street where we'd met just over an hour ago. I squeezed Sheena's hand before I let it go.

'Well, this is where I say "goodbye" until we next meet,' I told her, signing off.

We hugged each other, and I gave her a farewell kiss on the lips.

232

'Goodbye, Luke,' she said. 'I look forward to seeing you soon.'

We uncoupled ourselves and headed off in different directions. Before I turned the corner, I looked back and she'd done the same, and we waved once and walked on. Like lovers parting.

Graham

I've got my dream. That's all I could think once I got talking to Graham. He was *exactly* what I was looking for. I'd got this far in the game, after all, and I was at the stage where I needed someone to share it with me. Someone who could and would take me places.

Graham was a web designer who'd answered my ad. And I could see it in his eyes, as we met for the first time over a pint, that my line of work fired his imagination.

Well it would, wouldn't it? Any straight guy's fantasy.

I showed him the agencies I was with on his laptop.

'Nice pics,' he grinned after he'd cast an eye over my pages, 'but I can see how girls have got to go a way to track you down. I'll show you.'

He took a sip of his pint, which left a moustache of froth above his upper lip. He wiped it away with the back of his other hand and set the glass down beside his computer.

'Imagine you're some woman who wants to treat herself one night.' He brought up Google and tapped in the words 'male escort London'. A list of agencies I knew filled the screen.

'So she picks one at random.'

I pointed my finger at the screen.

'Try "Stagz". That's *exactly* what it says on the tin.'

234

He frowned slightly. 'We'll have to hope she's thinking the same way you are. That'd be a bold decision for her to make. She's sure to guess it's a gay site. Which means she's got to be up for the images she's going to be confronted with. That thought might scare her away to try somewhere else.'

He tapped into the main menu. I could see what he was saying right in front of me.

Dick – the lot of it.

But then again, a girl couldn't win. If she didn't want to wade through pages of hard cock before she reached the 'straight men' button, it would be pages of huge inflated tits she had to contend with. And either way, when she did find the guys she was looking for in the first place, she had no way of knowing whether any of the men offering their services to her were quite what they seemed.

I found myself laughing.

'Phew, it's exhausting, isn't it!'

'Yeah, but it does mean that those who manage to track you down are clearly determined girls. Gagging for it!'

I leaned back on the couch and put my hands behind my head, elbows jutting right out. 'You could say that,' I smug-smirked.

Which was only half the truth, though I wasn't going to let Graham know that. If I'd learned one thing in this game, it was that clients covered all bases, from shy first-timers through to up-for-it-in-all-four-corners-of-the-room nymphos. If he got my website up and running, as he said he could, he'd soon see what I was dealing with.

Seems he had something of the same idea. He took out a sheet of blank paper and a black Bic biro from his laptop bag and started sketching a series of empty squares joined to each other with a horizontal line.

'Now, Luke, just imagine all that pent-up female sexual energy aimed directly at you with no other guys getting in the way!'

I brought my arms down again, picked up my pint and shifted closer to the table, so that I had a clear view of what Graham was up to. I drank some of my beer and over the rim of my glass watched as Graham filled in the first box with the word 'Google'. In the next one along he wrote 'male escort, London'. His biro hovered above the third empty box and then he looked across the table at me and set the pen down, picked up his own pint and took a gulp of the gold liquid.

I frowned at him. *What the fuck?*

Graham set down his pint next to the biro so the sheet of paper, pen and glass were arranged in a neat line.

'*That's* the moment of truth in that third box, Luke. That's what comes up when the first two steps have been taken. At the moment it's a list of all the agencies you're signed up to. The trouble is that nobody knows they'll find you at any of those sites until they've found you,' he explained.

I nodded in agreement.

'Even at this stage they've still got an awful lot of searching to do before they track you down,' he continued.

It wasn't rocket science. I'd already got the gist of what having my own website might do. But it sure helped to have someone outlining my hunch right back at me, in a manner he'd clearly given a certain amount of thought to.

Graham carved my name in deep black capital letters into the third box.

'And that's what turns up once you've got your website up and running! It's that simple,' he smiled.

I was mesmerised by my name in that square. I blindly reached for my pint and gulped some back.

It really is THAT simple!

An image of a crowd of women falling over themselves to call me flittered through my head. *That* reminded me.

'You can't give any hint that I'm selling sex, you know that?'

Graham frowned. 'What else would you be offering?'

'It's your weird British law. It's fine to *be* a hooker,' I explained, 'only you can't go touting for business.'

Graham shook his head in disbelief. 'Talk about splitting hairs!'

'I know,' I laughed. 'That's why everyone calls themselves escorts. People are buying our *time*, and whatever might go on beyond that is between consenting adults. You'll emphasise that it's my time I'm offering.'

He nodded.

'Thanks, Graham.'

I shook his hand and he flipped down the top of his laptop and filed it back in his bag. 'You can call me Gray,' he said.

I nodded. 'Okay, thanks, then, Gray.'

We didn't speak for a couple of minutes. He looked down into his pint glass and I watched him.

'Graham –' I corrected myself, 'Gray, I'm not looking for a one-off. Y'know, someone who sets up a website and then takes the money and runs and that's the last you see of them.'

Graham had raised his glass to take another drink but stopped in mid-air before it reached his lips.

'I figured that,' he admitted. 'You need more than that for this to work, don't you?'

I mentally breathed a sigh of relief. We were on the same page. I spread my fingers wide across the table's dark wood and looked down at my thumbs touching.

'I need a website manager as much as a designer. Someone who keeps the thing updated and ticking over and fields emails and calls too?' I looked up at him across the table. 'That'd make a hell of a difference, I know it would,' I stressed. 'It would take a lot of the routine admin out of my hands, for one thing, and free me up to see more clients too.'

And since the website's sure to deliver more work anyhow, then that makes even more sense!

'Look, Luke, that's why I applied for this job in the first place. I can design websites. No sweat. But what you do *intrigues* me.

237

Probably intrigues most straight guys, to be honest. We're on your side, mate,' he smirked, then straightened up on his stool. 'But seriously,' he said, in a more professional manner, 'I see this site as a *real* challenge.'

'So do I, Gray. You set me up a basic site to start with that's workable, and we can go from there.'

'I'd love to,' he said.

We shook hands, and Gray finished off the dregs of his glass, picked up his bag, and I stood up with him and we said our goodbyes, before I watched him swish through the bar's swing doors.

I sat down again. I could barely contain my excitement at how things were developing, and I couldn't wait to see what Gray might come up with. I knocked back the remainder of my beer. Just wait until I told Mark and Si how things were turning out.

One giant leap for mankind!

A week later, Gray emailed me.

> Go on, Google yourself. I dare you! I don't mean Google yourself, of course. I mean, try a male escort search and see what comes up. ;0)
> Do let me know what you find and how you find things.
> Gray.

I did as I was told. When the Google list appeared, I *laughed*. There were two gay agencies listed above me. Stagz was one of them. Then third in line was little ol' me. 'Satisfaction with Luke.' And Gray had ensured too that the sub-heading made it *very* clear that my market was women and couples.

I shifted the cursor so the little hand appeared over my site, took a deep breath and pressed to enter.

Here goes.

I closed my eyes, fearful at what I might find. Then breathed out and opened them again.

No worries!

Gray had come up with the goods. I don't know why I had been frightened about what I might find. He'd taken copies of the photos I'd sent to the agencies and built a series of pages around them. I flicked through the site. It was a good start.

It was difficult to stop myself smiling. Now all I had to do was wait for the girls to roll in. I exited my website – *my* website – and dashed off a thank you email quick-smart to Gray.

Great, and so many thanx. The only way is up! L.

Ralph, Cindy and Us

Mid August

Ralph had arranged a party for him and his wife, and I was part of the entertainment. In fact, a quarter of it.

'Luke,' he'd instructed in an American twang over the phone, 'there is to be no touching my wife. We just want to sit and watch you four in front of us have sex.'

I was sitting with the other three now. Ralph had gathered us together in a restaurant in Wardour Street for a meal before moving on to his place.

Some gathering!

I'd been the last to arrive, and Ralph had stood up to greet me as I approached the table. He had sounded younger on the phone, I noted. He must have been about sixty, though he'd clearly done as much as he could to hold back time. He had dark dyed hair and a tan, and a sharp suit with subtle gold accessories that spoke of money. I had an inkling I *knew* Ralph. Not that we had ever met before, but his face was familiar, though I couldn't place him. He reminded me of Donald Trump, though with not *quite* as much money.

'Ah, Luke. That makes the full complement. Do sit down and I'll introduce everyone.' He'd directed me to the sole empty seat next to a Page 3 Stunnalike. Fake tits, tan, hair colour, the lot. But then again, something I hadn't tried before.

'This is Shannon, Luke, who we've paired you with,' Ralph had said as I settled into my seat.

I pulled my chair in and turned to face her.

God, her boobs are like Jordan's. Like she's just kept on pumping.

She sounded like Jordan too. 'Hello, Luke,' she said, and looked me over with a smile. Nothing in her body language suggested I hadn't met with her approval.

'Pleased to meet you, Shannon.'

Under the table, I took her hand in mine and kneaded it.

Let's start getting to know each other.

'Hello, Luke, I'm Sean, and this is Kelly, my partner.'

Sean sat opposite Shannon. He had an English accent difficult to pin down beyond south-west England, and bland good looks like the Hollywood actor Ben Affleck. His arm was slung over Kelly's shoulders as if it had worn a dip for it to sit in. She held on to one of his limp fingers.

'Nice to meet you both,' I nodded, with my eyes on Kelly opposite. She was a complete contrast to Shannon, which might have been the point. She was a classic English rose, with pretty, delicate features and her brunette hair flowing in waves down to her shoulders.

Wow, this is going to be some night.

I'd known that from the moment I'd put down the phone. Ralph had told me that there'd be another couple and that I'd be provided with a partner too. I'd been more intrigued about his proposition than anything, I suppose. I certainly wasn't nervous. For one thing, I couldn't see how it'd be much different from meeting new clients for the first time. Just more people at once. And for another, there was the money. On the phone Ralph had asked me my fee from eight to midnight, and when I'd told him four hundred and fifty there'd been a pause and he'd come back:

'I'll give you a thousand if you put on a *really* good show for me.'

And who was I to say no to that?

'And now you've met each other, may I introduce you to Cindy, my wife.'

Ralph had made his way from the head of the table, to behind me and Shannon, and was standing with his arm protectively around Cindy. I'd been so busy registering who I'd be playing with tonight that I had barely noticed this beauty.

No wonder there's a No Touching rule.

She was gorgeous and petite, and looked so much younger than her spouse. About thirty-two, I suppose.

She's better than either of the girls.

Cindy looked up at Ralph with a slight, satisfied smile and then turned to the four of us. 'It's lovely to meet all of you,' she declared in an American accent that had a Southern twang. 'We're going to enjoy getting to know you.'

The four of us in the middle of the table glanced at each other. We knew exactly what she meant. The night had only just begun.

We travelled to Ralph's home in separate cars, a couple apiece. I sank into the back seat and slipped my hand onto Shannon's stockinged thigh. She placed her hand on top of mine.

'Have you any idea where Ralph and Cindy live?' I asked.

I looked out of the window beyond her. I generally prided myself on my sense of London's layout but I had lost my bearings in the dark. We turned a corner and there was now the Thames on one side of us, a row of fine houses on the other. We'd left Chelsea, but I wasn't quite sure where we were, or, come to that, where we were heading.

'You haven't been there before either?'

I shook my head.

'But you've met them before?'

'No.'

'Oh, I have.' Shannon relaxed a little. 'They're an okay couple.

Friendly, you know. He's big in exports or something. Or that's what he told me, anyway.'

She shifted so our shoulders and knees now touched.

'Sean and Kelly seem nice enough,' I ventured.

'*Nice enough.* What's that supposed to mean?' she teased.

'Well, you know . . .' I smirked. 'They're partners, right?'

'They're escorts too. They come as a pair.'

I stroked from her thigh down to her knee and Shannon kept her hand on mine. She opened her legs a little for me to draw my hand back up again.

'So that makes all four of us,' I murmured, and gave her a sly smile.

She reached for my cheek and stroked it with the back of her hand.

'Am I "nice enough"?' she asked, half-joking, half-wanting me to say 'yes'.

I nodded, giving her thigh a playful squeeze. 'You're okay,' I chuckled, and so did she.

The car swung through an electrified gate and crunched to a halt. I opened the car door and eyed Ralph's house as I climbed out. My head just kept on tipping back.

'Oh my God, the size of this place!' I blurted to no one in particular.

The glass and steel and newness of the block was in a different league to all the others I had visited. From where I was standing I could see the river, and I imagined the spectacular view there must have been from the top floor. There was one of the Thames' bridges, highlighted in lights, though I couldn't for the life of me name it.

I went round to the car's other side door, opened it and took Shannon's hand, and she stood up and leaned slightly on my arm as she tottered in her heels across the gravel to the apartment-block door where the others waited.

'It's amazing, isn't it?' Shannon whispered with glee, because both of us knew without saying that you should never show your amazement to your client. We just looked at each other and I winked.

Ralph had plainly spotted me admiring his pad.

'There's a swimming pool on the top, you know. In the summer we take the roof off. Some other time, eh?' he smiled.

I didn't know what to reply without sounding like I was fawning over his wealth.

Ralph surveyed the little group at his front door.

'Now we're all here, I'll take you up.'

The four of us kept quiet and followed him and Cindy up to their penthouse apartment. It was as if the night became more luxurious the longer it went on and the higher the lift took us. It took us one button below the top floor. I thought of the weight of water above our heads. The lift doors swished open and my jaw hit the floor.

Oh my God. This place is unbelievable.

The lift opened directly out to the sitting room. The carpet was deep white, like one of those prize cats. The two sofas were massive and white leather. There was a huge plasma screen on the far wall, and a silver chandelier hung from the middle of the ceiling and dripped with glass that seemed to almost touch the floor.

Shannon's eyes, I noticed, were round like bull's-eyes.

'Do come through,' Ralph beckoned.

A young man seemed to appear from out of nowhere and took our coats. He said nothing but had the bearing and straight face of one of those soldiers that stand outside Buckingham Palace.

Fuck, a butler too?

The group of us followed Ralph through into a large lounge. Given the number of floors and the size of this one, his place, I calculated, must have been as big as three whole houses.

Ralph closed the door firmly behind us, as if giving the message to any staff that this room was out of bounds. There were deep armchairs edged like ring-side seats around the huge geometric-patterned rug that spread across the floor and gave plenty of space for the four of us to put on our show.

'If you can take your partners and undress each other,' Ralph instructed, taking Cindy's hand and settling down beside her in an adjacent chair along the length of the room so we were in full view of them.

Shannon stood before me. I unbuttoned and slipped off her blouse and she dropped her mini-skirt to reveal black lace lingerie, and stepped out of it. I was glad that the two of us had had the chance to grow comfortable with each other in the car. That we hadn't just been thrown together.

Shannon's hands began undoing my shirt and my hands were on her hips as she did. Sean came up behind her and unclipped her bra and his hands came under her arms and cradled her enormous breasts. She turned her head towards him and their lips met. Shannon's hands crept beneath my open shirt and swept my own chest.

At that very same moment, Kelly placed her hand on my own shoulder and drew me towards her so that I slipped away from Shannon and Kelly was now my concern. Sean and Kelly had a damn sight more confidence about playing this game.

They know exactly what they're doing.

Kelly drew my shirt off, and unbuckled my belt sharpish. Buoyed by how things had just revved up, I slipped my hands under her bra straps and lifted them off her shoulders and drew them down her arms, and then slid my hands down from her neck and beneath the lace. I now cupped her cute little tits in my palms and I brought my lips down to nuzzle them. The rest of my body came up to meet her.

Kelly's hands were tight on my ass and my trousers had fallen to my knees. I stepped out of them as my hands traced the edge of her ribcage round to her back and unclipped her bra. As my kisses tickled her shoulder, I could see the naked form of Cindy held by her husband. I made sure that Ralph didn't see me stare, but if I was gripped with pleasure when Kelly pulled away and stood undressed before me, it was as much for the American girl.

Does she know I'm watching her? Does he? Is that part of it?

All six of us were naked now. Cindy had shifted onto her husband's lap, and Sean had taken Kelly's hand out of mine and swapped her with Shannon. We had moved on to the next stage.

'You look great,' Ralph complimented, and Cindy nodded along with his words. 'Do please sit down,' he requested, and beckoned us onto the rug beneath our feet with a warm smile.

Anywhere else, it would simply have been a few words of politeness to make us feel comfortable. But with these two, everything was weighted with sex. It sounded perfectly fine and ordinary on the surface. Anyone could have said it. But there was a completely different meaning beneath it. They were speaking a different language and I understood every word.

The four of us unfurled across the rug, and I made love to Shannon, and Sean to Kelly. Even as I was enveloped by Shannon's curves, I couldn't get the svelte naked image of Cindy perched on her husband's knees out of my mind.

She's something special.

Sean had reached out and his hand was on my shoulder as I cradled Shannon beneath me. I momentarily froze.

No! This isn't part of the plan.

Had I misunderstood what Ralph *really* wanted?

Sean's lips were at my ears.

Oh God.

'Luke,' he breathed deeply, 'you take Kelly now. It's my turn with Shannon.'

I looked into his eyes.

Don't let it show that you thought he meant anything other than this.

246

'Shan,' I caressed her breasts and licked them, and then gave her mouth a deep lingering kiss. We unwrapped from each other, and I stretched and touched the tips of Kelly's fingers, and held her wrist and put her fingers in my mouth. Shannon had shifted towards Sean and now lay in his arms.

It would have been nice to throw precautions to the wind, to have gone with the flow, but a whole part of this game was making sure you kept yourself safe, hassle though it was. The trick was to take time out to sheath yourself with as much grace as you could manage. You didn't want to disrupt the evening's flow, though it was damn hard not to. I prepared myself for my next move.

Kelly felt entirely different to Shannon. She was lithe and almost delicate beneath me. I had appreciated Shan's curvaceousness, extreme though it was. The whole point of it, all that work on herself, it seemed to me, was to give as much as she could to a guy. You couldn't help but admire her enthusiasm.

It proved difficult to forget that Kelly came with her other half. That was intimidating to some degree. *He's right beside me. He could thump me now if I do wrong by her.*

But on the other hand, it raised the bar. I damn well had something to prove.

I'll show both you guys what I'm made of.

I held Kelly and bored into her. She moaned with pleasure. Her teeth bit into my shoulder and I buried my head between her breasts. My kisses traced hard up her cleavage and her neck, and my tongue tunnelled into her open mouth. She gave as good as she got.

Sean, it turned out, was lost in Shannon. All that could be heard through the lovemaking in that room in the rare moments that my hearing tuned into what was going on around me, was the breathiness of everyone and the movement of bodies meeting each other. Cindy let out a tiny yelp and my ears pricked up.

Presumably she liked what she was watching, but she was also enjoying Ralph too.

The sound of Ralph's wife's pleasure made me determined to put on a show for her. I barely gave a damn about *him*. Not that I didn't appreciate his contribution. He was paying for the night, after all, and he'd made the whole of it easy-going. But, for me, the bottom line was that I was doing all this for Cindy.

Sean and I swapped partners again, and then the rug turned into something of a mêlée, us guys together licking into both of the girls, Kelly and Shannon side by side and their arms round each other, all but joined at the lips, writhing and digging deep into the rug pile. Twice as much pleasure for the lot of us.

In the tangle, I looked up for a split second, and Ralph and Cindy were entwined in the depth of their armchair, and somehow getting off on us while they seemed just as engrossed in each other. Watching Cindy in action, even with another man, got me hotter than either of these girls wrapped together. Even though Shannon and Kelly were both something else, Cindy was in a different league altogether.

Which, I suspected, was what Ralph knew all along. If he and his wife enjoyed buying a couple of couples in to watch them at work, he probably got as much fun out of his 'Hands Off My Girl' policy. He *knew* it would have the guys *steaming*, and keep them as horny as hell for the floorshow.

And he was damn sure right about that.

A couple of weeks later, Ralph phoned again while I was speed-walking at the gym. I slowed the machine to a gentle stroll and trusted that my breathing would level off just as smoothly.

'Luke, you know how much I enjoyed the other night?'

'My pleasure,' I interjected, and caught my breath as I did.

'Well, I was wondering if you might do me a little favour?'

Shag your gorgeous wife?

I agreed to whatever it might be without a second thought. Ralph was the sort of guy you didn't say no to. The money, for one thing. He was Big Game. But there was an air he gave off that it wouldn't be good to get on his bad side. My head filled with images of Cindy too.

Anything to see her again.

I brought the walker to a stop and stepped off it so I could give Ralph my full attention. My eyes were on the view beyond the gym's floor-to-ceiling third-floor window. The building was on the corner of a busy intersection and pedestrians and cars vied with each other on the street.

'I can trust you, can't I, Luke?'

He was telling me, not asking, but it raised my hackles anyhow.

Why shouldn't you? It's all part of the service, isn't it?

'You met Cindy, my wife, last week, didn't you?'

'Yes, I did, Ralph. It was a real pleasure.'

You bet!

He'd set me off thinking about her again.

'The thing is, I'm off on business for a month . . .'

And you want me to fill in the gap while you're away?

'. . . and I've a friend who needs to be introduced to a girl until I get back.'

I wasn't quite sure what he was asking, or, come to that, where I might fit in. I didn't see its relevance to Cindy either. I held my phone to my ear and let Ralph fill in the pieces.

'The thing is, Luke, I'd like you to make the introduction. We'll meet at the same place as last time, in Wardour Street. I'll be there with Helena, and if you could turn up a little while later with Kim – we'll sort something out so you two meet beforehand – and when the girls are settled with each other, you can go.'

Ralph hadn't stopped for breath the whole time he was speaking, but I felt I needed to catch mine.

249

It wasn't about Cindy at all. He's got something going on with this Helena and he wants me to make a hot lesbian drop for him. Presumably so she doesn't stray with some guy.

I looked at the huge plate-glass window in front of me, but I wasn't really looking at anything. I was thinking of that time with Ralph and Cindy and the others at his place, and how it all seemed to run so smoothly.

He's sure as hell put the skids under that.

Kim and I made our way across the restaurant to Ralph and Helena's table, and he stood up to greet me as he had done the last time I was here, and I had to tell myself to forget that night and Cindy and all the rest of it.

I pulled out Kim's chair for her and peeled off her coat from her trim shoulders, handing it to a waiter, and she sat down. Her auburn hair cascaded down her back in enticing waves. I sat beside her and held her hand, so anyone looking on might think we came as a pair.

I was seated opposite Helena. She was pleasant enough. In fact, in any other circumstances, she'd have been fine.

Come on, Luke. You're not here to pass judgement on who's sleeping with who. Do your job.

I looked at her anew. Actually, she *was* pretty fine. She was even younger than Cindy.

There you go again. Shut the fuck up.

Helena wore her dyed blonde hair in a middle parting and the lot of it had been straightened to extreme. She was a tall size zero as far as I could tell, with the fake tits that required. A scarlet sleeveless shift dress showed off her deep tan.

'Pleased to meet you, Helena. This is Kim,' I introduced, and as I did I turned to my partner to see if I could gauge what she was thinking of her future date. Kim seemed to be taking in all of Helena in fine detail, though she looked like the Mona Lisa in what she gave away.

'Hello, Helena,' Kim offered, and looked her straight in the eyes. One side of her mouth had crept up to smile.

I returned my gaze to Helena, though she seemed more intent on Kim.

Looks like they've hit it off.

'And my name's Luke,' I declared to her, and she gave me a flicker of a gaze before returning her attention to my neighbour.

Don't mind me.

My job was done. I'd delivered the goods in one piece. I'd been instructed to order a starter, to eat it and then be called away. I had a slice of melon. I wasn't feeling very hungry anyhow, but I hoped too that it might take the remaining bad taste of this evening away.

When the food arrived, I didn't take long to demolish it. Ralph gave me a knowing 'get on your way' raised eyebrow across the table as he finished off his soup.

My BlackBerry suddenly went off. I'd set it so it would.

'Excuse me.' I nodded to the others and shifted my chair back and rose from the table. As I did, I noted that Helena and Kim were playing footsie beneath.

Fast workers!

I took my call in a quiet corner of the dining room. It wasn't a call at all. Just a lame excuse with little flair.

But hell, it gets me out of here!

I returned to the table with as apologetic a look as I could drum up. A waiter had cleared away the starter and Ralph had his head close to the two girls as they chatted.

'I'm sorry, I've just been called away. Urgent business, I'm afraid.'

Ralph looked up at me. 'It was good to meet you, Luke. Some other time?'

'I'd like that,' I said, though now not altogether sure that I would.

I went round to Kim's side of the table. 'Love,' I kissed her, 'you take care. I'll see you later,' I lied, as Kim had been told I would.

Helena rose to meet me over the table and I gave her a farewell peck on the cheek.

'Goodbye,' I smiled.

I stepped back from the table, gave a little bow, and turned on my heel and headed out of there.

Mission accomplished.

One-night-stand etiquette

The two of you have hit it off and have decided that this very same night you're going to go to bed with each other. But it's not as simple as that. Keeping to your role is very important. There are some 'rules' that it's worth knowing so that you can be sure about what you're getting into. And what you're getting out of tomorrow morning.

- Don't expect anything more from a one-night stand than a one-night stand.
- Nevertheless, the important thing is to treat each other with respect. It'll make for a far better night together.
- If you'll be staying the night at theirs, it's especially important that girls text a mate to let them know where they're going and who they're with. There's no harm in guys crowing about it either.
- At *his* house, if you meet his flatmates en route to the bedroom, be smiley and friendly.
- Don't expect breakfast in bed and morning cuddles the following morning.
- Don't overstay your welcome, and be prepared to leave early.
- At *her* house, make sure before you go to bed that you have directions to the bathroom, the front door, and the route home.
- Be careful not to bump into her flatmates or family to save possible embarrassment.
- If you're both happy to exchange numbers, do.

Myleene

I was having a lie-in on a Sunday morning in Manhattan, and I only had to turn my head to look through the ceiling-high window and out over Central Park. Myleene was stretched out beside me, twenty-six and a petite brunette, hands like butter-flies and as rich as shit.

'Oh man, that was one of the best night's sleep I've ever had. That was wonderful,' I burbled, still barely awake, and as much to myself as to her.

Of course the sex had been good. *Goes without saying.* But, God, I'd just flown halfway round the world in the last couple of days. And then Myleene had followed *that* with a proud whistle-stop tour of the city. Even though I hadn't quite got over the jetlag.

So, the sex had been good. But the high-weave sheets and the heaven of a mattress were what had taken me to another world. It had been like sinking into a warm nothingness.

Not that I'd tell Myleene that.

Still half asleep herself, Myleene reached out her hand and ran her fingers along my shoulder. Like petals brushing against me.

'You like sleeping here with me, Luke?'

We faced each other across the pillows.

254

'It's delightful,' I purred back, and leaned towards her.

We kissed a gentle wake-up kind of kiss, and I relaxed back on her pillow, my head touching hers. Myleene lay silent beside me, and I listened to her quiet breathing while her hand swept my chest, a backwards and forwards tenderness.

I didn't altogether get these women who hired a guy from across the ocean. And paid business class for me to reach them too. And then go home again. Like there weren't any cute escorts in their own country? Presumably not.

Not that I'm complaining. No way.

Myleene and I had at least got to know each other back in London. She'd been over there for some reason. Not work, I don't think. She didn't need to work. But anyhow, she'd called me out one evening. We'd gone to a restaurant in Mayfair, and then she'd invited me back to the Hilton. The night had gone well.

Well enough for her to think of me when she was back here.

And well enough to pay the mileage too. But then Myleene had money pouring out of her. She was a lovely, sweet girl too. Just not very good at relationships. She came from so much wealth that she'd spent her life surrounded by security in every country where her rich dad was assigned an executive post.

Not exactly conducive to a love life.

I fingered Myleene's dark hair, and lightly rested my chin on the top of her head. This was a morning for lounging around, for curling up in each other in the expanse of her bed, and acting like there was nothing worth looking at outside.

'I'm so glad we've become friends,' she sighed.

'Me too, Myleene. I've really enjoyed visiting you here.'

I had no problem being a friend to my clients. Not that it happened with every one of them. But getting on socially made the rest of the transaction all the more easy. It kept it fun for me for one thing, but it also made decent business sense too. Yet that wasn't what it was all about either. Some of these girls, I had to admit, I just liked. And Myleene was one of them.

You could tell pretty early on. Once they'd seen me on the website, and got up the courage to email me. How the messages flowed – or didn't – from there gave a pretty good indication of how we'd get on once we actually met. And that was how it had been with Myleene. There was an easiness in our online contact, and face-to-face the friendship had blossomed from there.

Yet with Myleene living in America I couldn't help being a bit nervous on the flight over. Would she be a different girl on home soil? You could be anyone you chose, after all, when you were in a foreign country.

And didn't I know that?

But I needn't have worried. She was waiting for me at JFK and we fell into each other's arms, all smiles, pleased to see one other again. She'd whisked my bags back to her apartment, and then after I'd had a wash and brush-up, Myleene had taken me up to the top of the Empire State Building and we'd first kissed looking out over the city. It was a cliché all right, but if she wanted me to fulfil some of her romantic fantasies, even in a race against time – *and God, it was some race* – then that's what I was here for.

Myleene's apartment was huge and open plan, and seemed all the more so when you were still getting your bearings. Seeing it for the first time had given me the weird sensation of feeling swallowed up by the place. Only for a moment, though. Myleene wanted me to feel at home in *her* home, and had done everything to put me at my ease. She'd poured me a large glass of quality wine and passed it to me, and that had helped ground me.

We'd peeled each other's clothes off and fallen into bed, and the sex, as far as I remembered, was as relaxed and loose-limbed as the sleep that followed.

Next to me, Myleene stretched her whole body as if she was limbering up for the ballet.

'You'd like breakfast, Luke?'

I nodded. She was already clambering off the bed.

'Yes, I would, thanks. But let me do that.'

Myleene stopped dead and turned and looked down at me, and her mouth made the disappointed shape of the letter 'O'.

Uh-oh, social faux pas alert.

So, this was part of her fantasy too. Making breakfast in bed, then sharing it with 'her man'.

Backpedal, quick.

'But the thing is, Myleene, I'm only just getting to grips with putting together an *English* breakfast. I tell you what, why don't you make me a *proper* American breakfast? I'd love that.'

Myleene visibly brightened as if all was well with her world again. She disappeared into the kitchen, and I sank back into the luxury again.

God, this is the life.

I was woken I don't know how much later by Myleene breezing back into the room, her arms laden down with a huge tray containing coffee cups, a large coffee pot, cutlery, hot waffles and a tiny jug of syrup. The clatter of the crockery brought me sharply to my senses and I jumped up to help her.

'Let me take that.'

She gladly handed it over, and reached for the bedclothes and pulled them straight.

'Put it down on the end of the bed, here, so we can get back in,' she instructed.

She's got it all planned out, just how she wants things. Just how she wants me.

I laid down the tray, and a second later Myleene had her arm around my waist and, laughing, was tugging me to the pillow end of the bed. I wrapped my arms around her and we stumbled in together, and the crockery chinked as we snuggled up together.

'Careful,' Myleene giggled as she reached out over the duvet and steadied the tray. 'You'd like a coffee?'

I sat up and crossed my legs and let her be Mother. I figured it was what she wanted.

While we eat, anyhow.

'Yes, please.'

A wave of tiredness washed over me, even as Myleene was handing me my cup and saucer. I had enjoyed visiting Myleene here, but I wasn't altogether sure it was good for my system. I had barely enough time to recover from the flight over, before I would be due on the flight home again tomorrow morning. And in between I had to give her my full focus, make her feel that there was nothing else at all on my mind.

My tired mind.

There was a relaxed silence as we ate our breakfast. Just the sound of the crunching into warm waffles, and the clink of the china. But I knew it was important not to let the quiet run on too long in case my client felt any unease or awkwardness.

All I had to do was ask the girl open-ended questions about herself, and the ball would keep on rolling. It might even make her feel comfortable enough to call me again, rather than tick me off and then go and find some other guy out there.

I shifted on the bed to survey the treetops down below the window.

'I can't believe what you can see from here.'

It was a vast green block of space and a lake surrounded by high-rise towers. Like this one. And because of all the concrete and steel around it, the colour appeared somehow greener.

Myleene moved too so she shared the view. I placed my arm around her shoulders.

'I know.'

Her voice was full of smiles, and she squeezed my thigh like we were sharing something all the more.

'It was a dream of mine ever since my father first worked here

258

when I was little. To live in an apartment that looks out over the park.'

'It's incredible,' I agreed, drinking the last of my coffee. I meant it. It was something most Americans could only ever dream of. Achieving it was something else.

Myleene pulled away from me abruptly to face me. She wore an intent and quizzical look.

'Do you live close to a London park, Luke?'

She's fishing.

'And you feel settled here, do you?' I parried.

'Yes, I do.'

I made a point of only giving out information about myself to clients on a Need to Know basis. The more I held back, I figured, the more they could create their own image of me. And the more they did that, the more likely I was to get them hooked. But it was about being professional too. I was on *their* time. It was enough that I turned up and was there for them. They had no need to know my life story too.

Myleene had set down her empty plate on the tray and had started stacking the crockery.

'So, there's no risk of you moving on again and me losing track of you,' I teased.

She looked mildly hurt for a second. 'I wouldn't let that happen. Even if I did leave here. But I wouldn't dream of leaving here. Or losing touch with you. You know that.'

I had an inkling. But I chuckled in a bid to reassure her.

'Hey, you,' I chirped, and placed my hands around her as she gripped the tray ready to take it back to the kitchen. 'Let's shift this stuff out of the way.'

I could feel her whole mood and body against me lighten with my playfulness. She let me take the loaded tray from her, and I set it down beneath the bed, out of harm's way, and rose up again in one clean move and lunged at her sitting cross-legged on the bedspread. I grabbed her round her tiny waist and pulled her over and we tumbled together like lion cubs.

'We don't have to go out at all today, do we, love?' I mock-growled into her ear.

'That's why I called you over,' she giggled.

'And why else would I choose to visit New York? There's nothing here!' I licked and kissed Myleene's taut swan neck, and she laughed.

Myleene was relaxed and putty in my hands, and ready for it, I could tell, so I slipped my hand beneath her silk nightdress, and my head followed. Her smell and the smoothness of her skin was tantalising. I kissed her belly and headed northwards. I burrowed between her breasts and suckled each in turn, and Myleene cooed and drew her legs around my back and, reaching through the nightdress's v-neck, she clung to my head and buried her face in my hair.

'God, you've a beautiful body, Myleene. It's delicate and strong at the same time.'

I heard myself say it. I sort of knew what I meant but it still came out not sounding right.

Shut the fuck up.

I pulled my head out from under the nightdress and frowned at her.

'That doesn't quite make sense, does it?' I quizzed.

Myleene relaxed her hold on me and shook her head, half-frowning, half-smiling. 'Well, it does and it doesn't,' she decided.

Which just about summed it up. It was what I liked about this girl. Somehow, across oceans and vast differences in backgrounds and wealth, for some unknown reason there felt a natural rapport between the two of us. Oh, I knew I had to be careful that Myleene didn't misinterpret our easy friendship as something more than what it was. But, certainly on my side of the equation, it made seeing her pleasurable and fun. As well as damn sexy.

Which reminded me. *Get back in the game, Luke.*

My body wanted more action. After all, wasn't that what I was here for? I reached again for Myleene's nightdress and edged it up her body. She got the message and pulled away from me, arching her back and tugging the clothing up her torso, then sitting up and dragging it over her head. There was a tight ripping sound.

My horror was instantaneous. 'Fuck . . .'

I felt part responsible, and I knew it showed on my face.

'Oh, Luke,' Myleene sighed, and gave me a pitiful glance from across the bed. 'Do you really think I can't get myself another, like I don't have any more in my closet?' She shook her head and laughed. 'You rich little poor boy!' she guffawed, and began pulling at the torn material, tearing it in two, all the while her eyes staring at me.

I reached out my hand to finger the flesh she had newly revealed, but as my hand went to touch her, she swept it away and then gripped that same wrist.

'No-oh,' she stated.

She kept on pushing, and I let her to see what she might do and where things might go, so my hand was now forced against my own chest and her face too was up close, examining my flesh with her own fingers and her tongue and her gentle kisses.

My whole body stretched out with the pleasure of it.

Oh, man.

I lay there and let her do whatever she wanted to me. I was on her time, after all, putty in *her* hands if she chose. And she very definitely had. The bed's warm nothingness turned hotter.

Since we had the whole day to ourselves, both of us knew to take our time about things.

This is a marathon, not a sprint.

It also suited my languid mood. We made love, unwound from

261

each other and relaxed, and spoke in quiet voices that wouldn't break the mood. And then crept closer to each other again. Full circle.

Delicious. This was sex in slow motion.

'Why do you have to live so far away?' Myleene sighed as she lay atop me, her light body rising and falling with my own.

Her head lay on my chest where she listened to my heartbeat.

'Ah, but if I was an American escort, you'd have hired someone else from the UK instead, wouldn't you?' I said to the top of her head.

She play-pummelled my gut.

'No I wouldn't!' Her mood shifted lower and she stopped pummelling and her hand rubbed my side. 'But you'll have gone by tomorrow morning. And then how long will it be till we see each other again?'

Myleene looked up at me from my ribcage with her large dark eyes that did their job and melted me.

'Whenever you want me to come again. When I can spare the days,' I conceded.

'That's just it,' she moaned, laying her head back against my heart.

It was important to keep a client's spirits raised. I never wanted to leave them on a downer, or even remembering that any of our time together had been anything but upbeat. So I tried to show Myleene the bright side.

'But while there are such big gaps between us seeing each other, it makes our time together really special, doesn't it?' I beamed down at her looking maudlin up at me.

'Yes,' she tried to smile, 'but . . .'

But nothing. I'll show you damn special.

My hands cradled Myleene's neat ass, and I shifted my body so she rolled onto her side and then her back, and now I had the upper hand as I rested on my side and surveyed her toned, tanned body. With two of the fingers of one hand I traced a path from the middle of her forehead and down the length of her nose. And then swept her lips each way, and her mouth opened and she sucked them in. Hard. Her own hands gripped my wrist like she was both guiding me but going with my flow. Wherever that might take her.

And then I drew my wet fingers from her mouth and continued on my merry way down her lithe neck. My kisses followed in their path. I encircled her breasts with my fingers, then my tongue, and headed downwards. She nestled deeper into the bed with a deep sigh of contentment.

Myleene knew what she wanted, what she wanted me to do. She pushed on my wrist so my fingers carved through her belly and down between her legs, and her moist lips parted for them and my own lips.

'God, Luke,' she breathed out in a half-strangled yelp, her hand tight round my arm and pushing and then relaxing her grip, pushing at my forearm and then pulling at me to let up as if she couldn't bear the force of her own passion.

Myleene's hips rolled with the rhythm and her pelvis thrust forward in pulses to meet me. I lifted my head just for a moment to look up at her strained neck and her jaw line, her whole head thrown back into her pillow, her pleasured groaning like she never wanted it to stop. For a split second I thought about going down on her again, flicking at her clit till sparks flew.

I changed my mind. With one hand reaching up to grip her slim waist, and my leg swinging over her so she was now lying between and beneath me, I arched my back and sank myself hard into her. We rocked together, clinging tight to each other, my chin resting heavy and jarring on her shoulder blade, she digging in, me digging down with our joint rhythm.

We were now one and the same, and I could feel the heat rising, my whole body pounding and taking Myleene with me in the rising passion. And then its wave crashed over us, and we were floundering, its wash flowing back over us, tugging at us. And then came the smaller waves in passion's wake, their furled edges lapping at us, then the stilling, the two of us flat out catching our breath, quietening, and the indent of the two of us beneath us. Beached.

We said nothing for a while. We didn't need to. I relaxed my hold on Myleene, my grip lightening into a touch, a tender caress. The flats of her hands stroked my back in great close sweeps, one following the other like an oar slicing through the wash.

I listened to our settling breaths. I nuzzled Myleene's shoulder and neck and she clung to me like she didn't want to let go, or let me go. We straightened out together on the bed, and I lay on my back with Myleene quiet in my arms.

'Luke.'

Myleene breathed out my name as if she didn't want to break any spell. I knew what she meant. It was like we were somehow wrapped in the experience of what we had just shared.

'Hmm?'

I was simply letting my body bathe in the sensations it had just enjoyed. I didn't need to say anything.

'I don't want to have to wait so long between sessions. I *miss you.*'

I looked down at Myleene, but she wasn't looking at *me*. Her head was level with my chest, and she was talking to my heart. Her emphasis on the word 'miss' set a tinkling of warning bells off in my head.

Uh-oh . . .

What could I possibly say that might put her at her ease yet not commit me to anything I couldn't possibly and wouldn't want to deliver? So I said nothing and let her fill the silence.

That was something I had to watch with wealthy, pretty clients like Myleene. They so easily fell for me, hook, line and sinker. I wasn't bragging. That's just how it was. Be nice to a girl who's missing a bit of male tenderness, and in her mind she all but had me walking up the aisle with her.

It was like walking on glass. Any kindness I might do for her – which, let's face it, was part and parcel of this job – she could so easily interpret as a sign of my love for her. And with their money and their looks, these girls couldn't work out why I wouldn't want to fall for them. But I didn't.

Myleene shifted onto an elbow and this time looked up at me and straight into my eyes. 'If I had a place in London, it'd be so much easier to meet. I could get somewhere!'

Her eyes shone bright with what she imagined our time together could be.

'You could, Myleene,' I replied, mirroring a little of her glee.

Myleene, after all, could throw money at anything or *anybody* she wanted to. If she wanted her own flat in London, then she could no doubt have it. Would have it.

We lay there for a while, me looking at her but trying not to look straight into her eyes, and neither of us saying anything.

What if she had a flat in town? How would that pan out?

If she was in love with me, as it seemed, then things could turn out awkwardly. For me, and for my other clients. Would I be able to shake Myleene off, if money to her was no object?

I shifted to take a better look at her.

Or maybe I'm just paranoid. She's lovely. Why wouldn't I want her around once in a while?

Once in a while. If only I could be sure of that. But the things Myleene said, the way she spoke when she spoke about *us*, made me very unsure indeed.

She wants me, and if she can't have me, I could end up with my own stalker.

My voice broke the silence like a cleared throat. 'The thing is, Myleene, if you came to live in London, I wouldn't be able to sink into this lovely deep bed in Manhattan overlooking Central Park. And then where would I be?'

I grabbed her by the waist again and our bodies and our laughter folded into each other, and the whirlpool of lovemaking began again and went on long into the night.

I lay in my bed, getting over my jetlag, adjusting back into London time, London life. Not like Manhattan at all. No girl or soft bed to sink into. I reached out and picked up my BlackBerry to check the time and my emails.

Gray had waited until I was back in the UK to forward any messages on. '*Good to have you here,*' he'd texted, '*they're queuing up, mate!*', along with a mass of attachments.

Among them I noted a text from Myleene.

'*Welcome back to England. I'm sending you money for your own special mattress to remember me by!*'

My eyes widened.

Shit. One of the perks of the job.

It wouldn't be the first I'd got a gift from a client. But however much it happened, I never quite got used to it. It was lovely, of course. Who wouldn't be happy to receive the latest designer gear and gadgets on top of the money they were paid? A mattress from Myleene was just one more present to add to the pile. Yet it somehow unnerved me too. Like it came too easy to me, just handed to me on a plate. Plus it made me stand out from my mates and was a world away from where I'd come from. Maybe *that* was the problem. Being reminded.

But all the same . . .

I lay back on my own bed, on my own standard-issue mattress, and closed my eyes. And then opened them again.

Hang on. What's she after?

It was a hunch I had. Something I couldn't quite put into words. That what looked like a gift plain and simple at face value was anything but. An inkling that there were conditions attached, though I didn't know what.

Or maybe I was just being paranoid. Myleene had that effect on me because I knew she had real feelings for me. So maybe I was doing her down. I should give her the benefit of the doubt. Because with her wealth, maybe she didn't even think of the kindnesses she could do for other people. It was the easiest thing in the world. She had so much money she didn't even notice when she was spending it. She did it because she could. It cost her nothing.

I rolled over onto my stomach, my elbows on my pillow and my chin resting on my knuckles.

Give the girl a break. She knows what you like and can afford to treat you. Don't look a gift horse in the mouth, for God's sake!

I shook my head a couple of times. In a short time I'd be sleeping in my own Manhattan apartment of a bed.

Myleene was back in London. Just for the hell of it. Just to see me, she said.

'*I'm in town,*' she'd written in her latest email. '*And looking forward to testing out our mattress.*'

I stopped dead in the street and rubbed the edge of my BlackBerry against my top lip. Myleene's message left me cold. It was good to hear from her, for sure. We were friends after all. But I didn't like that 'our' one bit. Those three little letters said far too much.

For one thing, Myleene was presuming that the mattress somehow belonged to the both of us. That although she'd given me the money to buy it myself, it involved her ownership too. More than cash was changing hands. That's what she seemed to be saying in that little '*our*'.

And since she partly saw the mattress as hers, then presumably she had every right to come check it out. At my flat. Which meant us sharing it. Sleeping together. And I hadn't bargained for *that*.

I shifted my shoulders to shake off the guy walking over my grave. I almost checked behind me to see if Myleene was there, or somewhere watching me.

267

I might bump into her. And then what?

Well, I'd say 'Hello', of course. That was what. But I still felt unnerved at the thought of meeting her. If it was unplanned, anyhow. Which was possible in a town like London, in spite of its size.

I set off walking again, but my head was now full of Myleene and the pressure I felt she was putting me under. Just because she was in the same city and wanting to track me down.

I looked into the front gardens of the houses I passed. Some of them were completely tarmacked over. One or two of them were full of flowers and colour. I thought of my home among all this, and how I was beginning to put down roots here. I'd enjoyed treating myself to the mattress with Myleene's money. It certainly made sleeping easier after a night on the tiles, and somehow transformed my rented room making it somewhere I really wanted to come home to. I just fell into my dreams. But all the same, no way was Myleene going to get an invite back to my place just because of that kindness. Not if I could help it.

It seemed she'd decided that the mattress was a bargaining tool after all. I should have listened to my gut instinct. She wanted a damn sight more than she was giving. It hadn't been a gift at all. It came too wrapped up in conditions.

My stride slowed as I thought things over, my feet avoiding stepping on the thin gaps between the paving stones. I pulled my 'Berry out of my jacket pocket and flicked it on again, and scrolled down to Myleene's message and read it again.

You don't have to answer it now.

That was the good thing about this new technology. I could use it anywhere, which meant she couldn't track me down. She could call me but I could physically be anywhere. She had no idea where. I didn't even have to reply. For all the perceived immediacy of these new gizmos, she had no way of knowing whether or not I'd even read her words. That gave me some leeway, some time to work out what I was going to do and how I was going to respond.

So, what was a guy to do? What does any guy do in this situation? I pull back, give her the hint of the cold shoulder. While not wanting to turn my back on her completely. We were friends, and she was my client, and for whatever reason, a number of good reasons, I didn't want to throw *that* baby out with the bathwater. But by the same token, neither did I want to give her any reason *at all* to think that we had anything more than that going between the two of us.

No way.

So, Myleene was in London. I could handle that. I enjoyed the mattress she'd given me. I'd continue to sink into it long after she returned home to New York. But while she was on this side of the Atlantic, then it was out of bounds for the both of us. I'd return her call and make that damn clear. Time spent together over the next few days would be on her territory. And definitely not mine. Not ever.

So I made the call.

'Myleene,' I said, 'it's good to hear from you.'

David and Charley

Early October

You never know what you're going to find behind the door. All the agency had told me was that I was to go to an address in Notting Hill, and that one of their girls would be joining me there.

My cab drew up outside a huge white mansion house, with steps leading up to it and a column each side of the door. I paid my fare and climbed out into the dank October darkness, hurried up the stairs and rang the bell.

A man opened the door. I took a step back.

I know you. Where the hell from?

He was older than me, in his early thirties, with crinkled, smiling eyes and dark cropped hair. And he certainly recognised me.

'Ah, it's Luke, isn't it? I'm David. We've been expecting you.'

We shook hands. 'Do come in.'

It was really bugging me. Where *had* I seen him before? He was better than average looking, though he'd need to be in the right light to be truly striking. He wore a collarless shirt and jeans. Presumably he was off the telly.

He took my coat and hung it up, and I followed him down the hallway. Directly in front of us was a huge staircase that demanded any hostess make a grand, sweeping entrance down it. Or escape to her boudoir.

David led me into a warm lounge. The floorboards were bare and polished, and two armchairs and a sofa were set around a solid square glass coffee table in front of a Victorian fireplace. He held back at the threshold and beckoned me in.

'Do make yourself at home. You'd like a beer?'

'Thanks,' I nodded, and sat down on the far corner of the sofa.

David returned a couple of minutes later with two chilled bottles. Handing me one, he went and sat down in an armchair. He put his feet up on the glass slab and took a gulp of beer. I followed suit.

'She shouldn't be long now.'

'It might have been better if we'd arrived together, but it wasn't arranged that way, I'm afraid,' I explained.

For a split second, David looked confused. He opened his mouth to say something and then thought better of it and closed it again. He looked at the bottle's label and took another swig.

'How long did the agency tell you to stay for?' he asked.

'They didn't. It's up to you. Whatever you want.'

'Oh, okay,' he nodded.

I wasn't sure what to do.

Where the hell is she?

I wanted to check my watch but knew I shouldn't look flustered, so I sipped from the bottle to keep myself occupied. I looked over at David, who didn't seem at all concerned at the no-show.

There was a creak from up above and footfalls could be heard crossing the ceiling to the top of the stairs. David looked upwards, his eyes following the sound of the tread. He turned back to me.

'Ah, here she is now. And Ingrid can join in when she arrives.'

His other half. Got it. Wonder what she'll be like? And what it's to be? They watch or we swap?

We sat and waited for his partner to come down. From where I was sitting I had a clear view beyond David and through the lounge door. She descended the stairs with an unhurried grace. First her bare feet appeared, below a fluid deep green dress, and her hand on the banister rail gripped it like a ballet dancer. And then her shoulder-length dark brown hair that haloed her pretty face . . .

God, she's the dead spit of . . .

And then I looked across at David, and I knew where I'd seen him before. These two were red-carpet fixtures. And I hadn't realised who *he* was because although he had kudos enough in his own right, it was *she* who gave him the glamour. It had been only a few weeks ago that I'd seen her on the *Jonathan Ross Show*, promoting her latest film.

She entered the room and it was like she'd walked straight off the screen. I fought the urge to jump up out of my seat out of respect.

Keep your cool, Luke. You don't want to look star-struck.

David swivelled in his seat to look at her.

'Darling, this is Luke.'

'Pleased to meet you,' I nodded, and stretched forward, reaching out my hand to shake hers. There was a lightness in her grip, though I only half-noticed. I was mesmerised by her deep blue eyes and willed myself not to blush.

'Hello, Luke. I'm Charley.'

Like I don't know your name. The whole damn planet knows your name!

Yet there was a reserve, or was it shyness about her – I wasn't sure which. Maybe she just didn't want to give too much away. Maybe she was just plain nervous. Why shouldn't she be? It was understandable either way.

Charley took a couple of steps towards the other armchair, then wavered. It was like she wasn't quite sure what to do with herself. She turned towards us. Her voice was quiet and measured:

'I've got some champagne chilling in the fridge. Are you boys ready for a glass?'

'Yes please,' we said in unison.

I watched Charley all but glide out of the room.

God, she's a dream.

I set down my beer bottle on the coffee table.

'How did you two meet?'

How lame a question was that? Truth was, there were so many things I wanted to ask the two of them, but what *can* you talk about to A-listers about without seeming to pry?

'We were the only English people in the whole of the Czech Republic so we couldn't do anything else but get together. That's not true, obviously, but it felt like it at the time.'

He stopped, his eyes glinting at the memory.

'About eleven years ago, it must be. We were in the depths of nowhere working on a film, and it was one of Charley's first acting jobs. I wasn't much more than a gofer so we were just as nervous as each other. And then we kept bumping into each other every couple of years on other projects. We just started from where we'd left off.'

'But doesn't that always happen? A group of people getting on like a house on fire on a movie set, and then going their separate ways when it's all over?' I stretched my arm along the ledge of the sofa.

'It does, it does,' David agreed with a genial smile. 'But every time Charley and I met we just got closer and closer, until eventually we decided to make it official. We've been married three years now.'

There was a deep warmth in his eyes as he looked over at Charley, who'd returned with a bottle of champagne and some glasses. I liked him. He wasn't up himself, as I might have expected someone so famous to be. He was just an ordinary guy talking to another guy he might have met down the pub. Only the situation was different. Very different.

Charley set the tray down on the glass block, poured the drinks, and, with a subdued smile, handed us each a glass.

273

'Thanks.' I nodded at her.

She picked up a glass for herself and settled down in the other armchair. She didn't say anything. She took a sip of the drink and seemed happy enough to let her husband lead the evening.

'Charl, Luke was asking us how we met . . .'

The doorbell rang. We looked at each other and David jumped up – 'Excuse me' – and left the room. I turned to Charley and gave her a close-lipped smile.

So there are two couples now. So where is it going to go from here?

There was talking in the hallway, mostly David by the sound of it, and then he returned, and behind him a girl I hadn't met before. She towered over him in her patent mauve four-inch heels. She was about twenty-one or twenty-two, and had long blonde hair, a pretty youthful face, and stockinged legs that went on forever.

'Meet Ingrid, everyone. Ingrid, this is Charley, my wife, and Luke.'

Ingrid sat down on the other end of the sofa and David fixed her a drink. I figured she must feel bad about the evening already having started. I know I would have. We could have been seated as if for an interview.

'Hi, Ingrid, the agency told me I'd meet you here,' I smiled, hoping I might put her at ease. And then I feared I might have rubbed it in that she was late. She took a sip of the bubbly and looked me up and down like she was mentally scrolling through the guys she'd seen on the website. All six of us.

'I trust you weren't hoping for the cute East European bisexual,' I quipped.

There was a leaden pause.

'And what if I was?'

'Don't worry, Luke. You were certainly the cutest in our book!' chipped in Charley.

'Well, thanks,' I grinned at her, taken aback.

Before I could say anything more, Ingrid had jumped in with both feet.

'I saw you on the *Jonathan Ross Show*. What's he like?'

I inwardly winced. How to squash an actress's fragile self-image. Tell her you noticed her but were more interested in the person she was with.

'He's just as you'd expect him to be. Warm. Friendly. Makes you feel relaxed in his presence. You know the sort of thing,' Charley lobbed with a tight-lipped smile, shooting a split-second glance at her spouse at the same time.

David jumped to his feet. 'Luke, come with me to the kitchen. You'd like another beer, wouldn't you?'

I heard the steel in his request. He was telling, not asking. I stood, and slipped past Ingrid, turning at the doorway towards the girls and bowing my head – 'Please excuse us.' Then I slipped out of the room.

The kitchen was large and decked out like a 1950s American diner, complete with tarnished enamel Coca-Cola signs on the wall, and a scarlet and chrome island table that was the room's centrepiece. The fridge matched. David yanked open its heavy door and pulled out another bottle and handed it to me. I stepped forward to take it, and caught a look at the inside. It was filled with not much more than beer, wine and champagne, and an assortment of expensive face creams, presumably to keep Charley looking so beautiful. Not that she needed much help.

David pushed the door shut and pointed to the bottle opener on the wall. I flicked the lid and put the bottle to my mouth. He brought his own bottle to the opener, and with his back to me asked:

'What do you make of Ingrid, Luke?'

I knew what I thought but I didn't dare say anything. I had to be damn careful in case I got it wrong. My job was to follow his prompting, but at the moment I couldn't see what he was thinking. Was this just small talk or did he want an honest opinion?

David turned and looked straight at me.

'How do we get rid of her?'

'Why's that?'

He shrugged his shoulders.

'I just don't fancy her. Charley's not happy either.'

'I sussed that,' I nodded.

'Luke, we don't want her here. Can you make her disappear?' As he spoke, he pulled open a kitchen drawer and fished out a wad of notes.

'Give her this, and do whatever you have to do.'

I nodded again but didn't take the money.

'Yeah, I can do that. No problem,' I stressed.

But the truth was there *was* a problem. Getting Ingrid to leave after such a short time could end up proving very messy indeed, however simple the rest of us wanted it to be.

'The thing is, David, she could feel very angry that she's been sent home after twenty minutes. I know these women. What I'm saying is that she could do something spiteful.'

I took a slug of beer, and watched him as I did.

I don't know what it was about Ingrid. Sure, she looked fine, but she didn't quite get the situation. Maybe she was simply out of her depth, not expecting ever to be asked to visit people like these two. I hadn't been able to believe my eyes either, in truth. But even so, you had to be sharp in this game. Pull yourself together fast and act as if nothing fazed you. And *never* faze the client. Day One, Lesson One. It is *all* about them.

David stood in silence and played with the notes like they were a flicker book while he looked at the floor. As if money could make everything right.

Maybe in his world it did.

An image of a tabloid front page flitted across my mind. Didn't David and Charley get it, that just because they were National

Treasures didn't mean they wouldn't be shot down in flames? That that was *all the more* reason. I wondered why on earth they would want to risk all they'd worked for for a paid fuck with a stranger?

'Look, what if she went to the press?' My words sounded dirty in such a clean space.

David's head jolted upwards and he stared at me.

'Be very careful,' I warned. 'This is the type of girl to do that.'

David paced the room.

'God, Luke, but she can't . . .'

'Tell you what,' I was thinking on my feet, 'just let her see you for an hour. You won't have to do anything, just keep her talking. And then you can pay her and see her off, but make some excuse as to why I have to stick behind. How about that?'

He'd stopped clattering across the floor. He let out a heavy sigh and nodded at me.

'Good idea. Thanks.'

'My pleasure.' I couldn't believe how naive he was.

We returned to the lounge.

'Hey, girls.'

Charley looked up and over my shoulder at David as we entered the room. She seemed to be searching his face for an update.

'You two been getting along, I hope,' he smiled as we settled in our seats.

'Ingrid's been asking me about Hollywood,' Charley replied, in a voice with just a little too much sunshine in it.

'You enjoy going to the cinema, do you, Ingrid?' David asked.

He made every effort to include her in the conversation over the remaining forty minutes. I don't know if it was guilt or fear, but it was as if he was going to make damn sure she went away feeling she'd got her money's worth. That she had no complaints.

On the cusp of the hour, I wound down the session.

'We'll have to be going shortly. It's been a pleasure meeting you both.' I smiled and stood up. Ingrid, I noted, looked a bit puzzled.

David stood up too. 'I'll call you a cab. Ingrid, where have you got to get to?'

She jerked herself to her feet as if she wasn't quite sure what was going on but was just copying everybody else.

'Acton Town.'

'That's a shame. I'm an EastEnder myself,' I lied, 'otherwise we could have shared a cab.'

'No problem. I'll sort out one for each of you.'

David made for the retro phone in the hall.

'Sit down, you two, and I'll get you your coats,' said Charley, and left us alone.

I sat opposite the fireplace and mentally traced the outline of the fleur-de-lys on the tiling at the base of the chimney.

'What the fuck was that all about?' hissed Ingrid.

I swivelled my head to look directly at her. 'What?'

'They hire us and nothing happens?' Her pretty features were spoilt by a confused frown.

'Er, that's what they pay us for. Our time. They can do whatever they want. Or not. Within reason, of course,' I explained.

'Oh, come *on*, Luke.'

She was right of course. It was invariably about sex.

'So they don't want anything sexual. They just want to sit around and have a chat. That's *ker-azy* celebs for you. Whatever.' I shrugged my shoulders.

She shook her head a couple of times.

'I get it, I get it. But it's not exactly Babylon, is it?'

'But if you just go with the flow, you never know. They might invite you back for something *really* hot.'

But I did know, and Ingrid wasn't going to get a look in. I sort of felt sorry for her.

Sort of.

Charley was back with our coats, and David craned over her shoulder as she handed them to us.

'Ingrid, your cab'll be here in five minutes.' He fixed me with an intense gaze. 'Luke, I'm afraid you're going to have to wait for another quarter of an hour.'

He slipped around his wife and began counting out money from a wad in his hand. Ingrid put hers inside a purse in her handbag. I folded the notes and pushed them into my back pocket.

There came a knock at the door, and Ingrid said her goodbyes.

'Some other time, I'm sure,' I called after her, as I watched her head down the hallway and out of there.

As the door slammed behind her it was as if the whole house breathed a sigh of relief. I stepped back inside the room. David was lounging in the armchair with his shirt half unbuttoned and Charley was sitting on his lap, with her hand on his chest and nuzzling his neck.

Fast workers.

I put my coat over the back of the sofa, and sank into the other chair, picked up my bottle and watched. David raised his glass to me. His other hand was up his wife's skirt, stroking her thigh. I caught a glimpse of her creamy flesh above her stocking.

'Let's get this party started, Luke.' He turned to Charley. 'You get more booze, I'll get the gear.'

She pulled herself away from him and David followed her out of the room.

Five minutes later they were back. It was as if Charley had emptied the fridge. A large ice bucket hung over one arm with a couple of champagne bottles sticking out. She clasped more to her chest and held a couple of beer bottles in each hand. I jumped up to help her, taking them from her before she dropped them. David was scoring some lines of coke with a practised hand in the opposite corner.

Now the glass slab made perfect sense. Who would have thought it? But then again, who *wouldn't*? I busied myself refilling our glasses, and prepared myself for the inevitable. Out of the corner of my eye, I watched David roll a note, bend down and vacuum up a line, and pass the note to his wife, for her to kneel beside the table and do the same. *The nation's sweetheart.*

I picked up a glass of bubbly and sank down into an armchair.

'Luke, would you like to join us?' David's hand surveyed the scene.

Charley wiped her nose with the back of her hand, and then she picked up the note and offered it to me. I put my hand up like a stop sign. I took another sip of champagne and raised the glass to them.

'Don't mind me. You just carry on. I'm fine with my drink.'

We relaxed into the early hours. The conversation and the drink flowed. At one point I was sharing a joke with David when Charley left the room. To the bathroom, I presumed.

But as fast as Charley was gone, she came back. Minus the green dress. She had on an ivory lace g-string to show off her hot ass, and naked breasts that were just made to sit in the cups of my hands.

I'd give you an Oscar any day, love.

'Fucking hell, what's going on here?' I shot at her. 'All those people who watch those catsuited science fiction films don't know what they're missing!'

Charley fired me a pout, placed her hands on her hips and stuck out her tits for me. Any reticence she might have had at our initial meeting had vanished a long while ago.

'Come here, love. Don't squander it on Luke.' David stuck his tongue out at me. 'She's mine, all mine,' he crowed, laughing. He seemed to like that I wasn't cowed by his gorgeous A-list wife.

Charley trotted over to him and climbed again onto his lap, then proceeded to undress him and covered every newly naked part with her kisses. She pulled off his jeans, then took him in her mouth and he was lost for words.

God, she's getting me going.

David dug deeper into his chair with every rhythmic nod of Charley's head. The chair screeched along with the moan of pleasure that rose out of his throat.

After he came, David bent down towards Charley and they snogged.

I started unbuttoning my shirt.

'I'm the only one who's got any clothes on!'

'So get them off, or why else are you here?' challenged David as he straightened himself in his chair. He whispered something in Charley's ear as he looked over at me. An impish smirk crept across her face.

Charley stood up and perched her ass on the arm of David's chair and watched me unbuckle my belt and kick off my trousers. She licked her lips. And then she slunk across the room towards me like a cat going in for the kill.

She swept herself onto my lap and I took her in my arms. Her skin felt like silk.

'She's all yours, Luke. Enjoy,' called David from what now seemed a long way away. But I could tell from the happiness in his voice that he was going to get as much pleasure from watching as partaking.

I kissed Charley's neck and her hands played across my chest.

'It's like somebody sculpted you. Yummy!' she exclaimed, and then traced a line of kisses down my torso that tickled like summer rain.

I ran my fingers through her hair. She reached the waist-band of my Calvins and looked up at me with her bewitching eyes. She hooked her right index finger over the elastic and pulled.

'Hang on, hold it right there,' I cautioned. I reached over the arm of the chair and levered up my trousers and dipped into the back pocket. I drew out four different coloured condoms. Because it was one thing for her husband to go commando; it was quite a different matter for anybody else who cared to join their fun. I fanned them out with one hand like a magic trick.

'Pick a flavour, any flavour.'

She selected strawberry.

As Charley pulled down my boxers, I rolled it on for her. Lips that were made for speaking the words of some spaceship commander character now traced their way up my dick.

'Beautiful,' I breathed out.

And then the words in my head shattered into pieces.

When I got my breath back, I knew it was my turn.

'I want to show you what this glass block is *really* for,' I grinned at them both like a wolf. 'Can we clear the decks? And we'll need a cushion for Charley's head. I'd hate her to hurt herself.'

'What are you going to be doing to my wife?' David asked with a look of mock horror, also making it clear that she wasn't *all* mine.

'It's okay, isn't it? *She* went down on me. I'm merely turning the tables.'

'Yes please!' squealed Charley, removing the bottles and lining them against the block's side.

'And David, you can hold her hand while I'm at it. We'll have some kind of threesome.'

Charley lay across the glass with her legs hanging over the edge so I could take those cute little peaches in my hands as I went down on her. I could practically hear her body's pleasure in the shrieking of the glass as she shifted across it, and when I eventually came up for air, all of us were grinning fit to burst.

'Mission accomplished!'

'Very much so, thanks,' said a pleased David, who seemed to have got as much out of it as his wife. His cock was saluting his appreciation.

I shook my head. 'I can assure you it was very much my pleasure.' I couldn't keep a laugh from burbling up.

'What? What's so funny?' David asked.

Both he and Charley were watching me, curious.

'Oh, I was just thinking. It's going to be a hell of a story to tell the grandchildren one day!'

It was a week or so after my session with David and Charley, and I'd got back home from my latest client at around midnight. I fixed myself a cup of tea and flopped in front of the telly to wind down before I went to bed.

I didn't bother checking the paper to see what was on. I turned on the TV and flicked channels for anything worth watching. My flatmates were asleep upstairs, so I kept the sound down.

And there was Charley before me. My finger hovered above the next button. She was tight against the curved wall of her spacecraft, laser gun in one hand cocked ready for whatever danger lurked around the corner. She was clad from her zipped ankle boots right up to the top of her neck in a skintight silver jumpsuit. I yearned to enfold her in my arms and whisk her away from danger.

I yearned to enfold her in my arms and shelter her from the rain. The glass of the screen separated us. I flicked to the image of her wrapped around me and seated on my lap. I winked at her in my mind's eye and thanked her and David for the memory.

A back-up unit had been sent to find her. I let him, and switched off the box. I didn't need them encroaching on my thoughts. I finished my tea and went to my room.

283

Ralph and Cindy's private island

Late October

I was strapped into my seat behind the pilot with a clear view of us rising above the end of the runway and Luton's rooftops fast diminishing below us. I breathed a mental sigh of relief.

Four guys, six girls cleared for take off.

That was the job Ralph had given me only a week ago. To round up a group of escorts, me included, for his and Cindy's delectation, passports cleared, and have us all flown over to his place off the coast of Spain.

The plane settled into its stride and I unbuckled my seatbelt.

'Thanks for letting me see that,' I motioned to the pilot.

'My pleasure,' he smiled back.

I hadn't told him what we were doing there and I suspected Ralph mightn't have either.

I halted at the doorway of the cockpit and surveyed the scene before me. This whole set-up was almost unbelievable. The place *stank* of money. The jet was a top-of-the-range G5 for one thing. For another, Ralph's monogram was on every available surface from the outside of the plane down via the mahogany surrounds of the TV screens and the cream leather upholstery to the champagne flutes we couldn't do anything else but celebrate with. Ralph had supplied us with a magnum of Dom Pérignon to toast the trip. It was out of this fucking world.

Mark, Simon and David were looking as sharp as hell in their suits and swivelling around in the recliners, not quite believing their luck. Around them swanned Emma and her friends, fixing themselves another glass of champagne.

What was a good time for, if you couldn't share it with your mates?

I'd figured as soon as Ralph got me the gig that while he asked for a planeload of escorts, I was going to do right by my friends and take them along for the ride. *And* they'd be getting paid for it too. It wasn't as if I knew any male escorts. What's more, if Mark and co. came along, then I'd have someone to laugh about it all with in five years' time, by which time I planned to have *long* been out of this game.

The girls on the plane were professionals. I'd mentioned to Emma what Ralph was after and trusted she'd know who to call. I looked at the other girls she'd collected together and had to admit she'd done me proud. Thoroughbreds, the lot of them.

Emma now made her way towards me with two flutes of champagne.

'Luke,' she said, handing me one, 'here's to the return trip!'

I touched her glass with mine. 'You bet, hon.'

When the plane touched down there were three limos waiting to meet us. I treated David and Simon to two of the girls each, and me, Emma and Mark made a backseat sandwich in the leading car with Louise up front in the passenger seat.

Few words passed between us on the way. Mark shook his head almost every time we turned a corner of the coastal road and a yet more impressive vista than the last filled the wind-screen. He'd give a high-pitched whistle and I'd wince. We didn't want to give the impression that we were *too* impressed. But then again, *this* was damn impressive stuff. Like we were in a Bond movie!

We didn't see Ralph's place until we were literally on top of it. The car took us to the edge of a cliff so we had a clear view over the hidden cove and its long, narrow strip of sandy beach far down below, and then we turned down a driveway to a gate concealed from the main road. The gate swung open, and we drove up to the white stone villa that spread out in front of us.

'This is the only way to the beach,' said our driver. 'You should ask him to let you visit it.'

It was my turn to whistle under my breath.

Our cars drew up together, and the lot of us piled out. There were a heck of a lot of eyes out on stalks. A white-suited guy came out of the villa to greet us.

'If you could follow me, I'll take you to your apartments where you can refresh yourself before dinner.'

Mark turned to me. 'This place is absolutely *stunning*!' he hissed.

We clattered up the steps to the main double door and filed through into the hall. Two flights of stairs curved up round the wall of the atrium to meet in the middle of the first-floor landing. The white of the building's exterior was repeated inside, and the marble floor gave the space a refreshing chilliness. We cut through the entire ground floor and out the other side.

Before us was a huge swimming pool, and I recognised Ralph and Cindy stretched out on recliners and sunning themselves at the far end. They watched us for a moment or two and then sat up, and both of them headed in our direction.

I set down my case and motioned to the others to do the same. 'Guys, this is Ralph. I'll introduce you.'

He walked up to us with Cindy in tow, and began schmoozing the others before I had a chance to say anything except my own 'Hello, Ralph.' Cindy, I noted, hovered on the fringes letting her husband do his thing. I felt for her, standing there like she wasn't part of the party.

'Emma,' I indicated to her, 'come with me and I'll introduce you. Cindy, it's lovely to see you. This is Emma.'

286

I read in Ralph's wife a hint of relief that somebody had taken the trouble to seek her out. Cindy looked Emma up and down and a small smile of approval crept across her face.

'We were just saying what a lovely place you have here,' Emma nodded. 'And the beach looks gorgeous,' she added, and held her look at Cindy just that bit longer than was necessary.

'Thank you. You had no problems on the flight over?' she asked.

'No, it was a pleasure,' I replied. 'It's a pleasure being here, Cindy.'

'Definitely,' purred Emma.

Ralph clapped his hands and the abruptness of it shattered the atmosphere like a gunshot. It worked. Each one of us turned sharply to listen to what he had to say. I noted that Cindy took a step back so she was on the outskirts of the group again, watching us.

'Welcome, everyone. I've no doubt you'll enjoy your stay here,' barked Ralph. His manner was more intimidating than what he was saying. 'My staff will show you to your apartments so that you can freshen up. Feel free to settle in and enjoy the facilities.'

He stretched out his arm to indicate the pool. Simon and David were looking at each other and grinning like they couldn't wait.

'Dinner will be served at seven.'

David was leaning against the aluminium doorframe of his apartment, his face shielded by sunglasses raised upwards to collect the rays. Mark, Simon and I were stretched out in adjacent recliners and also enjoying the sunshine, and the chance to breathe in where we'd found ourselves.

We'd been shown our rooms and unpacked and settled in and changed into our trunks and were fine doing nothing. The girls had taken their place at the other end of the pool.

David relaxed his stance a little and turned his head in our direction, though he was surveying the pool a metre beyond us. I took it as my cue and raised my head towards him.

'I know you think you look good standing there, David, but do you want some more sunscreen?'

'Oh, come on, Luke. Don't worry about me,' he scoffed.

'I was only thinking of you being too sore to get your end away. We wouldn't want that, would we?' I laughed.

He shook his head and reached up to the frames of his sunnies and pulled them down a little so he peered over the top at me.

'Thanks for your concern 'n' all, but I'll have you know I've got it all worked out. The necessary top-up of my tan to a level that is the most successful at pulling the birds without frying myself.'

Mark snorted. 'And that's a *very* fine line.'

I looked over at David. 'Are you going in the pool?'

'Nah. Later.'

'She said her name!'

It was shouted by Cindy at Ralph at the other side of the pool like a clap of thunder. The four of us shot looks at each other.

'Shit! What's that all about?' questioned Simon, rising from his doze.

'Just a domestic,' muttered Mark. He closed his eyes and let the sun soak him.

From where I was sitting I could see that Ralph had his hand gripped round his wife's arm like he was trying to stop her from storming off. I had turned my head, so with my sunglasses on it appeared as if I was looking in another direction, but I gave the couple my full attention.

Cindy knows!

The thought shunted itself across my mind. I didn't even have to engage my brain. It was just *there*.

Ralph was staring at me across the pool as if he'd heard my very thoughts.

'Luke! Can you come here please,' he called. Or ordered. He said it in such a way that it came as both a polite but firm request to me to join him and the stern direction to someone who had done wrong.

'S'cuse me a minute, guys,' I muttered under my breath as I slipped off the lounger.

Mark reached out and slapped the side of my leg as I walked past him. I looked down at him.

'Good luck.'

The depth of water was a trip away. If I kept my eye on it as I walked round its edge to reach Ralph it would be easy to be mesmerised and fall in. Cindy was now seated on the edge of a lounger, her feet flat on the ground together and her hands gripping tight to the chair's tubular frame. Her face looked furious and her lips were forced tight together. She was staring straight ahead and trying not to cry.

I still had a few steps to go, but Ralph was chomping at the bit to deal with me.

'What's going on?' he aimed at me.

I'd reached the two of them now, but Ralph stepped away and indicated with a finger that he wanted me right beside him.

'What's this about Emma saying "Hi *Helena*" to Cindy?' he spat. He said it in full earshot of his wife. I looked from one to the other. Cindy had her face in her hands. I wasn't sure what I was supposed to say.

'What do you mean?'

What's he talking about? Emma hadn't said that! I was there.

'Who's Helena?'

I looked from one to the other again and feigned complete ignorance. This was Ralph and Cindy's problem and I wasn't aiming to get mixed up in it. I also wanted to keep onside with Ralph by suggesting that nobody round here was aware of some 'Helena'.

'Cindy's just told me that Emma called her Helena,' Ralph fumed.

And then my eyes fell on Cindy. She might have looked crushed by her suspicions but she'd also found a very clever away of expressing them to Ralph.

This is the perfect way for her to let him know she knows!

And she'd managed to dump all the blame on me. Because Ralph had made it quite clear before I met Helena that I wasn't to let on to a soul about his girlfriend. And I hadn't. Which was why I was damn sure that Emma couldn't have let anything slip. But the way Cindy had put it made *me* look to Ralph like I was the weak link in his cheating games. And why wouldn't he believe what his wife had just told him? Even though she was talking complete bullshit.

I stood there, my hands by my side, not knowing what to do. My toes rubbed at the tiles beneath them.

'All I can tell you, Ralph, is that I introduced Emma to Cindy, and Emma said no such thing.'

I bit my lip. Ralph gave me a stern look but didn't say anything. Cindy got to her feet with a whimper that became full-blown tears and hurried away. Ralph went after her, and shot me an 'I'll deal with you later' look over his shoulder as the two of them headed down the path to the villa.

I stood there for a moment on my own among the sun loungers and turned on my heel and headed back round to the other side of the pool. Mark pounced on me when I was back beside him.

'What did he say?' he pleaded.

I knew I couldn't tell Mark all of it. I still felt some obligation towards Ralph, if only to ensure I knew where the truth ended and the lies began. Letting anything slip now, if only for the sake of a good story with my mates, wasn't likely to do me any favours.

I sat back down on my lounger and picked up my smoothie

and took a sip of it. I savoured its freshness, which took the heat off things a little. I looked up at Mark.

'Come on,' he said. 'What was all that about?'

'I can't tell you everything, you know that. Ralph's put me in charge of this thing. All I can say is that he's got himself a spot of girl trouble.'

Mark nodded in understanding. He knew well about girl trouble. He'd had a good six months of it. His relationship with Natasha had run its course back in May, and since I now had his old room he'd had to juggle getting over her with finding a new place to live. It'd taken until September, but although he was now settled and free to play the field again, his heart wasn't completely in it.

However, Mark's girl trouble wasn't quite in Ralph's league. Ralph was wealthy beyond most people's wildest dreams. He could do what he wanted with whoever he wanted. He'd hired a group of hookers to come to his own island, for God's sake! And that was going to have its advantages *and* disadvantages if he wasn't too careful.

David, who had been lying shaded under a huge umbrella, pulled himself up with a start.

'I don't know about you, but I'm ready for a dip. Coming?' He got to his feet and with a few steps had launched himself into the pool. A curl of water flew up and splatted on the deck beside us.

'David!' we chorused, but it had lightened the moment and reminded us of what we were getting out of being here.

Mark too took a flying leap into the water, and I slipped off the lounger and pottered to the pool's edge and watched the lads dive in the blue below me.

Louise was suddenly by my side. She all but spilled out of a tiny bikini that sure wasn't made for swimming in.

'You going in?' she asked.

'Thinking about it,' I smiled back. 'Probably in a minute or so when they have all calmed down a bit.'

All I really knew of her was that she lived with Emma.

'Tell you what,' I beckoned, 'you come and sit here and we can dip our feet in.'

She sat down beside me, the two of us perched on the pool's overhanging lip and our legs dangling below us in the water.

'Thank you for inviting me. It's a beautiful place, isn't it?'

'It's my pleasure that you're here,' I admitted, 'but you have Emma to thank.'

She nodded. 'Yes, but even so . . .'

I bent down towards the water and cupped my hand so it filled, then I lifted it up again and trickled a trail of drips from my own thigh across the flagstone between us and onto Louise's leg. She let me, and ran her finger around the little puddle on her flesh that I had made, then flicked some of it at me with that same index finger. I turned my head and allowed a smile to creep up my face. Because it was more than a piece of my mind I wanted to give her.

And then I froze in mid flow because she had turned still too, and there were now two feet standing in the gap between us.

'Luke, come for a walk with me,' stated Ralph.

I lifted my legs out of the water and pulled myself up. I placed a hand on Louise's shoulder, who'd remained seated.

'You stay here, girl. Something's come up.'

She nodded and bit her lip but didn't look me in the eye. *She was frightened of him.*

She was right to be. Ralph had started out the nice guy, but there was an intimidation about him that was unnerving. I could speak to most people but Ralph made me tongue-tied. The way he spoke made me feel that I had somehow done wrong by him.

We walked side by side away from the pool and the others. When we were out of sight and earshot of anyone else, Ralph stopped dead.

'Luke, what the fuck's going on?' he seethed.

My whole body tensed.

'Are you saying Cindy's a liar?'

'I didn't say anyone was lying, Ralph,' I stated, though it took all my nerve to stand up to him.

'Pff,' he sighed. 'No. Someone's lying. And it's not my wife.'

I defended myself. And Emma too. I'd brought her here, after all, and I knew all this had nothing to do with her.

'Well, I was standing with both of them and I didn't hear anyone mention the name Helena.'

Ralph snarled at me as if I was out of line just by the very fact that I'd answered back. There was evidently supposed to be no arguing with Ralph. Especially on his turf. His word was law. He stared harshly at me. I'd overstepped the line.

'Why are you standing there lying to me in my house, which I've invited you to?' he spat. His face had turned red and his eyes bulged. 'I'm on the brink of calling my pilot to send the lot of you back to wherever the hell you came from,' he snarled.

I felt the warm stone beneath my soles. I straightened my spine and took strength from what my height gave me. When I spoke my voice was calm and clear.

'Ralph, if that's what you want, it's completely up to you.'

Ralph stared at me. I waited for the earthquake but it didn't come. The air was hot and still and it felt stifling. I wanted to be back by the pool with Louise with my feet dangling in the water, its refreshing coldness washing away all this hassle I hadn't come here for.

'You're here to take instructions. That's what I employed you for, isn't it?'

I nodded but said nothing. There was nothing to say.

'Then get all the girls out here around the pool in five minutes. And the men,' he bossed. 'I want to meet everybody.'

He marched away and left me standing there.

I raced back to the water and called across to everyone to get their act together and come right here, right now. I pulled the loungers round so they created a semi-circle that gave the patio the air of a boardroom. I took a step back and admired the arrangement. And then it hit me.

Where's the fucking fun in all this?

Simon was at my shoulder.

'What's this all about? Is he going to be sharing out the sex?'

I shook my head. 'If only, mate. I haven't got the impression yet that he's even in the mood.'

A good seeing-to seemed to be very low down the agenda.

I watched as the seats filled. Emma sat with the other girls, who were joined by Mark and David. The water and the sun had done the trick and there was a relaxed, friendly air about this gang that was good to see. Especially after all the stuff with Ralph. Mark and one of the other girls seemed to be getting on, I noticed too.

At least somebody is.

Simon and David sat in adjacent seats on one side of me, and I left the one on my right vacant for Ralph.

His arrival was sudden and was an immediate dampener on the group, like a raincloud overhead. Ralph sat down beside me. He immediately had the full attention of everyone.

'They're all here, are they?' he asked me beneath his breath.

I nodded. 'Yes, they are, Ralph.'

He clapped his hands loud.

'Right, do you all know Luke?' he barked, with no build-up at all.

I felt everyone's attention fall on me like they were wondering what came next. And a moment later there rose up a chorus of 'Yes' from the lot of them. I swallowed a guffaw and focused on the water lapping across the pool to avoid catching any of the others' eyes.

Except one girl stuck up her hand.

'Ralph, my name's Anna, and this is the first time I've met him.'

What the fuck? Where did she come from?

Anna was telling the truth, of course. Except that hadn't been the game plan. Ralph had trusted me to sort *everything* out and make sure I met everyone face-to-face beforehand. And I'd trusted Emma to gather a group of friends of hers so I didn't have to do all that. But we were all supposed to be on the same page either way.

'How's that, Luke?'

'She came with Emma,' I blurted out, 'and I trust Emma.'

I said it because I didn't know what else I could say. I shot a scorching glance at Emma and mentally willed her to take my side.

Ralph surveyed the semi-circle. Everyone seemed to be holding their breath. Emma put her hand up the moment his eyes fell on her.

'I'm Emma, and I've worked with Anna and she's a good friend of mine,' she disclosed.

I winced.

Don't mention anything about 'mates'.

Ralph kept quiet like he was mulling stuff over. And then he blew.

'So why has Luke been lying to me and claiming he knows everyone?' he stormed. He swung round in his seat so he was facing me and the guys sitting next to me.

'So, how does Luke know you? You're not just friends of his he's brought along for a laugh?'

Each of them, well-primed in advance by me, shook their head.

'No, sir,' Mark offered in as professional a tone as possible, and Simon and David followed suit.

Ralph turned sharply and pointed a finger to Marie, a girl I'd met before. She had the hunched air of someone who hoped he'd pick on anyone but her. Which made him pick on her.

'What's your name?' he growled.

'Marie,' she mewled.

He laid into her. 'So why have you come out here? What's been promised you that you don't get back in London?'

Marie flinched as if he'd actually hit her, but said nothing. There was an appalled relief around the others that he wasn't taking things out on *them*. A couple of the girls were shivering.

'You know what?' continued Ralph, aiming his words directly at Marie. 'I don't like the look of you one bit. I'm thinking of sending you back.'

Marie shrank back and her eyes filled with tears.

'Ralph,' I blurted out. 'That's not fair. It's got nothing to do with Marie.'

Out of the corner of my eye I saw her visibly relax as our host turned his brute attention to me. He stared hard and crossed his arms like he was waiting for a very good explanation on my part.

'Look,' I went on, very aware that everyone else was counting on me to take the lead, 'you asked me to invite a good mix of people to create a nice atmosphere. And that's what I've done.'

His hooded eyes stared straight at me and he pursed his lips. He didn't say anything for a few moments. You couldn't tell what he was thinking.

'Right, everyone,' he suddenly announced, and everyone sat up straight. 'I want you all to go and get ready for dinner, and after dinner we'll all have some fun.' He pulled himself up from his lounger and walked away and left us sitting there. We looked at each other but nobody said anything, as if they were fearful somebody might be listening in.

I stood up to return to my apartment, and that seemed to be the signal for everyone to do the same. Marie sidled up to me.

'Thank you for that, Luke.'

I gave her a sidelong glance as we took the path back to our flats. Her trained sexiness made her appear surer of herself than she actually was. A trio of the other girls crowded round, looking to me for the same reassurance that Marie sought.

'He frightens me,' admitted one of them.

'Yes, I don't know what he wants us to do,' agreed Anna.

I stopped dead in my tracks and gazed at her.

You really threw us in it, girl.

But I knew that what had *really* got under Ralph's skin was that Cindy knew about Helena. He was taking it out on us. I turned away from Anna and grasped Marie's hand and continued walking.

'Don't worry,' I offered to them all. 'I'll deal with him. That's *my* job. The rest of you have a good time and forget what he said. That's what we're all here for, aren't we?'

I dressed in my best suit and shoes. I popped next door to Mark's. He was fixing his cufflinks.

'Very dapper!' I admired.

'Aren't we just?' he grinned.

I watched him check himself out in the wardrobe mirror.

'Look, it's our job to relax the girls,' I advised. 'You'll make sure there's one on each side of you over dinner and give them equal attention?'

He turned his head to me and nodded. 'Sure.'

I went to the door. 'I've got to let the others know too.'

I had my hand on the handle when I remembered what I was also there for. 'Have a good time yourself, y'know.'

'No worries,' he winked.

I stepped out into the early evening light and cut across the grass to David's place. Ralph was standing on the path watching me. I jumped back onto a paving stone in case he scolded me for ruining the lawn.

'Come over here,' he declared, and the hairs at the back of my neck bristled. I followed his order.

'Why the lies, Luke? Saying you know everyone here when you

don't?' Ralph's face was half in shadow so I couldn't altogether see what he was thinking. I decided to play things honest and straight.

'I'm sorry. Anna was the only one I hadn't seen face-to-face. I should have let you know,' I admitted. 'But Emma knows her, and I trust her choice. She won't have selected a stranger. And she hasn't.'

He eyed me with suspicion. I took it as a cue to explain myself more.

'It's not fair to be picking on everyone. We're all here to have a nice time. And make sure you do too,' I stressed.

In the half-light I still caught the look of shock across Ralph's face.

'But I haven't had a "nice" time, have I?' he fumed. 'Not since Cindy found out about Helena. And that was your fault in introducing Emma to my wife.'

That's not fair. I glared back at him, though I wasn't sure if he could see me either.

'Ralph, it *wasn't*. I don't know how Cindy found out, but it has absolutely nothing to do with me. And I'm not going to stand here and let you accuse me of something I'm not to blame for.'

Ralph sucked in air with a hiss.

'I might just send you home, Luke,' he growled under his breath.

'If that's what you want to do, then do it. But I'm taking everyone else with me. I'm not going to leave people here,' I countered, and stepped off the path to visit David.

'You can fuck right off,' he seethed after me.

I halted and turned right round so I was facing him squarely again. 'Ralph, *you* can fuck off.'

I heard myself say it and couldn't quite believe I had done. I turned on my heel and headed across the grass verge, expecting Ralph to come after me at any moment. But he didn't. I looked back as I knocked on David's door, and Ralph was heading back to his villa.

Cindy and Ralph were notable by their absence when we gathered for pre-dinner drinks. Not that it really bothered me. The girls *sparkled*.

'Look,' I made sure to tell each and every person there, 'you're here to enjoy yourself. Eat, drink and have a good time, okay?'

Mark had homed in on Susie, the girl he'd been getting to know earlier by the pool. That gave me an idea. I sought out David.

'Can you pair up with Marie? It'd be good to get each of the guys going in with at least one girl.'

'I'm not sure . . .' frowned David.

I got what he was getting at.

'*Not* for the whole night. Just for symmetry's sake, y'know?'

I sidled up to Simon.

'You and me are the lucky ones. We get to have a pair of girls hanging off our arms . . .'

He gave me a broad smile.

'. . . only I get to choose my pair,' I continued, 'and you don't.'

I'd already decided on Emma and Louise as my partners. To be honest, it wasn't as if any of the escorts was any less glamorous than any other.

'You'll look after Anna and Candice, that okay?'

'Def.'

As we entered the dining room, I observed my mates and the girls with them. I wondered whether Ralph had known that his harsh treatment of us earlier on by the pool would draw the ten of us together, make us tighter as a group. And so spruce up any play that went on.

Ralph and Cindy were sitting waiting for us at the head of the huge dining table.

* * *

The food was sumptuous, and afterwards we returned to the pool patio where an outdoor heater had been set up. The Jacuzzi bubbled away in the corner. I felt happy to sit with a glass in my hand for a while and relax into the night. Emma and Louise lay tangled together on the lounger next to me. I looked at the other recliners and there was a smattering of people getting it together in some way or other. Mark was snogging Susie. It was good to see my mates having a good time, but I wasn't altogether sure of what I felt about what was likely to happen next. It was one thing to see them getting off with a girl. That was a Saturday-night staple. It was quite another to be in their company when they were getting it *on* with one. And, come to think of it, they'd be seeing me too . . .

Ralph appeared, hand-in-hand with Cindy, and everyone sharpened a bit through the alcohol and food haze. The two of them were wrapped in a towel each, but disrobed before climbing into the Jacuzzi. We could see only their heads above its rim. I recalled Cindy's delicious body from that night over at Ralph's place, but I also remembered her husband's 'Don't Touch' rule. Given the distance already between him and me today, I didn't want to cause any more problems.

That hadn't crossed Emma's mind. She threw a look over at the Jacuzzi and stood up. In a moment she'd unzipped her dress all the way down the back and let it fall to the ground. She was now wearing only her Christian Louboutin heels and a tiny pair of silk briefs. She reached out a hand towards Louise, who rose from her lounger. The two of them, hand-in-hand, stepped over to the Jacuzzi. Emma undressed Louise and they kissed, while Cindy had hitched herself up so she could watch them over the rim.

That's why it's Don't Touch for the boys.

The girls climbed in, and just by their very doing it felt as if the rest of us were now on the outside with our faces pressed up against the window.

I looked across at the now empty lounger beside me. *Bummer. I was hoping for some fun there.*

At the moment I thought *that*, it was no longer vacant.

'Hello again, Luke,' purred Marie, who clearly knew an opportunity when she saw one.

'Why, hello, Marie. You're enjoying the evening?'

'Very much so,' she admitted, with just enough hint of flirtatiousness.

Marie retained an air of shyness about her, yet at the same time I could see that she had no fear about her escort work and it was that which held her in good stead when she approached a guy. She could play-act until she felt safe enough to no longer need to.

'Would you like to join me?' I beckoned.

She didn't reply. Didn't need to. She strode with purpose between the two loungers and perched on my lap. I wrapped my arms around her and pulled her down towards me so we were now lying together.

'Isn't this what we're here for?' I jested into her ear, as I started blindly unhooking her cocktail dress from behind, at the very same rate that she was working her way to undoing my own clothing all the way down.

I happened to turn my head to one side and my whole body stiffened. I gripped Marie to me without thinking.

'What?!' she struggled.

'Ralph!' I spat, and Marie held still.

He was standing feet away, though this time I wasn't his sole concern. *For a change.* He was waving a half-empty champagne bottle at all of us.

'Stay here and enjoy yourselves,' he commanded. 'We're going back to the villa but we'll be back later,' he explained, and pointed the bottle at the three girls wrapped around each other and already tiptoeing their way there.

He headed off to leave us to our own devices. The eight of

us took his words as a come-on. There was more than enough to go round.

It was *hours* later, and we'd entered the next day and Ralph hadn't kept his word. We'd seen neither hide nor hair of him, apart from the twenty minutes after dinner when he and Cindy were in the Jacuzzi.

'It's like he can't see the point of us,' pointed out Simon as he poured himself another drink. 'He's only interested in the girls . . .'

'And only because they happen to be into his wife and she fancies them back,' piped up Candice.

David tickled her and she giggled.

'Are you jealous that she didn't ask for you?' he teased.

'I'd rather have *you*,' she chuckled, nibbling his ear.

I couldn't help wondering what we had to do to please Ralph. And thinking that reminded me of how dog-tired I now felt. I slipped away from Marie and grazed her with a goodnight kiss, then announced my need to leave.

'Please forgive me,' I mock-bowed to them all, 'but I need to crash out, I'm afraid. I'll see you in the morning.'

Ralph's voice was booming me awake. *That* dragged me to my senses. I shifted in my bed so through my half-glazed eyes I at least had some view of him. He didn't let up one bit to take any account of my late-night wooziness.

'Do you reckon you can organise anything right over these few days? I want you to put together a proper party for us. Not like last night. Do you think you can do that?'

I sat up in bed and rubbed my eyes and willed my brain into gear. I pulled myself together as much as I could in the circumstances. Being butt-naked in bed while he was ordering me about wasn't exactly conducive to being a party organiser.

'Yes, Ralph,' I heard myself say, 'I can do that.'

I expected that to be all. He headed to the door, and I slipped out of bed and was on my way to the bathroom when he stopped and turned back to face me.

'There is one other thing.'

'Yes, Ralph?'

He ignored my nudity, though I found it hard to.

'After dinner tonight, this is what I want you to do.'

I concentrated hard through my sleepiness so I wouldn't miss anything.

'Me and Cindy, and you and the other young men, are going to go to the whitewashed outbuilding past the tennis courts. It's on the way to the beach.'

I nodded, taking it in.

'And I want you to collect one girl at a time, march them into that room, and I want all of you four guys to do her simultaneously *any which way*.'

I felt nauseous from his cruelty. He spelt it out.

'I don't want her to be able to *move* afterwards. And when she's completely spent, I want you to bring the next one in and the four of you to do exactly the same to her. Until you've worked your way through all six of them.'

You fucker.

I put on my dressing gown and tied it while I collected my thoughts, then swallowed hard and took a deep breath.

'Just because they happen to be hookers,' I spoke slowly, 'doesn't make them animals. They didn't come here to be treated like *that*.'

'Ah, but Luke,' he crowed, 'you told me when you organised things for me, you'd be happy to do *everything*. The girls *are* here, and that is what we're going to do tonight. You understand?'

I understood all right. He chilled me to the core.

He wants them DEMOLISHED.

I knew I had to warn the girls.

'I'll talk to them about your request, but obviously I can't promise you anything.'

That was the most I could say to him. It seemed to be enough. He opened my apartment door and stepped out, and through it I could see Cindy standing waiting for him and she had a huge smile across her face.

The truth of it hit me so hard that I had to grab at the wardrobe to stop me from keeling over. *The bitch knows. And she's fine about it.*

I watched Ralph and Cindy walk off hand-in-hand together and had to swallow hard to stop myself from throwing up. It was as if Cindy had sent Ralph into my apartment to do her dirty work. *She's more than up for seeing that happening to the girls. She's totally fucking sick.*

And when they were out of sight, I went to have a shower.

To make myself feel clean again.

I was standing in Emma's bedroom with all six of the girls seated around me. I hadn't told the lads. This was between me and the girls, because they were my responsibility. I'd got them over here and it was my duty to help get them back out in one piece.

I took a deep breath. I didn't know what to say. They could tell by the rush in which I'd gathered them together that something serious was going on.

'What I'm about to tell you,' I stuttered, 'it's dreadful and it's what Ralph and Cindy want of you, but I certainly don't and I know the other guys wouldn't either . . .'

I hadn't even mentioned what was required of the girls, but horror was already shadowing their faces. I closed my eyes, as if by doing that it might make it easier for me to say what I was about to say. It didn't.

'It's effectively gang rape, one by one. They want me and the guys to carry it out.'

There, said it.

One of the girls gasped in shock. Emma came towards me, tears running down her face, and I hugged her close. It was the last straw for her. She'd got the blame over Helena, which had unnerved her enough. Last night it had looked as if, with Louise's help, she had ironed out any differences with Cindy and Ralph. But now she knew she might as well be hanged, drawn and quartered.

I spoke to her, but I was speaking loud enough so they all heard it.

'I don't want that,' I said. 'None of you came here to be treated like that.'

Marie was weeping. 'No,' she pleaded through her sobs, 'please tell them we don't want to do it.'

'There's four of us guys with you,' I reminded her with an arm still around Emma. 'We're here to look after you. We won't do what Ralph wants. We won't let that happen.'

I looked down at them looking back at me for help. If I was going to do anything, then I had to do it as soon as possible.

'I'm going to go and visit Ralph right now and tell him that we all refuse to be part of anything so sadistic, okay?'

'Please, Luke. Thank you,' they cried, as I went to do battle over them.

I was alone with Ralph in his study, he on one side of his writing desk, me on the other, as if I was back in my headmaster's office. I felt almost as small, though I tried not to show it. For one thing, I stood the whole time I was there, so that Ralph might not think he had the upper hand just by the way we were seated.

'If you won't do what I ask when that was the reason I had you here, then I'm not going to pay you,' Ralph threatened.

I stood my ground. 'Ralph,' I said, to show that I wouldn't be intimidated by him, 'if you don't want to pay us, that's up to you.'

Ralph got out of his armchair and walked round to my side of his desk. He came within breathing distance of my face, and, looking me straight in the eye, ran a hand down my cheek and gave it a couple of light slaps.

'Who's in charge? Ralph is in charge,' he declared.

He said it clearly and quietly and I could taste the menace.

I don't know what possessed me. It was as if something deep down had made up my mind for me that I wouldn't be floored by this man's intimidations. I gazed right back at him.

'Ralph, don't *ever* touch me like that again,' I ordered. I'd had it up to my eyeballs.

It was the last straw for Ralph too. He didn't want us to stay the other night, and, what's more, he only paid half of what we'd agreed. Which made sense, though the girls didn't see it that way.

'But we were promised!' moaned Anna, and others nodded in agreement.

'But, you haven't done two days' work!' I tried to explain, though it was bloody tough trying to get it through to them.

I was stung by their attitude too. I'd done right by them by standing up for them so they didn't have to do what Ralph wanted – and they were turning on me!

We were all back in Emma's bedroom, but this time it was me who felt got at. I felt infuriated too. 'I tell you what,' I steamed. 'I'll pay you nothing. Ralph's only going to give me half the money because we did half the time. And most of you didn't do any work last night, anyhow, and now we're going back home. How about that?'

'No,' they caterwauled, 'we want our money!'

I stared daggers at them, though I felt cornered beside Emma's bed.

Of all the ungrateful . . .

It wasn't as if the half-rate wasn't good money.

They wouldn't have made THAT last night in London. AND

they had the flash jet trip, the champagne, sunbathing, the swimming pool . . .

But they didn't seem to see it that way.

We were seated on the plane, and this time I was following Ralph's instructions to the letter. He'd told me before we left: 'Make sure no one touches anything on the plane. Just sit in your seats, get back to London, get off the plane and I never want to see any of you ever again.' It was a little thing, but it was somehow important to me that the promise I'd made to him this time, I kept.

I hadn't banked on the girls. But then, by this stage we weren't even on speaking terms.

Once the plane was back in Luton, we were on the brink of leaving when I noticed the empty champagne bottle sticking out of the bin at the back of the plane. And not just any champagne either. This was worth a few thousand pounds.

'Where the hell did that come from?' I fumed.

The girls looked nonplussed. 'What's all the fuss about? We had a drink on the way here. We had one on the way back.'

And I could see where they were coming from. It was a fine end to a not-so-great time on a fabulous island.

I pulled the bottle out of the bin and showed it to them.

'I promised Ralph we wouldn't touch anything on our way back,' I sighed.

Fuelled by the quality champers, Marie piped up: 'Oh, forget it, Luke. Who cares?'

Oh, Marie.

She followed the others to the exit, leaving me standing there.

The trouble was, *I* cared. *I* hadn't touched anything because Ralph had asked me not to. The girls had not only emptied the bottle, they'd chosen to leave it in the bin as well. It was if they were saying, 'Not only have we drunk your fine champagne, but we expect you to clean it up as well.'

There seemed nothing else to do but tuck the bottle under my jacket so the pilot wouldn't notice. I held on to its smooth glass.

The guys were waiting for me at the bottom of the steps of the plane. The girls had gone on.

I never saw them again.

<u>Getting them to call you again</u>

You've hit it off but you know that you want more than a one-night stand. So, what do you do to ensure you hear from them again?

- Don't kid yourself that sex the first night you meet a guy will likely lead to a long-term relationship. If you give it to him on a plate, why should he stick around?
- Reveal just enough about yourself to keep them interested. Be a bit mysterious.
- And also be fun and upbeat.
- Don't hang around too long in the beginning and give the impression of being needy.
- It's good to be independent, but reveal a little vulnerability too. This mix works well for both men and women.
- Take their number and call them, or send a friendly text to get the ball rolling. The girl contacting the guy first won't be a turn-off.

Helen

Helen brought me back down to earth. Definitely. I'd only just got back from Ralph's island and she'd rung me and asked me to help her out. Because the last time Helen had sex, she was raped. Eight years ago.

You'd think by now that nothing would faze me, but walking along the hotel corridor to her room, I felt nervous because I knew that *she* would be nervous.

I reached her door, took a deep breath and knocked.

Here goes.

'Coming,' I heard her call, and her breeziness struck me. On the phone she'd been halting and shy, as she had every right to be. It was a hell of a thing to admit to anyone. But *this* sounded like the voice she might use to tell herself she was on top of things.

But if she was, then she wouldn't have called me out in the first place, would she?

I stood there, feet side by side, and waited for the door to open, very aware of the responsibility Helen had given me.

'Hello, Luke,' she smiled, and I sensed the chink in her cheerfulness as she said it.

'Hello, Helen, pleased to meet you.'

I hugged her as an old friend might do, as I was happy to

310

greet any of my clients, but as my arms held her to me I felt her whole body tense. We stood wrapped together for a moment and then she, bashful, pulled away. I was going to have to take it real slow.

I removed my jacket and she bolted to take it from me like she was trying to fill the gap and the silence.

'Thanks, Helen.'

I surveyed the room as she hung it on the hook on the back of the door. It was standard matter-of-fact middle range, neither scuzzy nor deluxe. There was the double bed, a chest of drawers that doubled as a writing desk, a chair, and a wardrobe in the far corner. And a minibar.

'It's a nice place you've chosen here,' I commented.

'You think so?'

I nodded. 'Yes, it is.'

I looked around the room again. It neither demanded an apology nor expected to live up to any occasion. In the circumstances it was the absolute right place to be.

I sat down on the end of the bed. Helen followed my lead and perched beside me, her arms stretched and hands pushing deep into the duvet. I left it a couple of minutes and then reached out and stroked the forearm nearest to me. She turned and gave me a nervous closed smile. It was like Helen knew what she wanted to do, but at the same time wasn't quite sure how much she *really* wanted it.

She took a deep breath. 'Would you like a drink, Luke?' she murmured, indicating the minibar with a nod.

'I'd like that. I'll have a red wine, please.'

I could do with a drink, and as sure as hell so could she. And anyhow, it gave her something to do as she relaxed into what I was there for. We had the rest of the evening and the whole of the night to ourselves to get things right.

I stood up as Helen lined up the two glasses on top of the bar. 'Let me help you with that.'

I uncorked the bottle she'd picked from the bar and poured the wine. The sound of it glugging into our glasses seemed to lift the awkwardness a bit.

I lifted the two full glasses and handed her one.

'Cheers!' I said and took a sip.

Helen followed suit.

You've got to guide her. Tread really carefully.

I touched her arm, and let my fingers slip all the way down to her hand, taking it lightly in mine and drawing her back to the end of the bed. We sat down side by side, but this time she sat further back. She hadn't let go of me.

'You okay?' I asked quietly a couple of minutes later.

She nodded. I set down my glass of wine by my feet and placed my now empty hand on her clothed thigh with gentleness. She took another sip of her red wine, and I noted its stain on her lips as she bent and put down her own glass and sat up again. My hand that had been on her thigh now took her other hand and squeezed it with lightness, to let her know I wasn't anything but on her side.

'I'm going to take care of you tonight, Helen.'

I spoke directly to her eyes. I saw her relax an iota and felt my own relief as she did. But I still couldn't help thinking of the fucking bastard who had stolen so much from her. And stolen so much from other men too, in making her so fearful of us.

I wrapped an arm around Helen's shoulders and she shifted so she was snuggling against me. I wanted her to feel completely at ease with me, but at the same time I was very aware that to draw attention to the care I was taking was likely to remind her of what had brought her to this place.

I changed tack.

'What do you do for a living, Helen?'

'Hmm?'

Her large blue eyes looked up at me looking down at her. There were warm creases around them.

'Oh, a nurse. Paediatrics – children.'

'Really? That must be tough.'

'Yes, it can be,' she conceded. 'But most of the time it's a pretty positive job. Helping kids get better again.'

I squeezed her. 'Well, it's certainly a job everyone appreciates, even if we haven't got the guts to do it ourselves. It's a good thing you're doing.'

'That's a nice thing to say, Luke,' she smiled.

'I mean it, Helen.'

I couldn't help feeling she needed to hear it.

We sat there in the full glare of the hundred-watt bulb above our heads. I knew I needed to move things along, and cutting the brightness a bit would certainly help, but I had to do it in a manner that didn't risk scaring Helen off. I needed to let her know what was going on every step of the way, so there was no reason for her to put up her guard at any time.

'I tell you what, Helen,' I spoke in a calm tone to her, 'I'm going to go and turn down the dimmer switch so it's a bit more cosy, and then I'm going to go to the bathroom to change.'

I stroked her hair.

'While I'm doing that,' I continued, 'if you could get yourself ready and into bed. You feel okay with that?'

She pulled herself away sharpish. 'If I could use the bathroom myself first . . .'

There was a nervousness in her voice, as if she expected to be shouted down.

I backpedalled *fast*.

'Of course. Of course. Do forgive me,' I said, and stood and gave way to her with a spread of my arm towards the bathroom, stepping out of her way.

I watched her leave the bedroom and shut the door behind her. I had to be *so* careful. I turned down the light and pulled my pyjama trousers out of the overnight hold-all I'd brought with me. *So I don't scare her off.*

I hovered beside the bathroom door, and when Helen walked out she was in a pale pink satin nightshirt that gave her an air of innocent prettiness.

'I won't be long,' I said, and watched her bare feet sink a path across the carpet to one side of the bed.

'Don't worry, I'll wait,' she grinned.

It was good to see her gradually relaxing. Or at least kid herself she was, anyhow.

I sorted myself out, and as I brushed my teeth, before I left the room I watched myself in the mirror above the basin. It was a chance to give myself a pep talk.

Keep calm and treat her well. Comfort at all cost.

I turned to make my way out, and felt like I was back standing outside the hotel-room door all over again. I took another deep breath.

Here goes.

I pushed open the bathroom door and stood for a second on the threshold of the now dimly lit bedroom.

Helen was sitting up in bed watching me. Her shoulder-length brunette hair was brushed so it shone and nestled against the lapel of her nightshirt. She held a nervous little smile, and her large blue eyes didn't blink as they followed me across the room to the other side of the bed.

I folded back the duvet and slid in beside her. We sat together and I put one arm around her.

'You look nice without your pyjama shirt,' she said.

'Thank you, that colour suits you, you know,' I replied.

I was very aware that we were at a crucial point. I suspected she knew it too.

I played with her fingers with my other hand.

'I'd like you to lie next to me, Helen.' I spoke softly to her at a level that seemed to suit the subdued light.

I noted Helen purse her lips.

'Are you all right with that, love?'

314

She said nothing but nodded her head just a little.

I waited a couple of seconds, just so she could get used to the idea. Then I lifted the bedclothes just enough so that both of us could slither down beneath them. I held Helen in my arms, and my fingers savoured the smooth satin across her back. Her own hand was on my chest, and she shifted her head so she was listening to my heartbeat.

'Ah, a good heart,' she concluded, and gave my breast a light rap with her knuckles as if she was joining in with my rhythm.

'I like to keep fit. Y'know, jog, gym, footie,' I told her, my chin resting lightly on her head and smelling the freshness of her hair. 'Do you do much sport, Helen?'

'It can be hard joining a club or classes because of my shifts, but I run when I can, and the hospital has its own staff swimming pool. I bike to work when the weather's okay.'

She pulled her head away so it now rested next to my shoulder and she was looking me in the eyes.

'Just working on the wards is good exercise enough, I can assure you,' she smiled. 'Like I bet all this keeps *you* fit.'

A sheen of pink blushed her face, and she ducked her head a little so she wasn't looking me in the eyes any more.

I was as surprised as much as she seemed to have surprised herself. I wondered if something of her old self, before the rape, had just slipped through. A little flirtatiousness. Though if that was true, it was clear that she wasn't quite sure how to deal with it when it did shine.

Helen spoke with calm as she fiddled with my fingers.

'It's funny, Luke, isn't it? That we're both sort of in the caring professions.'

She looked up at me again as if to emphasise the point. I wouldn't have put it like that myself, but she needed to think it so.

She's telling me what she's after.

315

I leaned towards her and kissed her on the forehead, and then moved closer towards her. Her face rose up to meet mine and we kissed on the lips. As we did, I slipped one hand down her back to cradle her butt, and shifted my whole body from under her, setting her beside me so we were now lying eye to eye.

One of my hands was now on her shoulder closest to the bed, and I stroked her neck with my thumb. Her head twisted lightly so she was nestling into my gentle pressure. She didn't say anything but her mouth opened just a little. She watched me all the while.

My hand that had cupped her ass now stroked her free arm with a steady rhythm. I moved at the same pace to now stroke her dark hair, all so that she would come to feel at ease with me being there for her.

'Helen,' I whispered, 'I'm now going to unbutton your nightshirt.'

'Yes,' she breathed out, in just as quiet a voice.

'If at any time you feel any discomfort, you let me know and I'll stop what I'm doing, okay?'

She nodded, her lips now pursed. The buttons ran almost the whole way up to her neck. I undid the top one, which bared the dip at the base of her throat. Just the sight of her pretty pale skin felt like letting some air in.

Helen's entire body remained stiff.

Is this what they mean by lying back and thinking of England?

I wanted the occasion to be something more for her. Given all that she'd been through, it damn sure needed to be something special. The last time she'd been made completely powerless. It was important, then, that this time Helen felt involved.

I was now raised up onto one elbow so my body shadowed hers.

'I tell you what, Helen,' I suggested. 'How about you hold my hand as I undo your shirt, so that you're doing it with me, eh? That'd be better, wouldn't it?'

She nodded and her lips released into a slight smile that was a pleasure to see.

Helen's hand reached up from its hiding place among the bedclothes and clasped mine like it was holding on for dear life. I waited a couple of minutes until she felt more comfortable and the pinched grip subsided into a warm cover to my own hand. I kept my eyes on Helen's as the two of us one-by-one released the buttons free from their holes all the way down to the final one, a few inches shy of her knees.

I released my hand from hers and changed places and lifted her hand to my lips and gave it a tender kiss.

'What I'm going to do now, I'm going to open your shirt, and when that's done, then you could take it off, all right?'

She looked puzzled.

'But we've already opened it?' she stuttered.

I looked her straight in the eyes.

'I mean *open* it. There's nothing to be afraid of. I *will* take care, I promise,' I assured her.

I slipped my closed fingers under the pink satin that lay over the plain beneath her collarbone and fanned them out as I felt my way, so that the cloth fell away and my fingertips rounded the edge of her breast and followed its curve downwards so that it sat in my cupped hand.

There was a flurry of Helen's own hand and she gripped my forearm, not to push mine away, as I'd feared, but to feel part of what I was up to all the more. It was as if she might feel she was directing my hand over her body. I bent my head and kissed the slope of that same breast, and her hand that had held my wrist reached for my hair and her fingers rippled my scalp. I ran my tongue with lightness across her cleavage and up the incline of her other breast, and her left hand slipped under me and drew back the rest of her nightshirt like she was giving her permission.

I nibbled my slow way down the rest of her smooth torso so that she began to shake with the pleasure of my light touch on her skin. I reached the edge of her bikini line and stopped short of going any further.

Just rev her up so she's in the zone . . .

I pulled away again and smiled down at Helen. She was already peeling off the remainder of her shirt. As she did so, I slid off my pyjama trousers so we were now naked together.

'I just need to get some protection. I won't be long,' I explained, as I swung my legs over the edge of the bed and slipped out from between the covers. She watched me cross the room and trawl through my trouser pockets and pull out a condom, then return to climb onto the bed beside her. It was a routine operation that had to be done, but it was one way Helen might see the whole of me and relax into the lovemaking we were about to embark on.

I nestled up to her and wrapped my arms around her, and she did the same to me.

'It isn't just the sex, Luke,' she breathed into my ear.

'I know, I know,' I replied, stroking her back with my hands and nuzzling her neck as I did. Her fingers seemed to want to cover every available space of me. Because of that bastard's legacy, he'd also left her devoid of any physical intimacy these past years too. She deserved a huge bout of TLC, and I was going to make sure that this night was as memorable for her just being held as it was about making up for the eight years' lack of sex. And I wanted there to be a natural flow from one to the other.

We kissed again, and Helen's fingers held my jaw line and then slid down and round to the back of my neck. I placed one arm round her shoulders again, and with the other hand traced down her to her slim waist and further, to settle on her thigh.

'I'll just get myself ready,' I explained, as I pulled away to sort out the protection.

Helen lay in waiting.

It was difficult not to break the momentum right now, and with Helen I was even more aware of that possibility. And the more I worried about *that*, the more likely one or the other of us might lose it.

Keep calm.

I was as much wishing it for me as I was for her.

I edged my body closer to her and ran my hand down the length of her thigh again, then slid it down between her legs and let my fingers skitter there then slip between her lips, so she knew my cock was next in line. Her own hands slid down my torso and I lifted myself up and sank into her. She gasped and her hands tightened their grip on my flesh like she was holding on for dear life. Our bodies rose and fell in unison, and all the while her wide blue eyes stared right back at me. She said nothing but she was taking everything in.

What IS she thinking?

I reached forward to kiss her throat as our rhythm subsided and we relaxed back into each other. Our faces were now cheek to cheek, and half my chest lay against her left breast, so our heartbeats echoed each other and one of my legs remained entwined with hers.

Helen was looking up at the ceiling and a tear had crept out of the corner of one eye. I stroked it away with the tip of my index finger. Her lips quivered just enough for me to notice.

'Are you okay, Helen? Was that okay?'

She rubbed her thumb down the length of my upper arm to the elbow and then did it again, but otherwise didn't move. She didn't speak. And then her head turned a degree in my direction, though not enough to look me in the eye. She sniffed once, and then it was as if the dam burst. Her whole body shivered as the tears rolled down her face. She buried her face in my shoulder, and it was my turn to hold on tight.

'I'm not going anywhere, Helen,' I breathed, as I rested my cheek lightly against her head and let her cry herself out.

'I didn't know . . . I didn't know . . .' she snuffled, when there were no more tears left.

I brushed away some damp strands of hair that clung to her cheek and kissed her forehead.

'What didn't you know, hey?'

She bit her lip and coughed, and her voice came out deeper, like she was holding everything in to say what she had to say.

'I didn't know that it could be so good. I never imagined . . .'

I looked at her with tenderness but chose not to say anything. It wasn't my place, for one thing. For another, I feared I might have a real go at the shit who had stolen such a huge chunk of her joy. And thinking *that*, it struck me that I'd already answered the bastard, right here and now in Helen's arms.

'If you feel like crying, Helen, you cry. I'm here through the night. You've got nothing to fear,' I reassured her.

'Thanks,' she whispered, as she burrowed herself into my embrace and rested her head above my heart again and her legs tangled themselves around mine.

'Uh-uh,' I shook my head and looked down at hers settling in for the night. 'It was my total pleasure.'

I woke with the sun coming up and closed my eyes for a split second and remembered where I was. Helen had shifted apart from me in her sleep, though she still had a light hold of my arm. I took a deep breath and began to draw myself away from her, though I was on tenterhooks in case I woke her.

I slipped out of the bed and crept across the room to the bathroom, then shut the door behind me and dressed. I threw some water over my face to refresh myself, and gave myself a quick look over in the mirror.

It was time to leave now. When I went back into the bedroom, Helen had shifted and looked on the brink of being fully awake herself, though she was finding it hard to keep her eyes open.

'I've got to go, love.' I shot the words across the room, yet in a voice I hoped wouldn't shatter the peace. I tiptoed over to her and bent down to her head on the pillow, giving her a gentle farewell kiss on the lips.

'On the desk,' she muttered with wooziness.

'I know, love,' I whispered back, and paced back across the room. I put the cash into my wallet, and took one last look at Helen lying there, blew her a final kiss, unhooked my coat from the hanger and let myself out.

I peeled the lid off the carton of milk and up-ended it into my cup of black coffee. I picked up another carton and did the same. I stirred my coffee and took a look round the railway station bar. The tropical fish wafting round the bar's aquarium looked as languid as I felt.

I took a sip of coffee and imagined Helen having breakfast at her hotel before she went back to work. I'd email her later today just to check things were okay.

I shook my head a couple of times. Both to clear it and at the realisation that *that* wasn't something I'd got into escort work for. It was funny how things worked out. I'd expected it to be about lots of hot sex and money, and never imagined I'd end up *here*.

God, I was SO naive back then, assuming that girls were just there to fall at my feet.

Though I'd since realised that to some extent that had been true! Because, before I turned up on the scene, a lot of my clients had found it difficult even getting hold of a straight male escort. The internet had certainly helped them start their search. Before that they'd simply had no chance of tracking down a gigolo. They needed someone like me to be available, someone they felt comfortable calling.

I sipped some more of my coffee and set the cup down. My clients had been so different from each other, but I got on well with most of them anyway. A good number like Jenny and Sasha, and Myleene and Mae, became good friends. For the time I knew them, at least. I hadn't expected that out of it at all. To have made those sorts of connections with clients.

Jenny. I wonder what she's doing now?

On the outside, everyone seemed to assume that escort work was just about having sex with lots of people.

I certainly did.

But it wasn't.

There's all the other stuff. Being there for people. Being a good listener. Not judging the clients. Like a confidant, I suppose.

Before I'd got into this line of work, I'd also believed – presumably along with most other people – that because of the money involved, there couldn't possibly be any meaning in what went on between me and my clients.

How wrong I'd been!

Of course, there were plenty of times when I was just there because I was paid to be. The sex was fine, but that was it. But there were a good number of clients I recalled with fondness. I was there for more than some financial transaction. And they reaped the benefits of that. But the funny thing was that so had I. I'd done right by them, by providing them with what they wanted or needed, and that made me feel like I was doing something worthwhile.

I sliced through a bacon rasher, speared one half with my fork and dipped an end in the yolk of my fried egg. I had it halfway to my mouth when my BlackBerry rang.

Oh man, not just yet.

And that was another thing. The phone never seemed to stop ringing these days. Not that the far fewer call-outs in my early days hadn't seriously buggered up my social life. It would have been wiser to have had a separate phone back then so it

322

would have made it easier for me to have a break. I could never make any plans because I never knew when I'd get a call-out. And I lost track of the times when I was just out the door with my mates and the phone rang. Given that the girl would be paying me over a hundred quid for my time, there'd been no contest.

Getting Gray on board had taken a lot of the stress from my work by allowing me a bit of breathing space between clients calling in and me returning their calls. He was my firewall. And help from people like Janice and Bob at Stagz had certainly upped my game early on. I couldn't be sure that escorting would have proved such a success if they hadn't given their support.

I rubbed the bridge of my nose between my fingers to help me concentrate, and fished the 'Berry out of my coat pocket and flicked it on. There was a message from Gray.

'*Morning, L, hope Helen went well. Julie would like to hear from you, G.*'

She'd left her number, but hers wasn't a name I recognised.

I took another sip of coffee and swilled it around my mouth and looked at the 'Berry's tiny screen. There was a time when every call was a completely new experience. I had no idea what I might be letting myself in for. But I'd soon taken to sex work like a duck to water. Even though I had not yet met Julie, I had no fear of what she might require of me.

My mind flipped back to the Sasha and Chloe incident right at the start of all this, when I had been so full of nerves that my cock almost gave up the ghost. I shivered thinking about it. That was one of my biggest regrets. That I hadn't been more confident and experienced at that once-in-a-lifetime session so I could have really let rip with the two of them and enjoyed myself even more! I was so much bolder these days.

I tapped Gray a reply.

'*Helen fine. Will touch base, call Julie later, L.*'

I checked Julie's number but hadn't a clue where she might be calling from.

Okay, Julie. Sometime today. But just let me get my breath back.

I switched the 'Berry off, put it back in my pocket and carried on eating my breakfast.

The Secret Diary of a Sex Addict

Amber Stephens

Starved of sex but forced into a sex addiction clinic. How will Shelley ever survive...?

Shelley Matthews is married to her job as a journalist at a glossy women's magazine. Which is just as well as she hasn't had sex for over a year. But when her editor decides a re-vamp of the magazine is needed, Shelley is forced to go undercover as a sex addict . . .

Attending therapy sessions, Shelley meets a whole host of extraordinary characters. There's:

Cian, lead singer of a hot new band, enjoying ALL the trappings of fame.

Dominatrix Abigail, who finds that inflicting pain has become a necessary part of sex.

Will, family man and serial adulterer. He knows his marriage is in jeopardy but he just can't help himself.

Former porn star Rose who is only aroused when the cameras are rolling.

Cliff and Cheryl, a swinger couple who prefer sleeping with strangers rather than with each other.

Can Shelley keep her secret from the others as well as writing the story of the year? And most importantly can she keep her cool – and chastity – intact? And does she really want to?

ISBN: 978-1-84756-085-8

A Brand New Me

Shari Low

For anyone who makes resolutions on January 1st – only to break them all by January 2nd . . .

Leni Lomond isn't one of life's risk-takers. A creature of habit, she's been stuck in her comfort zone for so long she's almost asleep.

So, on December 31st, she vows that things will be different – new job, new man, new life.

Less than a month into the New Year, Leni's first resolution is fulfilled when she accepts a job as PA to astrologer and TV celebrity Zara Delta. And her new work assignment – to date men from every sign of the zodiac and then report back to her batty boss – looks like it might just help her with the second one.

But the men she has to date include wannabe rockstar Matt who sees Leni as his ticket to fame and fortune, overgrown teenager Harry – a man whose idea of a good date is a night down the amusement arcade – and therapist Craig, whose patronising attitude is even more of a turn off than his long straggly beard . . .

But just when Leni's ready to give it all up her fortunes take a turn. Has Lady Luck finally deigned to shine on her – or is she being hoodwinked?

Can Leni control her fate, her feelings and fulfil the promise she made to herself at the start of the year? Or is her destiny already written in the stars?

'Great fun from start to finish.' Jenny Colgan

ISBN: 978-1-84756-017-9
Out in December 2008

The Trophy Taker

Lee Weeks

A serial killer is on the loose. His target? Lone Western women lured to Hong Kong by the promise of easy money. As **The Butcher's** killing spree escalates, bags of mutilated body parts are found all over the island – and more girls are disappearing.

Taking on his first major homicide case, **Detective Johnny Mann** is determined to stop The Butcher's brutal reign. Haunted by the memory of his father's death by the Triads, he's the only man who can track down a killer who's paralysing the city with fear.

Georgina Johnson has left her tragic past in England to start afresh in Hong Kong. But soon her life is in peril as she is sucked into the sinister world of the city's hostess clubs – magnets for the rich and perverted.

Venturing into darkness and dangerous places, Mann unearths chilling evidence about the killings. and then another body is found, one which brings the murders close to home . . .

Bolt the doors, turn on the lights and pray for mercy – you'll be up all night with this disturbingly addictive debut from a writer being hailed as the female James Patterson.

ISBN: 978-1-84756-078-0

Confessions of a Lapdancer

Anonymous

City girl by day, city stripper by night . . .

Geri Carson is fed up with life in the City. Forced to act as one of the boys in order to climb the ladder, it seems however hard she tries, she's constantly sidelined.

Struggling to keep up with an increasingly lavish lifestyle, Geri gets deeper into debt. She needs cash – and fast.

A company night out leads her to a lapdancing club where she is presented with an offer she can't refuse. A chance to earn a fortune performing in one of the hottest clubs in town.

At first petrified, once the lights go up, Gerry has never felt more alive. She's a natural.

Then she becomes involved with a millionaire client. The sex is mind-blowing but then she discovers a seedier and scarier side to life as a lap dancer. A world where anything goes and only the strongest survive . . .

Sexy and provocative, this tantalising tale will seduce fans of *Belle de Jour* and Tracy Chan.

ISBN: 978-1-84756-084-1